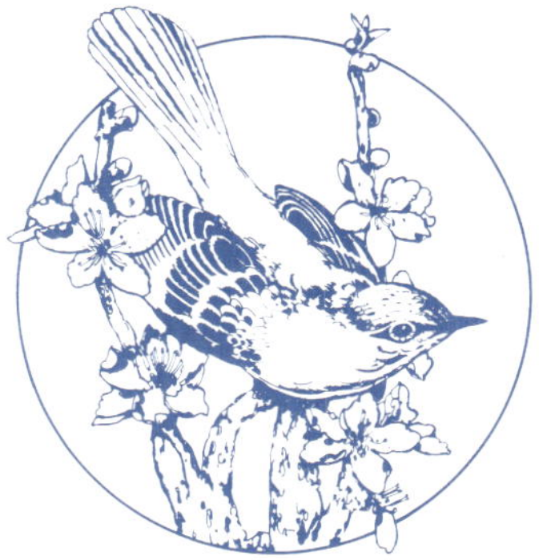

BIRDS IN ART
THE MASTERS

Inga Brynildson
and
Woody Hagge

Leigh Yawkey Woodson Art Museum
Wausau, Wisconsin

Library of Congress
Cataloging-in-Publication Data

Brynildson, Inga.
Birds in art: the masters/by Inga Brynildson and
Woody Hagge.
p. cm.
Includes bibliographical references.
ISBN 0-945529-05-8 : $24.95
1. Birds in art – Exhibitions. 2. Wildlife art – United States – Exhibitions. 3. Art, Modern – 20th century – United States – Exhibitions. 4. Wildlife artists – United States – Exhibitions.
I. Hagge, Woody. II. Title.
N7665.B79 1990 90-43625
704.9′432–dc20 CIP

CONTENTS

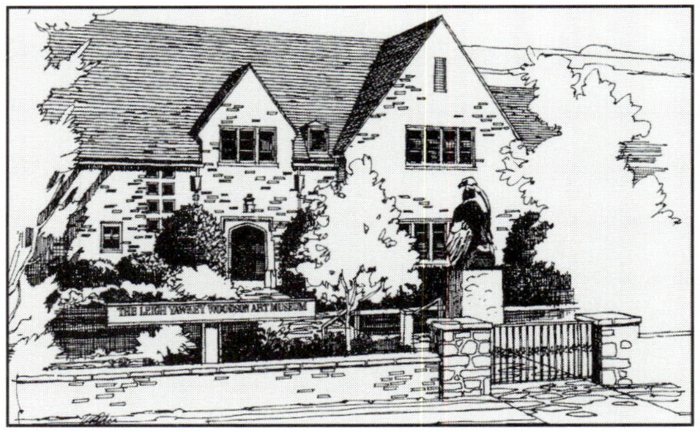

FOREWORD

Kathy Kelsey Foley
Director
Leigh Yawkey Woodson Art Museum

The 1990 *Birds in Art* exhibition marks the commencement of the Leigh Yawkey Woodson Art Museum's fifteenth anniversary. Since opening its doors in September 1976, the Museum has annually organized *Birds in Art*. The exhibition has grown steadily. Initially featuring artists from North America, it is now international in scope. The quality and variety of artworks have improved and increased remarkably, challenging the expertise of the jurors who convene each spring. Reflecting the growth of the exhibition, the catalogue has expanded into an information-packed, full-color publication.

What has remained constant each year is the designation by the Museum of a Master Wildlife Artist. The fourteen artists so honored collectively boast hundreds of years of experience both in the field and in front of the easel. As a group, their importance and influence are daunting. Though their lives and work often cross – at exotic birding spots, in conjunction with conservation efforts, or at art exhibitions – they are further united by the honor of receiving the Master Wildlife Artist Award and by their association with the Leigh Yawkey Woodson Art Museum.

The Museum's anniversary provides an ideal opportunity to celebrate the achievements of the Master Wildlife Artists. In fact, the idea to compile a book devoted to the Masters began simply as a suggestion to publish the remarks of the fourteen artists made in conjunction with the presentation of their awards. Regrettably, in the early years their public lectures were not recorded and, without question, humorous anecdotes and sage advice were lost.

Fortunately, the inventiveness and determination of Inga Brynildson – also to be credited for the initial suggestion of the publication – and Woody Hagge created the comprehensive volume presented here. Not fazed by the lack of readily available material, Inga and Woody sorted through previously published accounts, conducted lengthy interviews when possible, and reassembled both the reminiscences and collective wisdom of the Master Wildlife Artists. The text for each artist is comprised of quotes compiled from their review of thousands of printed pages and countless hours of taped interviews and lectures. *Birds in Art: The Masters* documents the exhibition through the philosophies, experiences, and representative artworks of the Masters, within the context of the Museum and *Birds in Art.* To Inga and Woody, we extend our profound appreciation for proposing such an undertaking and for possessing the vision and fortitude to produce this consummate anniversary volume.

Numerous individuals and institutions supported the efforts of the authors. The Museum staff worked with characteristic efficiency and dedication. Art dealers, publishers, and private collectors graciously checked records and made photographic materials available for our use. The artists, their families, and studio and office assistants answered questions, responded to requests, and cooperated in every way. To all, we convey our heartfelt thanks.

The decision to undertake this publication required not only vision but also financial commitment. The Museum's Board of Directors, in particular Alice Woodson Forester and John E. Forester, and the Aytchmonde P. Woodson Foundation have again demonstrated their leadership roles; the initial authorization was followed with the requisite financial support. *Birds in Art: The Masters* is the best expression of our gratitude.

Please join us in celebrating the achievements of the Museum's fourteen Master Wildlife Artists – Robert Bateman, Charles Greenough Chase, Guy Coheleach, Don Richard Eckelberry, Owen J. Gromme, Lars Jonsson, J. Fenwick Lansdowne, Roger Tory Peterson, Maynard Reece, Peter Scott, Keith Shackleton, Arthur B. Singer, George Miksch Sutton, and Kent Ullberg. They have helped to make *Birds in Art* the "institution" that it is, recognized virtually around the world. At year fifteen, the Leigh Yawkey Woodson Art Museum has already covered tremendous ground, with the promise of even greater things to come as *Birds in Art* continues to soar.

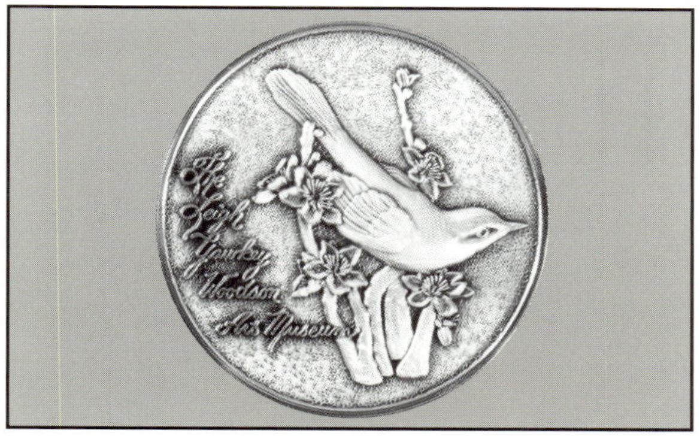

PREFACE

Birds in Art
Master Wildlife Artist Medallion

Birds in Art: The Masters commemorates the fifteenth anniversary of the Leigh Yawkey Woodson Art Museum's annual exhibition *Birds in Art*. In those years, it has become the most prominent annual exhibition of contemporary wildlife art in the world. Such acclaim is reason to celebrate. However, the success of *Birds in Art* has significance beyond the Museum. It reflects a phenomenal and rapid change in the history of bird art and, perhaps, in the values of American culture.

The 1990 *Birds in Art* exhibition was juried from works submitted by more than 600 artists – roughly the number of bird artists who had lived prior to the middle of the twentieth century, according to the calculations of one art historian. Moreover, most of the 600 artists who painted birds prior to modern times did so as illustration for natural history texts, sport hunting prints, or as designs for decorative arts. Today, there is great popular interest in gallery paintings of birds, realistic and impressionistic, portraits and landscapes. There is also an audience for sculpture depicting birds, even monumental sculpture for public art. These modern avian images express a vital contemporary artistic vision of nature and echo the passionate voice of environmental concern intensifying throughout the world.

Birds in Art was inaugurated in 1976 – the heart of the "Eco-Decade." It celebrates its fifteenth anniversary in 1990 – "Earth Year." In the mid-1970s, the U.S. Fish and Wildlife Service estimated that 57 million Americans enjoyed wildlife watching, wildlife feeding, and wildlife photography. A 1985 survey boosted that number to 135 million people. A 1990 poll by *The New York Times* and CBS News surprised even environmentalists with 71 percent of Americans favoring environmental protection at the cost of increased taxes, and 56 percent at the risk of lost jobs in their communities. Eighty-four percent of Americans now view pollution as a serious problem that is getting worse. Clearly, the past two decades have seen meteoric growth in concern for the environment and interest in nature. The profusion of new agencies and legislation safeguarding air, water, wilderness, soil, and wildlife is testimony to an emerging American value for environmental quality.

Is current interest in art depicting birds and wildlife an outgrowth of this emerging cultural value? Ecological concern is an artistic motive voiced in unison by the Master Wildlife Artists celebrated in this book. One cannot be certain whether the present popularity of wildlife art is a reflection of popular environmental concern among art consumers. However, there may be insight in artist Keith Shackleton's observation, "We find beauty, quite simply, in what we love." Perhaps, too, it reflects an underlying human need for nature surfacing in an increasingly paved wilderness – an inborn longing for the Garden. As artist Don Eckelberry theorized, "Some of it may be what Carl Jung would call, 'the unconscious in search of its roots.'" Eckelberry added, "I think people need paintings of what they miss."

If this is true, it is appropriate that *Birds in Art* celebrates its anniversary in Wausau, Wisconsin, just upriver from Portage – the birthplace of Frederick Jackson Turner. In his seminal essay "The Significance of the Frontier in American History," Turner observed that the 1890 United States census had done away with a frontier boundary on the American landscape. No longer, noted Turner, was there a chafing line of savagery against which the pioneer American character was hewn. This celebration of *Birds in Art* falls on the hundredth year since the closing of the American frontier.

Wausau is also just upriver from the nineteenth-century boyhood farm of John Muir, renowned visionary of American wilderness preservation. A few miles farther downriver is the "shack" from which, in the 1930s and 1940s, Aldo Leopold penned the foundations of an American land ethic, calling for conservation to be an integral part of our human system of morality. And in 1976, the Leigh Yawkey Woodson Art Museum, in Wausau, founded the world's foremost exhibition of art devoted to the beauty and message of birds. The banks of the Wisconsin River have been fertile ground in America's conservation heritage.

Former Leigh Yawkey Woodson Art Museum director David Wagner sees the Museum as an anomaly in the art community. "I don't see many other art museums hanging wildlife art on their walls in the trappings of high culture," noted Wagner. Indeed, wildlife art, contemporary and historical, is nearly always exhibited in natural history museums. When author Martha Hill showed transparencies of impressionist paintings by Swedish wildlife artist Bruno Liljefors (1860-1939) to a curator of European painting at the Metropolitan Museum of Art in 1977, the curator responded, "We would never consider an exhibition of his work – it is genre painting." (This, Hill writes, while the Met's walls hung with Dutch and Flemish still-life paintings.)

Many of the Master Wildlife Artists express similar dismay that art depicting birds and other wildlife has so rarely been recognized as authentic artistic expression. In 1980, however, the Smithsonian Institution's National Collection of Fine Arts (now the National Museum of American Art) exhibited selections from *Birds in Art* 1979 – an exhibition which *National Wildlife* magazine deemed the "coming of age" of wildlife art.

In the fifteenth anniversary year of *Birds in Art*, the Leigh Yawkey Woodson Art Museum is exceptional among art museums. Future generations may view *Birds in Art* as a bellwether of change in American values and aesthetics – a continuation of Wisconsin's legacy in the vanguard of the conservation movement.

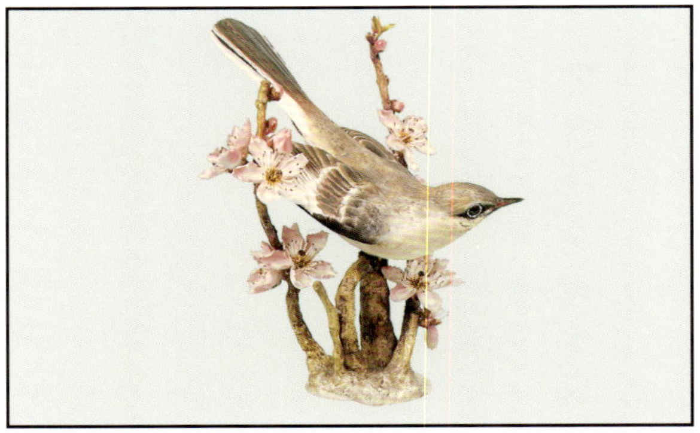

BIRDS IN ART – TAKING FLIGHT

Dorothy Doughty, Mocking Bird and Peach Blossom, *1940*
Porcelain, 10½ inches
Collection of the Leigh Yawkey Woodson Art Museum

Birds in Art took flight on wings of porcelain. Ninety-five delicate, life-size birds comprised the first permanent collection of the Leigh Yawkey Woodson Art Museum when it opened its doors in Wausau, Wisconsin, September 11, 1976. The birds on floral perches, collected by Leigh Yawkey Woodson, are one of only a few complete sets worldwide of Dorothy Doughty's *American and British Bird Series* designed between 1935 and 1962 for the Worcester Royal Porcelain Company. The Museum was dedicated to the memory of Mrs. Woodson by her three daughters – Nancy Spire, Alice Forester, and the late Margaret Fisher. The Woodson daughters decided to keep the porcelain set intact and agreed "the birds belong in Wausau." Alice and John Forester donated their English Tudor home to house the Museum. "It had been a dream for a long time. We wanted to create a little world of beauty," recalls Alice Forester.

Prior to the 1976 opening, the Foresters visited artist Owen Gromme, who agreed to "call a few friends" and to put together a show for the dedication. *Birds of the Lakes, Fields and Forests* opened with seventy paintings and sculptures by twenty-three artists, all from the United States with the exception of one Canadian. The catalogue cover of the premier exhibition featured Gromme's painting of whooping cranes, *Salute to the Dawn* – a fortuitous foretelling of the exhibition's ultimate significance in advancing wildlife art.

Artist, naturalist, and field guide author Roger Tory Peterson observed, "The *Birds in Art* exhibition, in my opinion, has raised the standards of wildlife art. It has done a great deal for young and unheralded artists of artistic diversity ranging from impressionistic paintings to highly detailed realism. At the same time, it has shown the works of Old Master bird artists. *Birds in Art* seems to have shaken the complacency of even the best bird artists."

Canadian artist Robert Bateman agrees. "*Birds in Art* has had a very good influence on wildlife art. The traveling exhibitions and the high profile have helped make bird art, and wildlife art in general, more important and more respectable in North America and other parts of the world. The exhibition has high standards and shows more artistic integrity each year. It encourages artists to take risks and puts younger artists in touch with experienced artists."

In its fifteenth year, *Birds in Art* is juried from over a thousand works submitted by more than 600 artists from around the world. *Birds in Art* has twice toured internationally. The 1981 exhibition traveled to the Royal Scottish Academy, Edinburgh, and the British Museum of Natural History, London, with support from Gulf Oil Corporation. The 1986 exhibition flew to China's Beijing Museum of Natural History with help from Northwest Airlines.

Birds in Art has exhibited at more than twenty museums throughout the United States. Among them are the Rochester Museum and Science Center, Rochester, New York; the Arnot Art Museum, Elmira, New York; the National Geographic Society, Washington, D. C.; the Carnegie Museum of Natural History, Pittsburgh; the Houston Museum of Natural Science, Houston; the Missouri Botanical Garden, St. Louis; The High Desert Museum, Bend, Oregon; the Anchorage Museum of History and Art; the California Academy of Sciences, San Francisco; and the Bishop Museum, Honolulu. Chicago's Field Museum of Natural History estimates that its 1988 exhibition of *Birds in Art* attracted 300,000 visitors.

Perhaps the finest feather in the cap for *Birds in Art* was the 1980 exhibition at the Smithsonian Institution's National Collection of Fine Arts (now National Museum of American Art), in Washington, D. C. It marked the first exhibition of contemporary wildlife art at a major American art museum. "Walking up the steps at the National Collection was one of the finest moments of my life," recalls John Forester.

The founders of the Museum did not anticipate the popularity and success which *Birds in Art* enjoys. "We had no thought of it becoming an annual event; we just needed something to hang on the walls in time for the dedication," explains Alice Forester. "It was autumn and, in the northwoods, that means birds to a lot of people."

David Wagner, who served as Leigh Yawkey Woodson Art Museum director from 1977 to 1987, observed that the success of *Birds in Art* rode the updraft of changing values and interests in American culture. "The exhibition opened a year after the famous *Animals in Art* exhibition at the Royal Ontario Museum in Toronto. It opened in the midst of the environmental decade, and collectibles featuring wildlife, such as limited edition art prints, were already quite popular. I don't know how much these things played into the selection of a bird art exhibition. I think the Museum founders simply felt it would serve the people of central Wisconsin and surrounding areas because of the love for nature and the tradition of ecology in Wisconsin."

Birds in Art, too, has become an autumn tradition in Wisconsin. The exhibition annually attracts upwards of twenty thousand visitors, including hunters right out of the duck blind. According to Kathy Kelsey Foley,

Museum director since 1987, "Some people come for the birds but they come back for the art, while others come for the art and delight in the beauty of the birds."

The exhibition traditionally opens the weekend following Labor Day with festive events for the artists and their guests hosted by the Museum. The gala opening weekend draws artists from around the world to central Wisconsin, even though, as British artist Keith Shackleton observed, "Wausau, Wisconsin, is a long way from a lot of other places."

Wagner, who left the Museum to become director of the Colorado Springs Fine Arts Center, remarked, "Wherever I go, there seems to be a mystique about the Leigh Yawkey Woodson Art Museum. It's not just the *Birds in Art* exhibition, but also the hospitality shown the artists."

Many of the artists agree. East Coast artist Guy Coheleach attests, "Artists are treated with dignity here. They don't have to stand beside their artwork trying to get the public to buy. They are treated like kings and queens."

Marcia Theel, public relations coordinator for the Museum since 1977, credits the Foresters with setting a tone for gracious hospitality at *Birds in Art*. "Mrs. Forester spends countless hours learning the names and backgrounds of the artists so they feel at home."

This "little extra" is now a proven formula for the success of *Birds in Art*. Of the twenty-three artists who participated in the first exhibition, thirteen attended the opening. Of the 105 artists featured in the fifteenth anniversary *Birds in Art* exhibition, more than eighty journeyed to Wausau for the opening celebration. For the artists, the opening weekend provides a valuable opportunity to meet with peers.

Swedish artist Lars Jonsson remarked, "For me, getting together for discussion with other artists is as important as the exhibition. Every time I leave Wausau, I think of a hundred things I meant to talk about with other artists."

Bateman adds, "It's a rallying place for artists that stimulates the exchange of ideas. I'm always amazed at the generosity and good feelings and swapping of ideas among artists at *Birds in Art*. The personal benefit to the artists is very great."

The highlight of the opening weekend is the presentation of the Master Wildlife Artist Award, given to an artist who has made outstanding contributions as a naturalist and conservationist, and who has created important bird art. Gromme was the first honored with the title in 1976. Peterson presented Gromme with a scrolled declaration signed by the other twenty-one men and one woman whose artwork comprised the original exhibition.

After the success of the first exhibition, the Museum Board of Directors decided to present *Birds in Art* and the Master Wildlife Artist Award annually. A medal was struck, depicting Dorothy Doughty's *Mocking Bird and Peach Blossom*, which has since graced the necks of fourteen artists whose lives and work are celebrated in this book. The Master Wildlife Artist is selected by previous award winners with the approval of the Museum Board.

When asked what it means to have received the Master Wildlife Artist Award, Coheleach responded, "It was a tremendous honor to be in the company of artists I have admired all of my life." Iowan Maynard Reece, the only five-time winner of the Federal Duck Stamp Competition, said, "The Master Wildlife Artist Award is one of the highlights of my career." Don Eckelberry thoughtfully responded, "It was very gratifying to receive the award. It would have been even more gratifying twenty years earlier if there had been a museum to give out such awards. You need these things when you're young, when you're working in the dark and need encouragement."

George Harrison, field editor for *National/International Wildlife* magazines and nature editor for *Sports Afield*, served as consultant to the first twelve exhibitions. The Foresters and Wagner attribute much of the success of *Birds in Art* to Harrison's ideas, knowledge of birds, and enthusiasm for wildlife art. Harrison began the tradition of including the work of an Old Master bird artist in each exhibition. The paintings of Audubon, Fuertes, Thorburn, Liljefors, and others provide a historical context for contemporary bird art.

Now celebrating its fifteenth anniversary, *Birds in Art*, which began with a dream and a vision of beauty, has spread wings of paint, bronze, stone, and wood across the globe and into the hearts of millions of people throughout the United States, China, and the British Isles. Through the morning shadow of a plover on sand, the gleaming power of an eagle's talons, and a lyrical strand of goldfinches in grass, the exhibition displays a varied artistic vision of nature and of ourselves. It is more than the beauty of the birds which stirs us; it is the ancient truth which stares back through the asking eyes of an owl; it is the renewal of wonderment sparked by the delicate riddle of color in the feathers of a mallard; and it is the recognition of self shimmering through an egret's reflection in a pond. At *Birds in Art*, with artistic vision expressed in images of birds, thoughts preen and souls take wing.

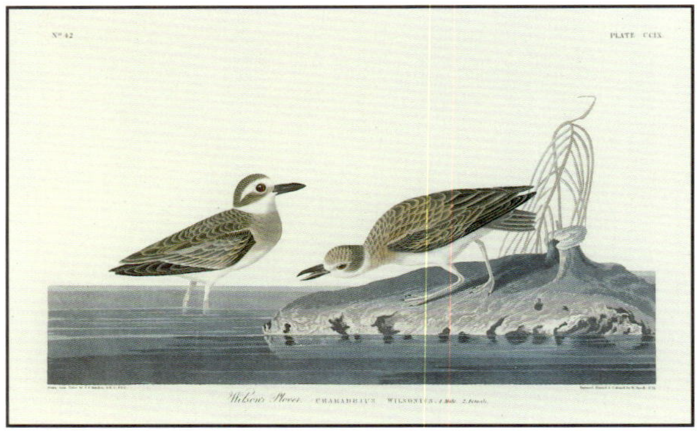

THE FLIGHT OF THE PAINTED BIRD

John James Audubon, Wilson's Plover *from* Birds of America
1826 - 1838, hand-colored engraving, 25 x 36 inches
Collection of the Leigh Yawkey Woodson Art Museum

The painting depicts a long, nervous flock of geese, necks stretched in anticipation of take-off, as seen through the eyes of a hunter. This composition is not a contender in a state waterfowl stamp competition, nor is it a numbered and signed print awaiting purchase in one of the many galleries in the United States specializing in wildlife art. These geese are painted with earth pigments on the wall of a cave in southern Spain. The artist, who likely hoped to conjure sympathetic magic to empower him as a hunter, lived 4,000 to 6,000 years before Christ. His ancient rendering is among the earliest records of humankind's artistic vision of birds.

In the ensuing 8,000 years, where has our artistic interest in birds taken us, and what course has the painted bird followed throughout the history of art?

Ancient Egyptian frescoes and low reliefs are rich with images of birds. The concept of the soul as a bird can be seen in the decoration of ancient tombs.

Aristotle (384 - 322 B.C.) wrote the first descriptive ornithological text. His *Historia Animalium* includes an elementary drawing of a bird, or rather, its internal anatomy. From Aristotle to Audubon, and even to Fuertes in this century, the history of bird art closely follows the history of bookmaking. Increasingly beautiful and life-like bird illustrations became possible with advances in printing methods. Why the history of bird art is traced through the pages of books with only rare references to the framed contents of art galleries and museums is a matter of speculation.

In *The History of American Ornithology Before Audubon*, Elsa Guerdrum Allen suggests that the bestiaries of the Dark Ages, which ascribed powers of sorcery to animals, cast suspicion on the whole of nature and stagnated scientific and artistic inquiry. Others blame the Renaissance rift between science and the humanities, furthered by Copernicus, Galileo and, later, by Darwin. Robert Mengel, in his 1980 article "Beauty and the Beast: Natural History and Art," writes: "As the revealing word implies, the humanities, closely reflected by their arts, were almost exclusively concerned with contemplating, and especially with glorifying, 'God's image' (that is, man) and his works . . . . Although the mainstream of Art grew apart from Science, the artistic spirit remained in some of those who pursued Science . . . . The result was the birth of wildlife art, which even in maturity has remained more a province of natural history than of Art."

Whether due to Dark Ages superstition or Renaissance anthropocentrism, if Western art became an inhospitable environment for birds, historians ultimately blame the rise of Christianity. Just as the contemporary environmental crisis is said to have its roots in the traditional interpretation of human "dominion" over the earth, the book of Genesis is also held responsible for the apparent condemnation of nature's wild creatures as subjects worthy of art. While contemporary Biblical scholars argue that Genesis was never intended to justify disregard for nature, traditionally such interpretation placed Occidental man and his cultivated stock above wild forms. Not so Oriental man, whose art remained rich with images of cranes, songbirds, pheasants, and other wild fauna.

Consequently, in the West, exhibitions of bird art antiquities are more often assembled from natural history libraries and rare book collections than from art museums. Examples include the New York Public Library's 1988 exhibition *The Bird Illustrated: 1550 - 1900*, and *The Bird in Natural History: Before, During, & After Audubon*, organized by the University of Wisconsin-Madison's Elvehjem Museum of Art in 1982, from the Chester Thordarson Collection of rare books.

One of the oldest manuscripts in which the painted bird appears is *Ornithiaka* (512 A.D.) by Dionysius Exiguus. It includes forty-eight paintings of birds.

The notes from thirty years of bird study by Emperor Frederick II of Hohenstaufen (1194 - 1250) comprise one of the earliest richly illustrated ornithological texts, *De Arte venandi cum Avibus* (The Art of Hunting with Birds). It is thought to have been compiled and illustrated by Frederick's son Manfred (c. 1232 - 1266) after his father's death. The Vatican copy includes 900 vivid illustrations. The manuscript was not widely circulated until it was published in Augsburg in 1596.

Falconry was a common theme in medieval tapestries and embroideries. Oil paintings portraying nobility with falcons as symbols of victory and triumphant scenes of courtly hawking parties were popular throughout the sixteenth and seventeenth centuries. In the mid-seventeenth century, the Dutch gamepiece (or, hunting still life) flourished as a symbol of prestige. These sumptuous panels are cluttered with limp-necked fowl of all sorts – swans, geese, pheasants, partridges, and songbirds – hanging by their feet or piled beside copper bowls of fruit and hunting horns.

In England, the Game Act of 1671 largely restricted hunting to the wealthy, landed class. That same year, Francis Barlow (1626 - 1704) began the tradition of the sporting art print by publishing twelve plates entitled *Severall Wayes of Hunting, Hawking and Fishing, According to the English Manner.* Sporting art depicting the chase and quarry became a status symbol and enjoyed popularity for well over a century. One source lists ninety painters who specialized in sporting subjects in eighteenth-century England.

The tradition of sporting art continued through the nineteenth century in the works of such artists as Arthur Fitzwilliam Tait (1819 - 1905). Born in England, Tait's paintings depicting hunting dogs, and hunting and fishing scenes from America were popularized by Currier and Ives.

In the twentieth century, American waterfowl hunting and art were united in the federal duck stamp program. Pulitzer Prize-winning cartoonist Jay "Ding" Darling (1876 - 1962) designed the first stamp in 1934, featuring a pair of alighting mallards. Since that time, every waterfowler in the marsh has carried a postage stamp-size reminder of the long legacy of sporting art which ultimately began on the rock walls of caves.

Despite this sally to the canvas of the sporting artist, the bird as an object of art continued to evolve on the pages of books, with few exceptions. One exception is the finch which appears in Renaissance paintings as a symbol of the Passion of Christ.

Birds figured prominently in the decorative borders of fourteenth-century illuminated manuscripts devoted to religious texts and herbals. Although sometimes realistically drawn, birds were incorporated into the margins of these texts largely for beauty and symbolism rather than as natural history illustration.

The fifteenth-century invention of the movable type printing press, advances in paper making, and the discovery of the New World provided the means and motive for renewed interest in natural history. *Das Buch der Natur,* printed in 1475 in Augsburg, is the earliest known printed book to contain illustrations of birds. It includes 103 bird drawings in twelve full-page woodcuts.

The latter half of the sixteenth century in Europe saw publication of three encyclopedic works of natural history, each with hundreds of woodcuts depicting birds. Of particular interest is *Historia Animalium* (1551 - 1558) by Swiss physician Conrad Gesner (1516 - 1565). The third part, devoted to birds, was published in 1555 and describes and illustrates 217 species. Interestingly, the bird illustrations with short descriptions were also issued separately under the title *Icones Avium* (1555), which remained a household reference for 200 years.

One of the first bird books printed in English with copper engraved illustrations was John Ray (1627 - 1705) and Francis Willughby's (1635 - 1672) *Ornithology* (1678). Metal engraving brought a delicacy and elegance to bird illustration not possible under the coarse line of the woodcut. Bird illustration, however, continued to suffer from the artists' general lack of field experience and the standard practice of drawing from dried, stuffed specimens instead of from living birds. This encouraged mistakes, such as the portrayal of grebes and loons standing erect like penguins instead of squatting forward in the manner of ducks and geese.

Mark Catesby (1682 - 1749) of Essex, England, set a new standard in bird illustration with publication of his two-volume work *Natural History of Carolina, Florida and the Bahama Islands* (1731 - 1743). Catesby, who some historians favor as rightful bearer of the title "Father of American Ornithology," not only produced the first extensive portrayal of American flora and fauna but also inaugurated the practice of drawing birds against a background of characteristic foliage and fruits.

Catesby was a field naturalist sent to America in 1722 to collect botanical specimens. His observations and collections extended far beyond plants, and he made watercolor sketches and compiled meticulous field notes of many life forms – frogs, fish, snakes, and insects, as well as birds. As Catesby writes: "In designing the Plants, I always did them while fresh and just gather'd: And the Animals, particularly the Birds, I painted them while alive (except a very few) and gave them their Gestures peculiar to every kind of Bird, and where it would admit of, I have adapted the Birds to those Plants on which they fed, or have any Relation to."

Catesby's birds, illustrated in 109 of the 220 plates, show an unprecedented vitality and beauty. He etched all but two of the copperplates himself and supervised the hand coloring for the first printing.

Although methods for color printing existed in the 1700s, hand coloring remained a cottage industry, practiced mostly by women, until the late nineteenth century. Throughout this period, elaborately illustrated bird books were highly popular and introduced those who could afford them to the wonders and beauties of nature. Perhaps none was more treasured in England than Thomas Bewick's *History of British Birds*, issued in two volumes – *Land Birds* (1797) and *Water Birds* (1804). In its day, it was the nearest thing to a popular bird guide. Bewick (1753 - 1828) refined the inexpensive process of wood engraving to produce a delicacy of line comparable to the detail of metal engraving. Toward the end of his life, Bewick was visited by an American, John James Audubon.

Audubon (1785 - 1851) is indisputably the most famous pioneer American ornithologist; however, his contemporary Alexander Wilson (1766 - 1813) published *American Ornithology* (1808 - 1814) well before Audubon's classic *Birds of America* (1827 - 1838).

Wilson fled Scotland for America in 1794 as a disgruntled silk weaver and poet. As customary for nineteenth-century bird books, Wilson's nine-volume book was issued in sections, the last two volumes published after his death. His sketches, in ink, pencil, and watercolor, were etched and engraved onto copperplates by Alexander Lawson (1773 - 1846) of Philadelphia. The plates included 320 figures of 262 American bird species, some drawn from specimens collected on the Lewis and Clark Expedition.

Wilson walked extensively throughout the eastern United States, collecting and drawing birds, and later, soliciting subscribers for *American Ornithology*, which sold for $120. In 1810, Wilson tried his sales pitch on a young storekeeper in a frontier store in Louisville, Kentucky. After intently examining the sample drawings, the storekeeper pulled a case from a shelf and showed Wilson his own bird sketches. Wilson asked the storekeeper if he had any intention of publishing his drawings and was surprised, and probably relieved, to learn there were no such plans. The storekeeper was Audubon.

Financial hardship changed Audubon's mind. He sailed to England in 1826 in search of a publisher when he failed to attract one in America in the wake of Wilson's success. After several exhibitions of his paintings, one French artist exclaimed, "Who would ever have expected such things from the woods of America." While Audubon enjoyed the romantic image of the woodsman artist, he had been raised and schooled in France and claimed to have studied under the famous artist Jacques Louis David, a matter which historians have since questioned.

Between the years 1827 to 1838, approximately two hundred sets of Audubon's *Birds of America* were published in a double elephant folio format with plates 39½ by 29½ inches – the largest bird book of all time. Most of the 435 hand-colored aquatint plates were etched by Robert Havell, Jr., London, from Audubon's watercolor and pastel paintings. The original set cost $1,000.

Audubon's birds were life-size on the double elephant folio plates. He stooped the neck of the lanky flamingo and turned the head of the bulky wild turkey cock to fit them on the page. Audubon had a flair for dramatic composition. His artistry quickly overshadowed the renderings of Wilson, who, ironically, may have given Audubon the idea to publish.

Audubon's success rode the wave of Victorian zeal for natural history inspired in the late 1700s by the journeys of Captain Cook and other explorers. In Europe, zoological gardens and private menageries of exotic plants and animals had gained popularity and aroused curiosity in natural history. The production of lavishly illustrated bird books was accelerated by the invention of lithography in 1798, which allowed artists to draw directly onto stone instead of relying on the often limited artistic skills of an engraver. No one appraised the public's appetite for natural history books as keenly as John Gould.

Gould (1804 - 1881) is better known as an entrepreneur publisher of folio bird books than as an artist. Some of the best bird artists in Europe worked at Gould's London "bird factory," producing forty-one folio-size volumes with 2,999 hand-colored lithographs. They worked from Gould's rough sketches and detailed notes.

German-born artist Joseph Wolf (1820 - 1899) painted some of Gould's finest plates. Unlike many bird artists of the day, Wolf had studied painting in his youth. He once complained, "If you paint a dead linnet or red poll, it is admissible to the Royal Academy. If you paint it alive, it is a transcript of an object of Natural History, unfit for exhibition."

This prejudice was less pronounced in Sweden, where Bruno Liljefors (1860 - 1939) painted birds with the free hand and eye of an impressionist. Trained at the Royal Academy of Art, Stockholm, Liljefors is frequently hailed as the greatest painter of wildlife of all time. Although his paintings are seldom exhibited outside his homeland, Liljefors was a sublimely talented impressionist, whose hand was on the mysterious heart of nature and who could echo its beating onto canvas.

In America, the bird portraits of Louis Agassiz Fuertes (1874 - 1927), of Ithaca, New York, were in great demand by book and magazine editors. In the first two decades of the twentieth century, Fuertes brought new vision to American bird painting by capturing the attitude and vital spark of a species. Fuertes left a lasting impression on the painted bird in our time.

In the last half-century, the painted bird has swerved from its course through the pages of natural history texts, or as strictly an object of food, talisman, or sport, and has alighted on canvas as an inspiration of beauty. Through the centuries, the bird occasionally emerged from the brushes of artists such as Dürer, Fabritius, Monet, Picasso, and Wyeth, but only in recent years has the painted bird evolved and flourished in great number on canvas. The current popularity of limited edition art prints has made it possible for more artists than ever before to earn their living painting birds and nature scenes as gallery art instead of as book and magazine illustration. The painted bird is still seen in well-worn pages of field guides, but now it also thrives on canvas. Just as declining populations of wild birds are living barometers of a changing environment, so too might the recent abundance of the painted bird be a sign of changing cultural values and aesthetics. Risen from the ochre of the cave painter and evolved from the field pencil of the naturalist, the painted bird wings its way into the hearts of all who see beauty in nature. While the wild bird struggles to survive, the painted bird has found new life in art.

THE MASTERS

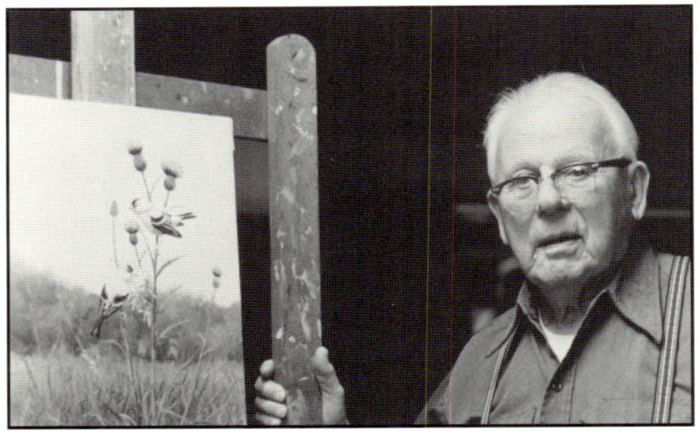

OWEN J. GROMME

Master Wildlife Artist 1976
Born: 1896, Fond du Lac, Wisconsin
Resides: Portage, Wisconsin

Bird art is man's highest expression in color and form of his appreciation of one of God's most beautiful creatures. In the various mediums it portrays those feathered marvels without whose help the delicate biological balance of all living things on our planet would indeed make the fragile human tenure short lived or impossible.

I love to paint and I am fascinated by the beauty of nature. My favorite subject is wildlife – birds, mammals and their environment. Emerson stated, "If eyes were made for seeing, then beauty is its own excuse for being." I try to put on canvas some of the lovely things I see in nature. I paint for pleasure and the pleasure of others, and I am very happy if what I paint causes them to relate to some happy experience they have had or something they have seen, such as a leaping deer or the majestic flight of an eagle.

I like birds. They are so special that without them life wouldn't be possible on earth. They are an important part of our existence – the way they keep insects in check. So, because I admire birds, I wanted to paint them.

My emphasis is to depict something pleasing to the eye. To me, nature is pleasing, even in its most violent aspects. I want to do paintings that are uplifting. I want to tell a story, stir the imagination, trigger an emotion, spark a memory.

I want to show people the beauty of a bird or a mammal in an ecological setting, but I also want them to learn something about what they are enjoying. From that I hope they gain a greater appreciation of that particular bird or animal's place in the scheme of things.

If a naturalist doesn't *do* something with the knowledge he acquires out in the woods, what the hell good is he? To punch and punch and punch on behalf of the environment is *applied science*, the *job* of the naturalist.

I spent forty-three years with the Milwaukee Public Museum, and we strove for absolute scientific perfection. When we created an environmental group, we wanted to show that bird in its environment for that particular season. I'm trying to do with paint what I used to do with mounted birds and mammals. I try to create a moment in time, with the idea that it will do some good for humanity.

To do the kind of work we did back then, you'd have to be a jack-of-all-trades and damned near a master of them all. A good museum man must have a solid background as an all-around scientist, artist, carver, sculptor, lecturer, writer, photographer, cinematographer, bookkeeper, taxidermist, and hunter.

We have to preserve the past to create the future. A museum, in my opinion, should serve as a storehouse of references to the past. It should link the past to the present. . . . That's how we make progress. It's the same in every field of endeavor. We are standing on the shoulders of the giants who have come before us.

I don't say Audubon was the greatest bird artist, but let me put it this way: He did more with what he had than many of the living artists are doing with what they've got now. His gun didn't go off half the time, he had no transportation, he didn't have any binoculars, the brushes he had were questionable, and he simply did a wonderful job with what he had. And Fuertes, in my opinion, was one of the finest watercolor artists who ever lived.

[When I was growing up] I found sketching wildlife subjects to be so enjoyable that I often did it at the expense of my homework. Now, as I look back on my life, I would say that egg collection, pencil sketching, and some early trial and error taxidermy were the influences that led to my museum work. That, in turn, eventually led me to become a wildlife artist.

I'm a hell of a lot different than most other artists. I'm not motivated by what other artists have done before me. I think one main reason that I am different is the simple fact that I didn't have formal art lessons and all that sort of thing. I paint because I love it. It's as simple as that. I figure my paintings speak for themselves.

You know, it's a funny thing. I read about what all these artists try to put into a painting and into people's minds. I can reduce the whole thing to a very simple common denominator. I don't worry about the "blue period" or the "green period" or the post-impressionists or the pre-impressionists. That's all more or less hogwash. I paint because I like to paint, and I want to produce something of beauty and at the same time something that will, I hope, teach a lesson: That everything in life is connected, that we're made of the same stuff the stars are. I try to teach a lesson in conservation.

I paint what I want, when I want, on my own time. I never tire of painting. I've always got ideas for scenes I want to paint. It's always a challenge for me to start out with a wooden frame, stretch a piece of canvas over it, and begin painting.

Owen J. Gromme

I study the material in my file and then begin making progressive sketches until I get my final sketch for the picture I want to paint. I begin drawing with a pencil on paper and then transfer the final sketch to the canvas before painting with watercolor or oils.

An old printer from Munich, Germany, told me that the great nature painters used three primary colors – pale cadmium, ultramarine blue, and alizarin crimson. That's what I wanted to do too. It's hard, but you can mix everything with these three colors.

I never know exactly how a painting will look once I begin. I have a fairly good idea because I make a pencil sketch and draw in my reference points, but a lot of things can change between the time I start and the time the painting is completed.

You have to be careful when you're working hard on a painting that it doesn't take control. A lot of people don't believe this, but I know it's true – a painting can hypnotize an artist. You have to get back from a painting once in a while and look it over.

When I am creating a painting which will eventually belong to someone, I approach it differently than a painting for reference only. If I am depicting canvasbacks, for example, it might be interesting to show them in a setting that stirs the emotions, one that moves the person viewing the painting to experience something special. I might want to show these canvasbacks bucking a storm and depict the fury of the storm as well as the bitter cold and the force of nature – things an outdoorsman can relate to.

Before I'm done with a painting, I call in people to look at it and to see what they think. I try to call in children because they give you a real, honest opinion.

I've been criticized for putting in too much detail. But to me, if the detail isn't there, then the picture has very little scientific value, and I'm always striving for scientific accuracy.

I try to improve my technique, to do a better job with fewer brush strokes. I don't paint into a picture microscopic things anymore, because they're not necessary. I don't try to put into a picture what you can't see at a distance of six feet. There's just no sense in it. The average person doesn't go up to a painting and look at the barbs in the feathers. If you want to do that, you can use a photograph. You could call it an experiment, but it pleases me to do it that way, and after all, the artist has himself to please as well as the people who view his paintings.

A lot of these duck stamps are little more than traced photographs. I can almost tell if they used a telephoto or a wide-angle lens. They have no experience in the field. A lot of them have been doing commercial art, and now that there's money in wildlife art, they're trying to climb on the bandwagon.

When I paint. . . I call on the experiences of a lifetime. . . . When I look back, it seems to me that my concern for the environment came about as part of my job at the museum. I was always interested in birds, animals, and the outdoors because I was a hunter and a taxidermist. But I could see how it all fit together once I started working at the museum.

The old high school in Fond du Lac was a four-story building, and, when I was fifteen or so, it was as high a point as there was from there to Lake Winnebago. From the assembly room, you could see the steam-powered log boats coming down the western shore from Oshkosh. The steamers were all coal burners and belched out thick black smoke. The ducks on the lake would part and take flight, and there would be so many of them that you couldn't tell the clouds of ducks from the clouds of smoke.

One afternoon, I saw a line of ducks three miles long and a hundred yards through. I figured that I was looking at three quarters of a million canvasbacks and redheads in one flock. I went home and told my dad about it. He said, "You should have seen the ducks on this lake forty years ago, before they built the dams up by Neenah-Menasha." I'd seen all those birds, and he was saying that was nothing!

We suddenly wake up to the fact that, in building our present day culture, we have seriously upset a delicately adjusted natural balance. . . . We owe a great deal to those who came before us, and it is our duty to pass on to posterity a world morally and physically as good or better than the one we live in.

I'd like to be remembered for having made a contribution to the environmental movement. Everything we eat and everything we use is a product of the soil, and if we don't have fresh air to breathe and fresh water to drink, and if we don't conserve our soil, what will be left for our children and grandchildren? I feel that my ability, to the limited degree it is, to paint will enable me to get that message across to future generations. I try to demonstrate in paint what Aldo Leopold so beautifully demonstrated in words. That just about says it.

In my ninth decade, I have found reason to hope, and my hope is fully embodied in my painting. There will always be new beginnings as long as we are sensitive to nature's ways and needs.

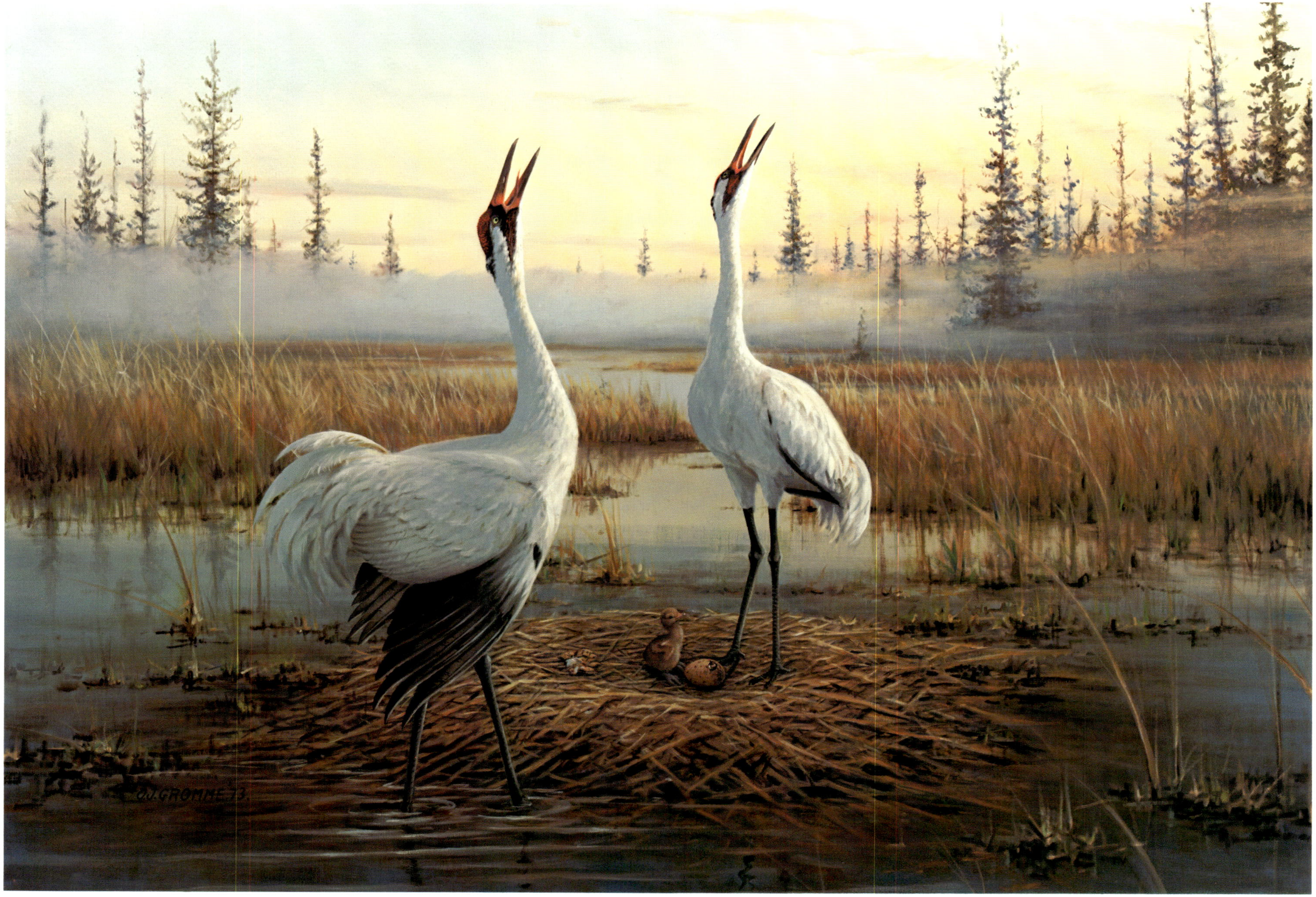

Salute to the Dawn (whooping crane) 1973, oil on canvas, 41 x 58 inches, collection of Mr. and Mrs. Norman Sauey. *Birds in Art* 1976.

I want to do paintings that are uplifting. I want to tell a story, stir the imagination, trigger an emotion, spark a memory.

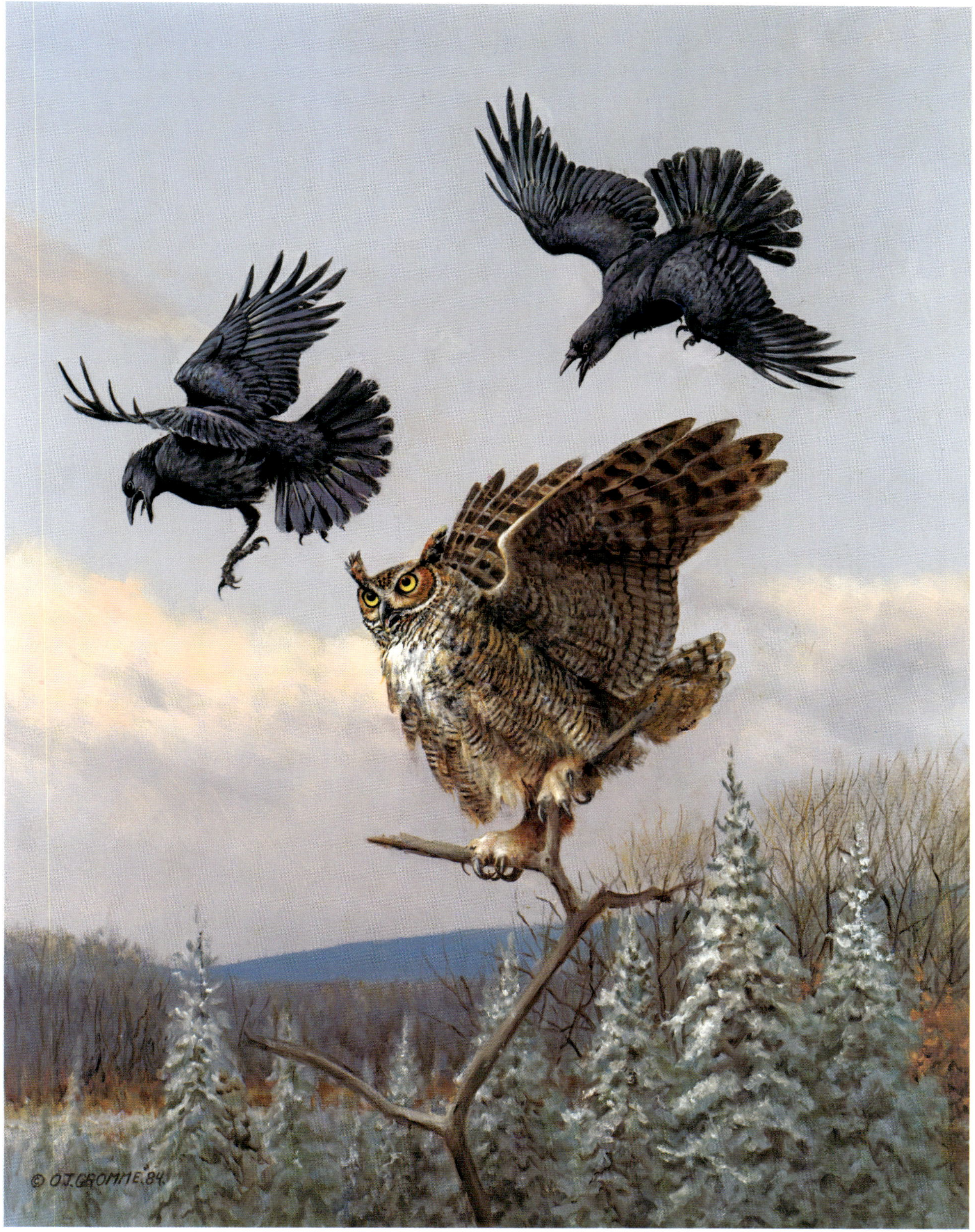

I paint because I like to paint, and I want to produce something of beauty and at the same time something that will, I hope, teach a lesson: That everything in life is connected, that we're made of the same stuff the stars are.

Getting Even (great horned owl and crow) 1984, oil on canvas, 35¾ x 30 inches, private collection. *Birds in Art* 1984.

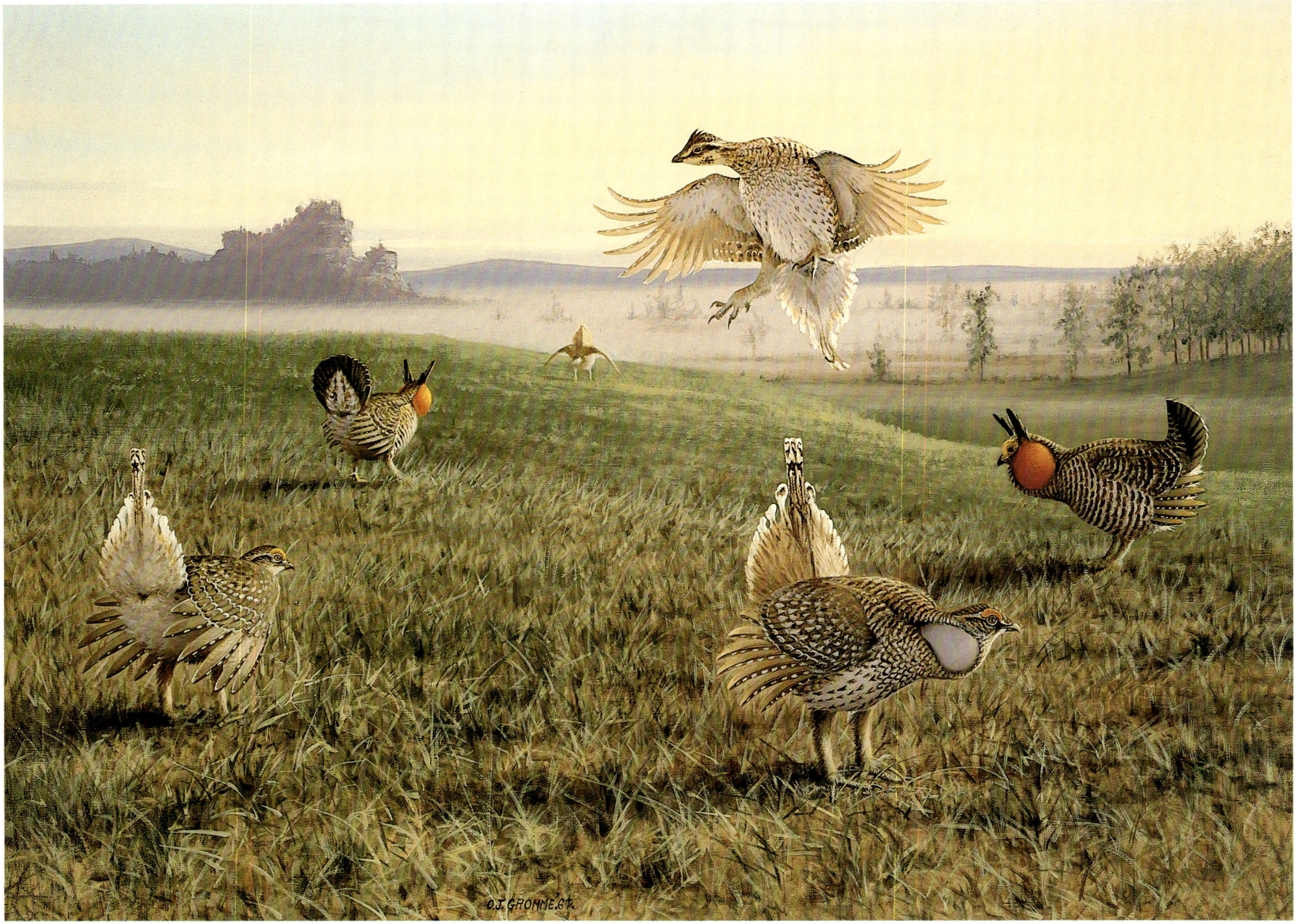

Sharptails Dancing (sharp-tailed grouse and greater prairie chicken) 1967, oil on canvas, 30 x 40 inches, collection of M&I Marshall & Ilsley Bank, Milwaukee, Wisconsin. *Birds in Art* 1978.

Everything we eat and everything we use is a product of the soil, and if we don't have fresh air to breathe and fresh water to drink, and if we don't conserve our soil, what will be left for our children and grandchildren?

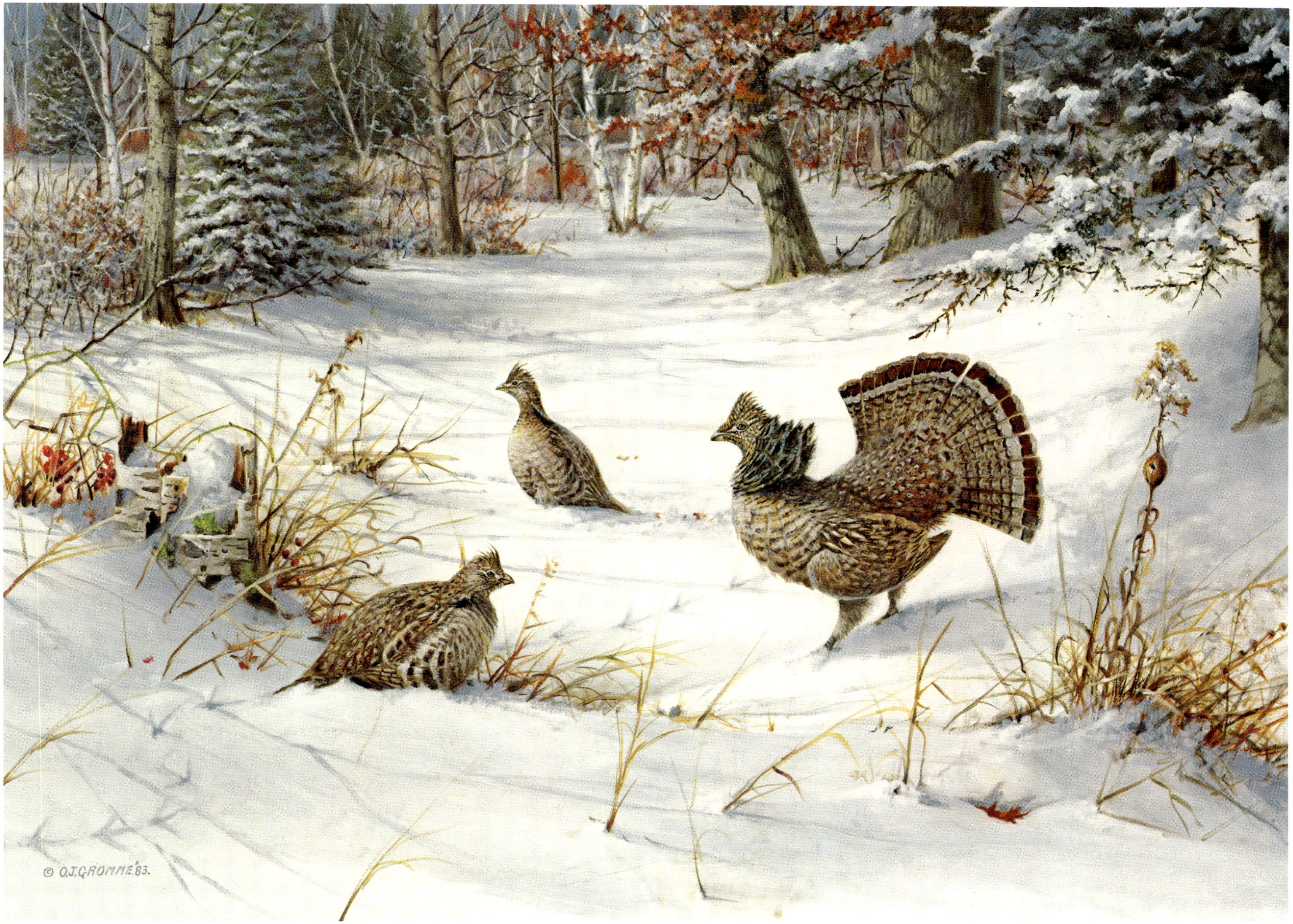

Ruffed Grouse 1983, oil on canvas, 30 x 40 inches, private collection. *Birds in Art* 1983.

Bird art is man's highest expression in color and form of his appreciation of one of God's most beautiful creatures.

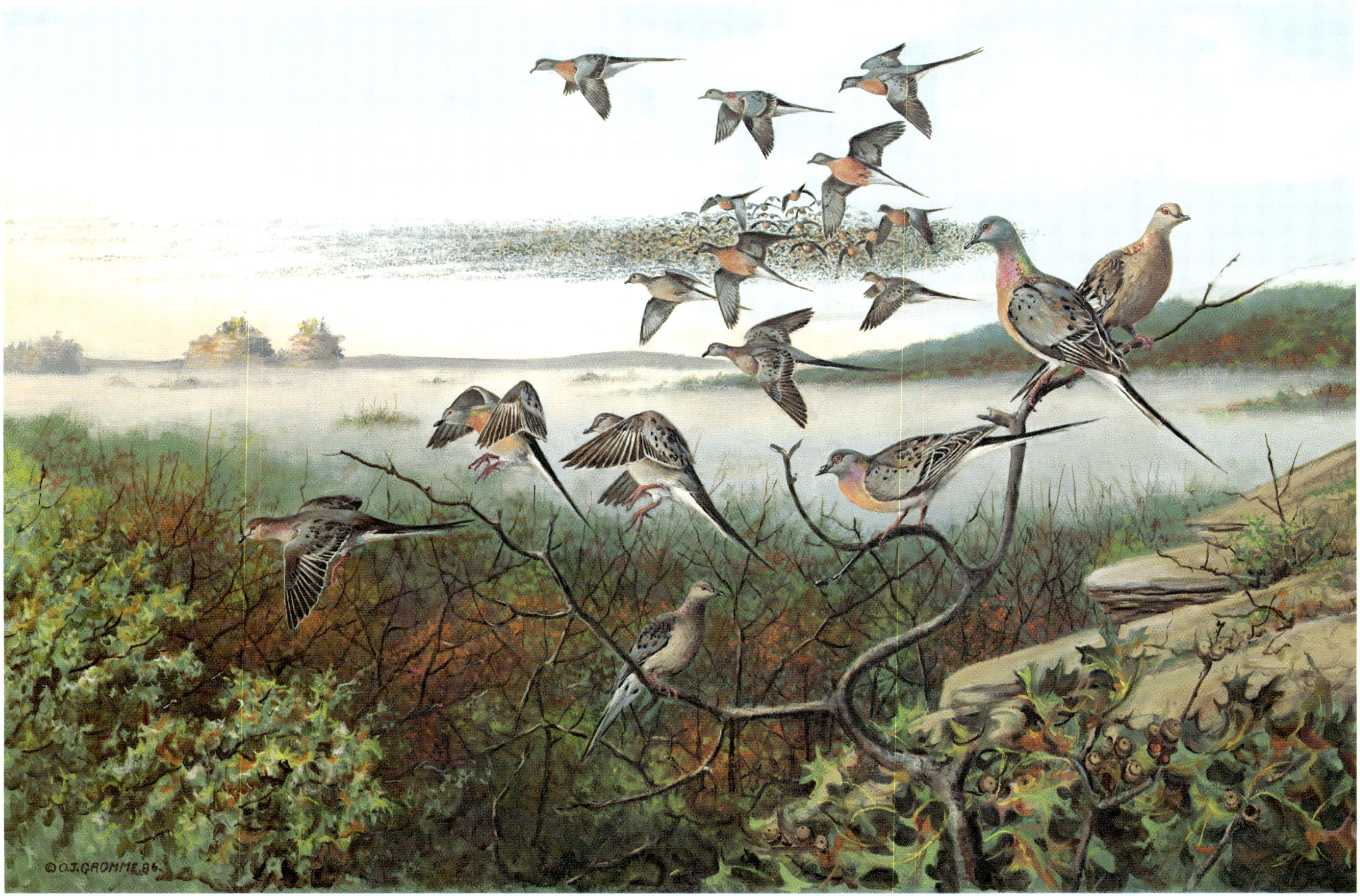

Distant Thunder (passenger pigeon) 1986, oil on canvas, 31 x 48 inches, collection of Stanton & Lee, Madison, Wisconsin. *Birds in Art* 1987.

Look closely, it is all there on my canvas. It is what we must remember. The passenger pigeon is the *symbol of extinction, an extinction we all face if we do not act.*

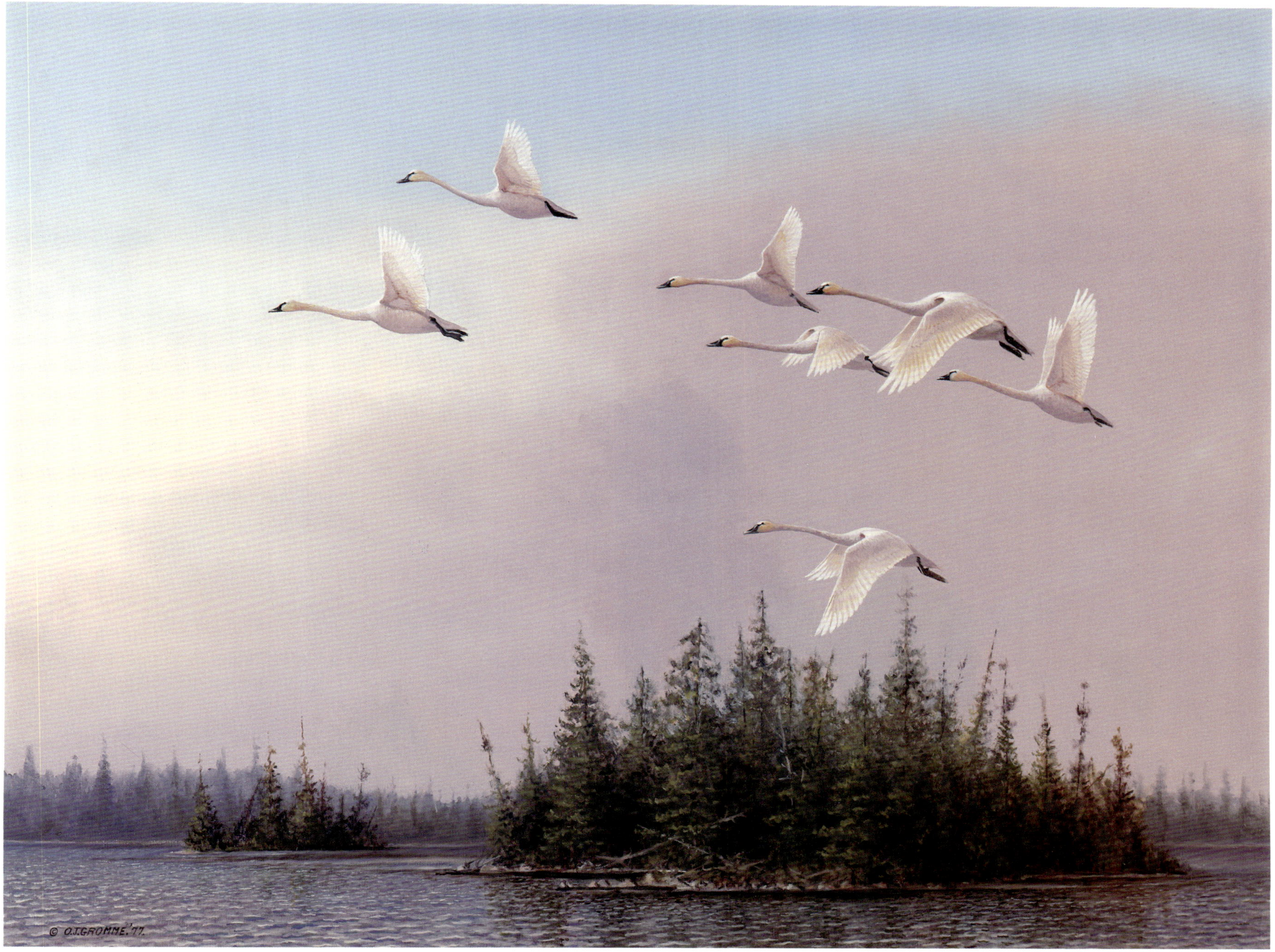

Departure From Lake Katherine (tundra swan) 1977, oil on canvas, 32 x 44 inches, collection of the Leigh Yawkey Woodson Art Museum. *Birds in Art* 1977.

Because he has envisioned flight from the dawn of his existence, it is man's nature to express this interest in various art forms by showing the freedom of flight in birds.

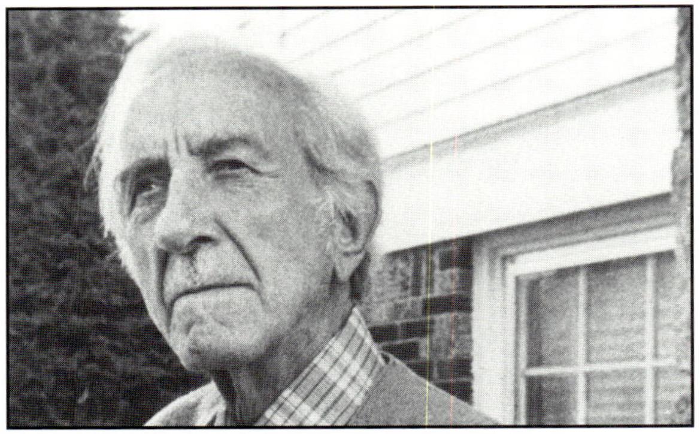

George Miksch Sutton

Master Wildlife Artist 1977
Born: 1898, Bethany, Nebraska
Died: 1982

Don't blame me for this restlessness. Blame the birds. You'd understand me if ever you'd seen a white gyrfalcon sitting by himself on an iceberg, his regal image sharp against the grayness of the sea; or a roseate spoonbill perched on a mangrove bough, wings half-lifted in readiness for flight; or an ivory-billed woodpecker flashing his black and white and scarlet plumage across the sun-shafted darkness of the swamplands that are his home.

As ornithologists, we observe a new bird half fearful that we may not see it again, and fully aware that we may never in our lives have a better look at it than this. Every move it makes, every cry it utters is important to us. Observing it intently, we ascertain as quickly as possible what it is; not what its name is – that can come later – but how it compares with species we already know, what attitudes of body and expressions of face it repeats most frequently, what facts about it are so indubitable that we can safely add them at once to our personal store of knowledge.

When I was very young, I loved birds dearly, but I don't remember being puzzled by them. The handsome ruffed grouse that came to our cabin in the woods near Aitkin, Minnesota, to drum every day on the sill of the big window in the living room came because it had found that sill a good place for drumming. . . . The year was 1901. I was three years old. I didn't even know that drummer of ours was a male bird. Its drumming entertained me in a way that I find impossible to describe. Every blessed thing it did on that windowsill gave me a feeling approaching ecstasy. But I was not puzzled. Grouse drummed. It was their way.

[A few years later,] I decided that the time had come for me to make good drawings. . . . So I found paper and crayons and proceeded to draw redbirds, blackbirds, and bluebirds, contenting myself with images that were in truth red, black, and blue and not much else. . . . I peddled them from door to door, selling them at a penny apiece.

My first serious drawing was of a prize rooster at a Nebraska State Fair, a drawing for which an admiring passerby paid a dime.

My first bird book [was] Frank M. Chapman's *Bird-Life,* with its colored pictures by Ernest Thompson Seton. Those beloved parents of mine, wondering what to do with a son who obviously doted on birds and didn't seem to be interested in anything else, had ordered it for me. It became a focal point of my life [and] gave direction to my every thought and move. Never did I read it from cover to cover. Indeed, I read in it very little; but I looked at the color plates over and over, often wondering why I had failed to see so many of the species pictured. I did not realize that the book was really about eastern, not midwestern, birds.

My interest in delineating birds took a serious turn. I had neither crayons nor paints, but I made a series of pencil drawings that I decided were good enough to keep. These I pasted together, end to end, making a roll of them. . . . The drawings are folded now, not rolled. But they are pasted together end to end, just as they were seventy years ago. I enjoy looking at them – and I smile as I look.

All the drawings were crude, crude beyond belief, but they were the result of sincere interest, and I am glad now that I was conceited enough to save them. The prize of the lot was the redwing, whose legs each had a tibiotarsal bone, a tarsometatarsal bone, and a fine short "extra" bone in between the two – providing the bird with a grand total of four ankles (and heels) rather than two. What a bird!

In the January/February 1915 issue of *Bird Lore* appeared my drawing of a pet roadrunner "in an attitude of fright." At the front of this same issue was an exquisite color plate of juncos by Louis Agassiz Fuertes. Publication of my drawing convinced me that somehow I had become a bird artist. It convinced me that I had a right to make myself known to Fuertes, to become personally acquainted with him. Perhaps, through knowing him, I could learn to impart life to my drawings. . . . I decided to write Fuertes.

I had felt for a long time that Fuertes would understand me; that he might, indeed, be the only other person in the world who felt as I did about birds. He would know all about my desire to draw them well, to capture their beauty.

Had Fuertes not said to me. . . that I was "going ahead nicely," might I have decided to give up drawing birds? Questions of this sort cannot, of course, be answered.

The very force which drives me, at times relentlessly, to do the best I can at drawing birds *is* Fuertes.

[One] letter from Fuertes was, in its way, the most beautiful I had ever received from anyone, for on its second page were three exquisite pencil drawings – one of a snowy owl, one of a deer's head, and one of a great horned owl holding a squirrel in its foot. I have looked at these drawings again and again, each time deriving inspiration from them and each time marveling. The hand that had drawn them was the hand of a genius. And that genius had gone out of his way to guide me.

George Miksch Sutton

I recall how amazed I was when Louis Fuertes showed me the trick of working out in detail the dark parts of a bird's folded wing, then of bringing the wing to life by covering all of it, except for the parts that needed to stay untouched, with a pale, swift wash.

Fuertes himself gave me one of his old paint boxes – a treasure I was to take with me four years later down the whole of the Labrador coast; seven years later down the Abitibi River to James Bay; ten years later down the Missinaibi River and the east coast of Hudson Bay; eventually time after time to the New World arctic, repeatedly to Mexico, once to Iceland. Never since the summer of 1916 have I painted a bird without having that battered old paint box somewhere close by. . . . There was something mystical about that paint box. Having it near me warmed my heart and gave me confidence.

I've never been able to dissociate painting from bird study. It's all part of the same thing. Putting things across in one way or another is the real thing. . . . I work directly from life in order to make my studies as authentic as possible.

On my Mexican trips, I made a point of drawing either live birds caught in nets or freshly killed birds. I wanted there to be a scientific record of exactly what the colors of a bird's fleshy parts are – the color of the legs, the eyes, the linings of the mouth, and around the beak. This is especially important for the rarer species, where the colors are often altered by age in museum specimens. Even photographs can distort the colors, depending on the quality of the light at the time or the angle from which the picture was taken.

Throughout virtually the whole of my career, I have used a well-sharpened hard pencil in drawing the outline of my bird before putting on any paint. I have learned that all too frequently there is such a thing as thinking that the outline is right, then charging ahead with adding details, only to discover that the whole bird is oversize. . . . A bird too big in outline may be ever so attractive when colored in, but it will still be too big.

Most of my paintings are watercolors. Oils are hard to take into the field, especially to areas where the moisture and temperature are uncertain. Also, there are problems reproducing oil paintings for publication because there are a lot of little glittering spots on the rough canvas that reflect the light.

The more details of plumage [the artist] shows, the less the bird figure moves. The human eye cannot see much detail in a flying bird; therefore, when the eye perceives every little feather, it tells the brain that the bird has stopped.

A bird artist cannot and, therefore, must not try to tell everything in a given drawing. He cannot show every feather as he knows it to be. If every tiny marking is to be the point of the representation, then why not work out a technique of gluing feathers to paper?

Queries that have crossed my mind over and over since that long-ago day when a fine arts department director informed me that my paintings were material for display ("a very nice display, too") in a natural history museum, but not in an art gallery, are these: Is bird art really art at all? What do we bird artists do to our drawings that keeps them from being art? Can it be that we who long so desperately to capture some of the beauty we have seen, and that we want others to enjoy, are not artists at all?

Is there anything basically wrong, basically dishonest, in showing jays of normal shape and color? Is such representation plagiarism? Does a bird artist prove himself a mere imitator if his blue jays are instantly recognizable as blue jays? Must a bird artist declare his "freedom," . . . his imaginativeness by making their bills and feet twice as large as they should be?

I recall deciding, once upon a time, that it would be good fun to paint a lot of snow-white birds in a cornfield and call the picture *Crows*. . . . A crow can, with wings spread horizontally in such a way as to form a mirror, become the exact opposite of black.

[As Fuertes told me:] "Remember what I've said about light, shadow, and reflected color. Black feathers struck by sunlight aren't really black. You know they're black, of course, but blackness is not what you see. . . . Black spots struck by sunlight are gray, not black, and the gray may have a blue tone if the sky is blue or a green tone if there's green vegetation close by." Never have I made a bird drawing since that day without bearing in mind those important statements.

I have no false notions about my standing today as a portraitist of birds. I have made many bird pictures, some good, some less than good. Many of them, even several of the poorer ones, have been reproduced so I have won for myself something of a reputation.

[Bird art] is a record of man's tussle with self. The beautiful creature, like the mountain, is there – the bird to be painted, the mountain climbed. The bird's beauty must be acknowledged, understood, captured. *I am the one to capture it*, says the bird artist. *I shall do the best I can.*

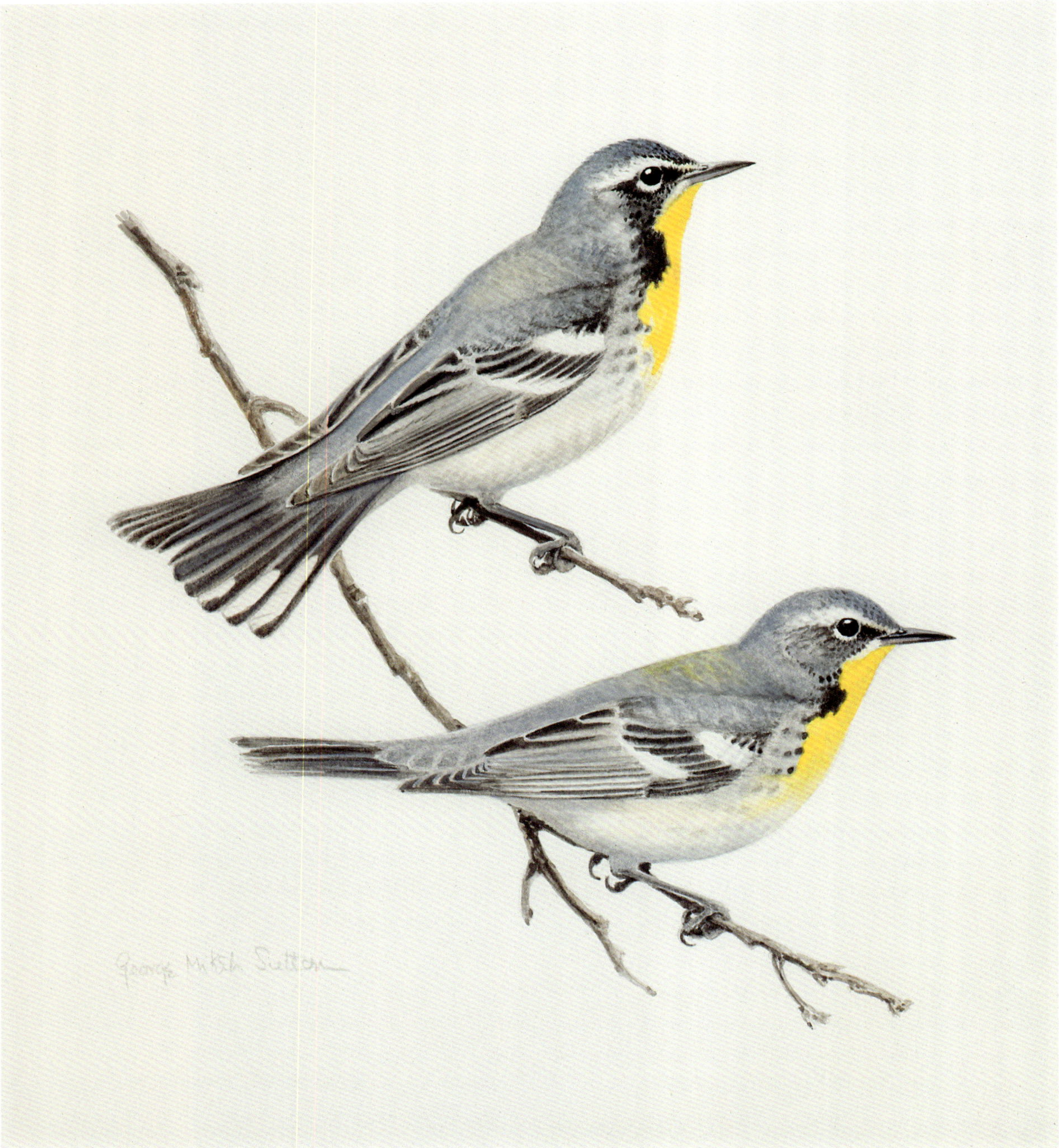

As ornithologists we observe a new bird half fearful that we may not see it again, and fully aware that we may never in our lives have a better look at it than this.

Sutton's Warblers 1939, watercolor on paper, 16 x 12 inches, collection of the Leigh Yawkey Woodson Art Museum. *Birds in Art* 1977.

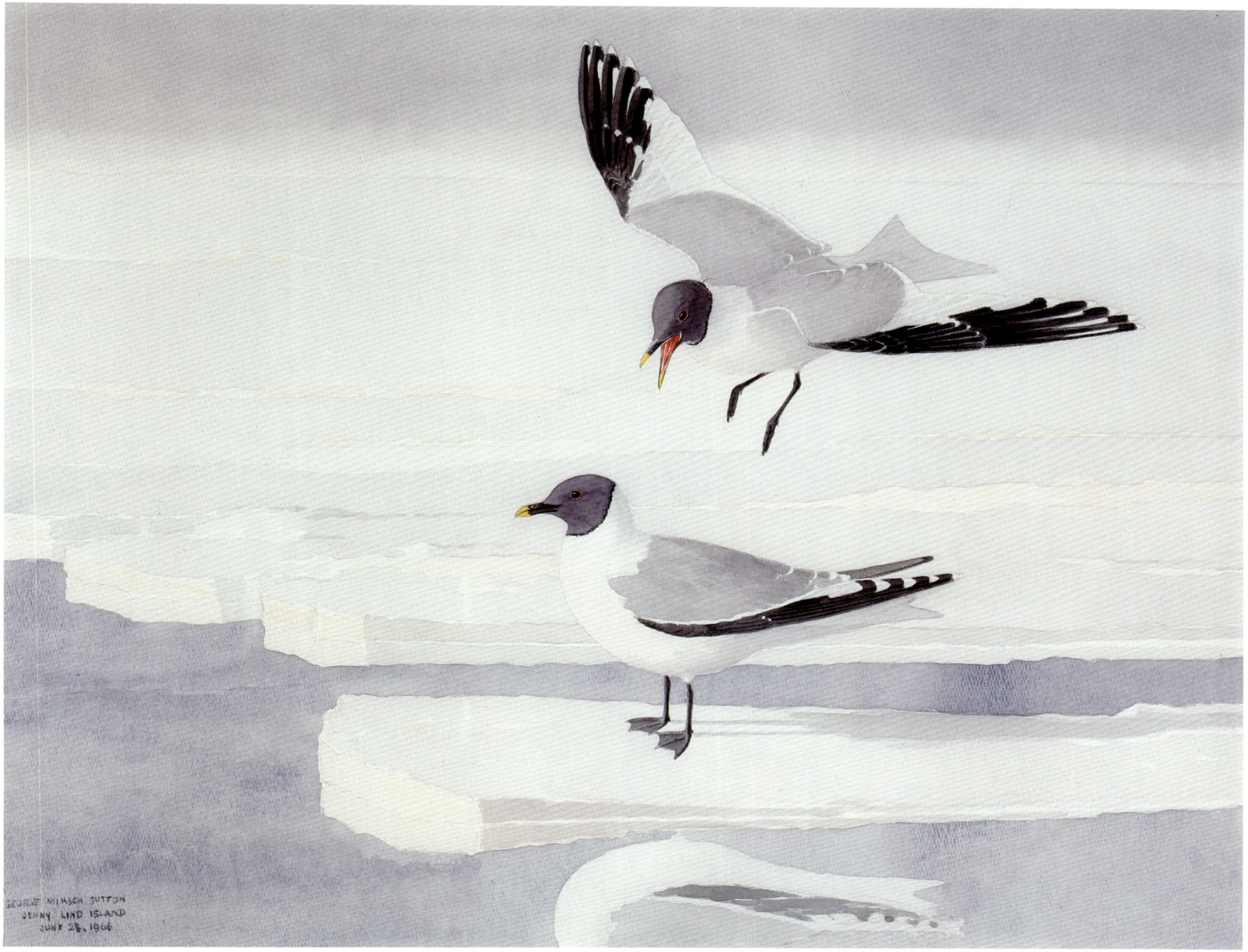

Sabine's Gulls 1966, watercolor on paper, 20 x 26 inches, collection of the University of Oklahoma Foundation, Inc., Norman. *Birds in Art* 1978.

What is a man to do when his purpose is to make other human beings see and feel what he has seen and felt?. . . Since he doesn't know exactly how birds feel, or what goes on in their brains, he has to set down what they seem to him to do – and let it go at that.

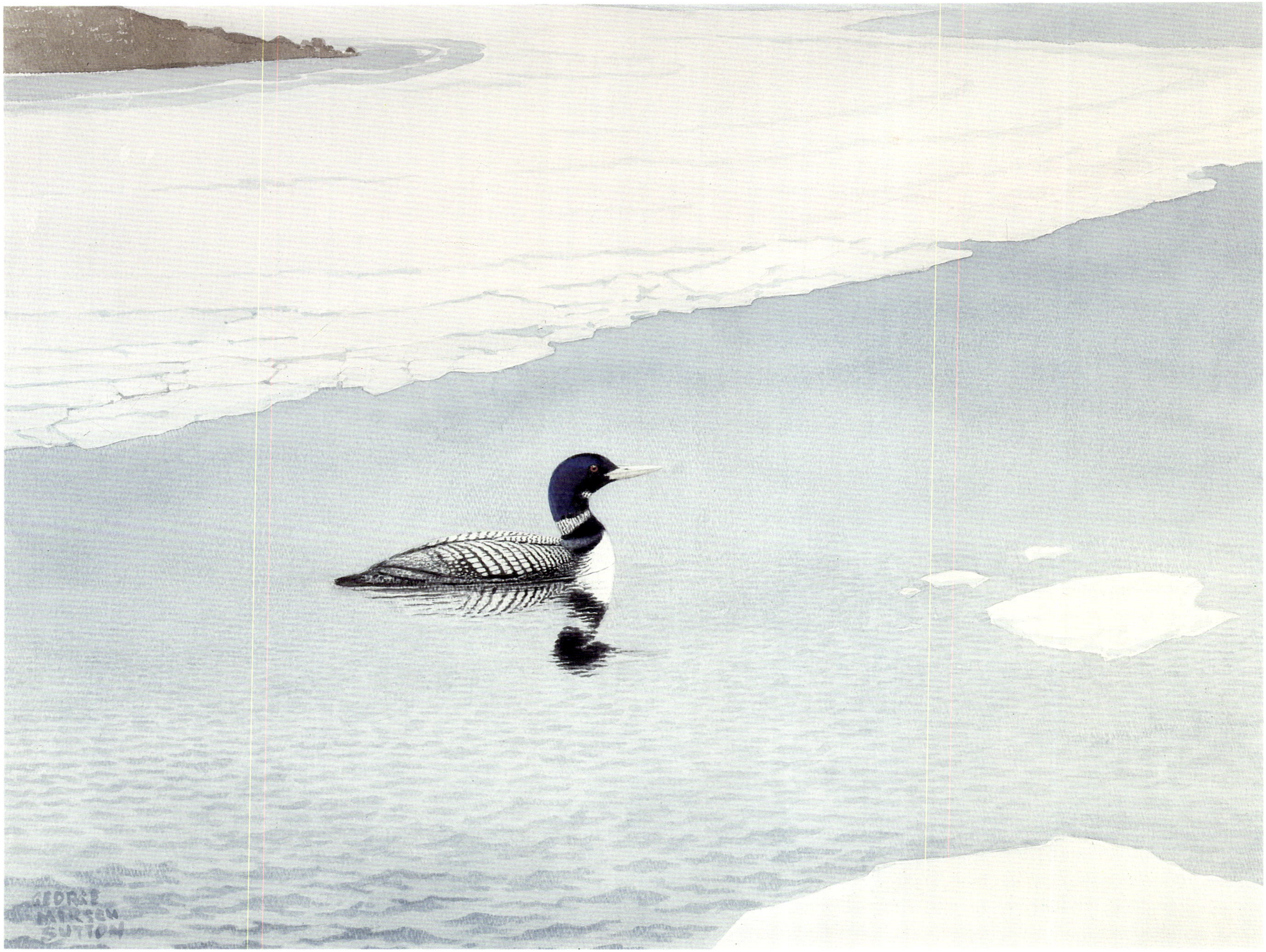

Yellow-billed Loon 1966, watercolor on paper, 18 x 24 inches, collection of the University of Oklahoma Foundation, Inc., Norman. *Birds in Art* 1978.

The human eye cannot see much detail in a flying bird; therefore, when the eye perceives every little feather, it tells the brain that the bird has stopped.

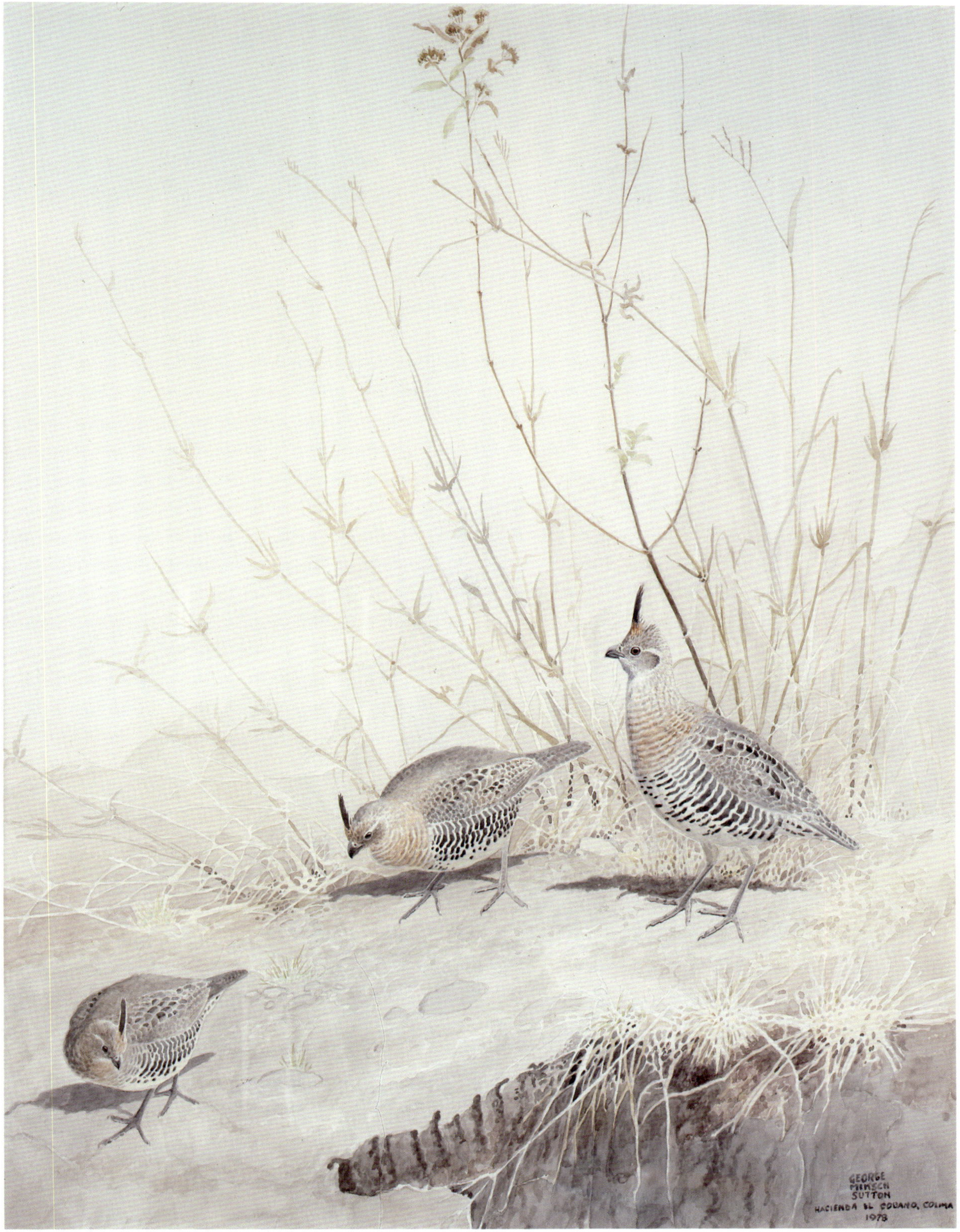

A piece of art should be an intensely personal declaration of what the artist sees and what he feels about it.

Barred Quail 1978, watercolor on paper, 30 x 24 inches, collection of the University of Oklahoma Foundation, Inc., Norman. *Birds in Art* 1979.

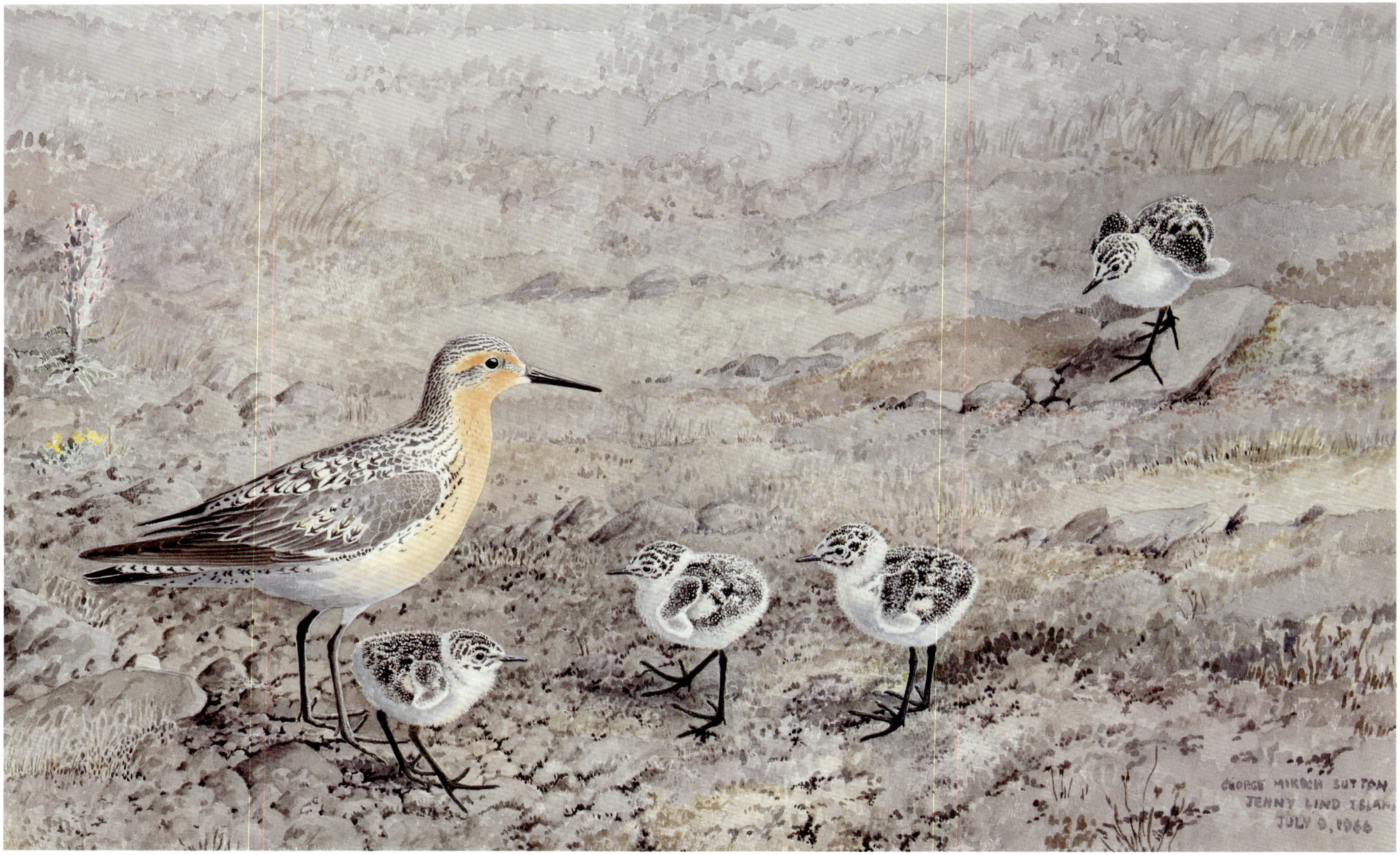

Red Knot and His Brood 1966, watercolor on paper, 14 x 24 inches, collection of John S. Shackford. *Birds in Art* 1982.

Through struggling to portray birds well, I am, in my way, arguing for their protection.

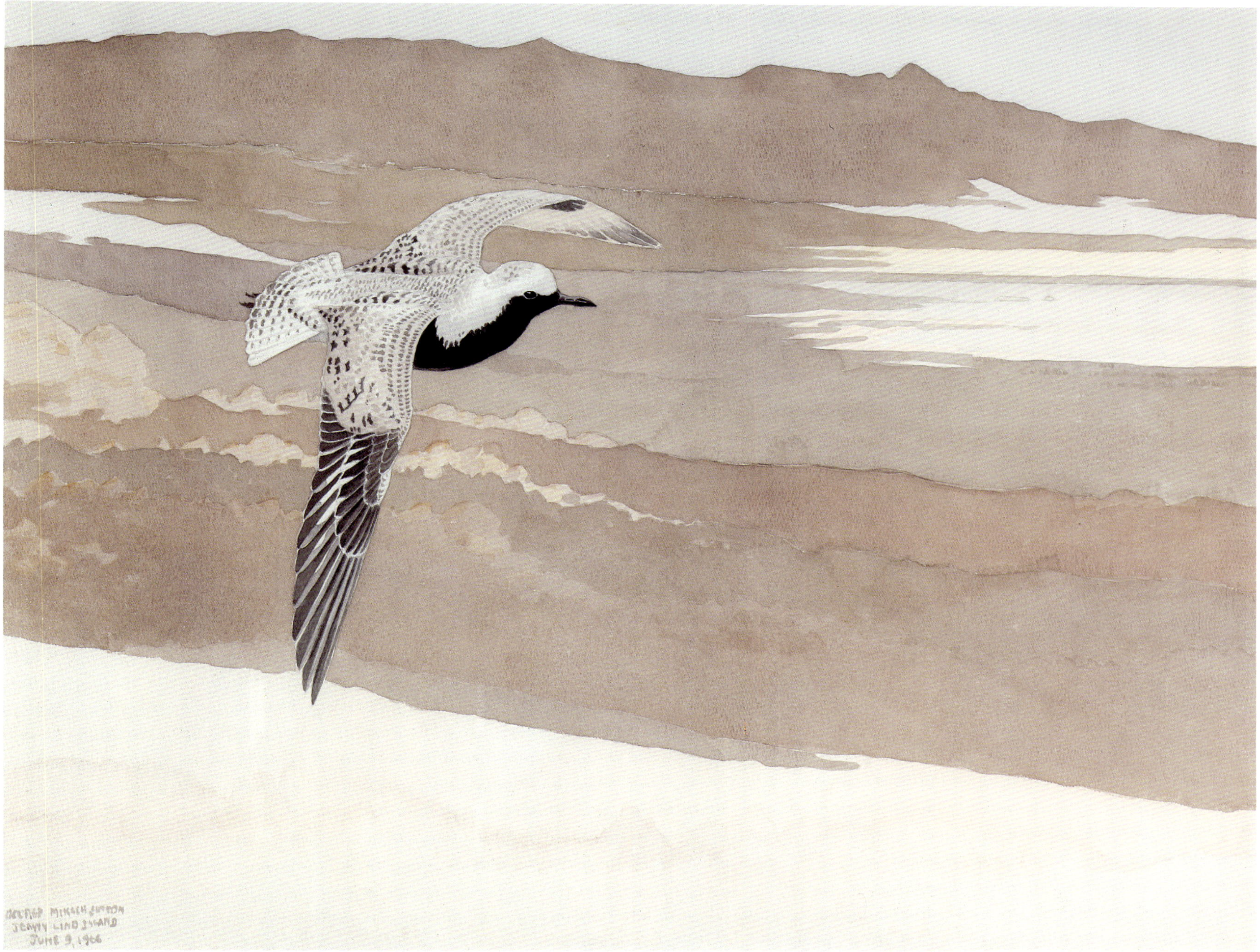

Black-bellied Plover 1966, watercolor on paper, 20 x 25 inches, collection of the University of Oklahoma Foundation, Inc., Norman. *Birds in Art* 1976.

No bird of passage shall fly north or south / Breasting the stiff wind or pushing through the fog,
But I shall be there, feeling the deep urge / That drives it otherwhere at summer's ending,
And otherwhere once more with spring's return; / Ever so thoroughly I shall learn
The signs a bird must travel by, / The many ways in which a bird can die.

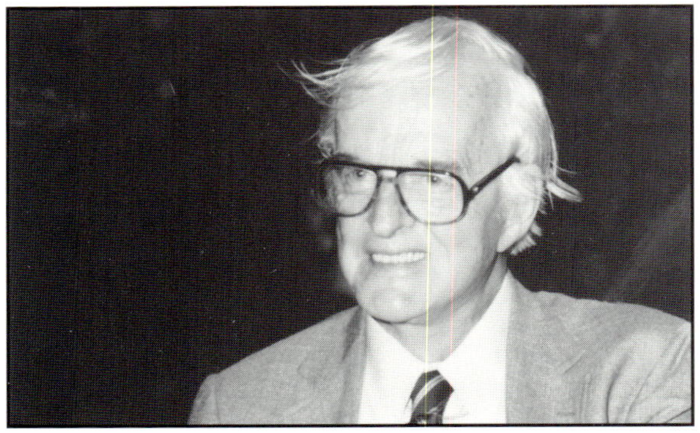

ROGER TORY PETERSON

Master Wildlife Artist 1978
Born: 1908, Jamestown, New York
Resides: Old Lyme, Connecticut

Birds have been the focus of my existence since I was a boy of eleven. For more than seventy years, they have occupied my daily thoughts, filled my dreams, dominated my reading.

My seventh grade teacher, Blanche Hornbeck, started a Junior Audubon Club. For a dime, we each got Audubon leaflets with a drawing to be colored. Our teacher also gave each of us a little box of watercolors, a brush, and a color plate from Fuertes' *Birds of New York*. I was given the blue jay to copy, and I thought I'd done very well. Later, when all the paintings were put on the blackboard, mine was credited to the girl across the aisle. I was very upset, and I made it plain the blue jay was mine. That was my first attempt to draw birds – copying Fuertes' blue jay. I've always rather liked blue jays.

Another critical event happened about that same time. One Saturday, a friend and I went exploring south of town. We crossed the railroad tracks and climbed up Swede Hill into a woodland. I saw a bundle of brown feathers on a tree trunk and, thinking the bird was dead, I touched it. All of a sudden, wild-eyed and in a splash of color, the bird flew away. It was a flicker that was sleeping, probably after migration. Something I had thought was lifeless was very much alive – like a resurrection. It hooked me on birds. Ever since, for me, birds have seemed to be the most vivid expression of life.

When I was a teenager, I read Ernest Thompson Seton's *Two Little Savages*. There was a character, Yan, who saw some ducks mounted in a showcase. He sketched them so he could recognize their colors and patterns at a distance in the field. I thought that should be done for all birds, so in a way that was the germ of the idea for my field guides.

Later, when I was becoming more and more obsessed with birding, I tried to locate a book that would treat *all* birds in this manner. . . . I wished for a *visual simplification*, a boiling down, so that any bird could be quickly named with certainty in the field. No such book existed.

It was during the succeeding years, while I taught natural history and art at River's School in Brookline, Massachusetts, that I prepared my first field guide.

You might say Bill Vogt was the midwife to my field guide. He knew flowers very well, so when we went on field trips, he taught me the flowers and I taught him the birds. One day he said that if I put my knowledge of birds into a book, he would take it around to different publishers. We took the book, which was rather crudely done, to five publishers before Francis Allen, a senior editor at Houghton Mifflin and a very fine birder, saw the potential and the validity of it. But one editor voted against it. This was during the Depression, 1934, and he didn't think enough people were interested in birds to pay $2.75 for a book. The first printing of 2,000 books sold out overnight. Today, a copy of that first printing brings over $1,000 in the collector's market. I don't have one myself.

There was a great leap forward in bird watching in the mid-1930s, partly because of my field guides, partly because of the Audubon movement, and partly because of the National Wildlife Federation.

Up until then, the only way an ornithologist could make a positive identification of a species in the field was to shoot it and examine the carcass. My idea was to identify each species by physical characteristics which could be seen through binoculars so the birds wouldn't be harmed.

The "Peterson System," as it has been called, is a visual one consistent with field birding. It is based on patterned drawings with arrows that pinpoint field marks. These rather formal illustrations and the direct comparisons between similar species are the core of the system, unlike the more traditional bird portraiture found in most bird books. My illustrations are deliberately schematic and in similar profile for the sake of direct teaching or communication.

Field guide paintings have been called another art form. I call them illustrations, and they take a lot of discipline and knowledge. The paintings are done double size because detail is very critical where bird identification is reduced to simple patterns and marks. The first edition was almost too elementary – I reduced speckled birds to two simple patterns. I have since modified the paintings because we have better binoculars now.

For reference, I use my memory, my notes, and specimens, and I usually make a lot of sketches. I might study photographs, but I don't copy them. Photography can be very useful, but a photograph is the record of one moment, a split second, whereas a drawing is a composite of your experience. When you draw, you can edit and showcase to the best advantage. For field guide paintings, I start out with transparent watercolor and some gouache, and I might pull myself out of the fire by using acrylics. But my proper paintings are usually done in oil.

When I am painting for the field guides, I try to portray the character of the bird rather than my own character. But, when I paint more environmental pieces, I try to reveal my reaction to the bird. For me, the bird is most important. Every bird has a personality. They're very different. They're not all chickadees at the window.

Roger Tory Peterson —

A naturalist, to be honest with himself, cannot stray too far from realism or representational drawing, regardless of what the "art establishment" has to say. Now that the public is more environmentally aware, good bird art is no longer dismissed simply as "bird illustration."

Until recently, however, wildlife painting had seldom been considered "Art" (with a capital A) by the galleries and curators who dominate the art scene. But, I submit, those of us who paint wildlife, because of our fascination with the other creatures that share our planet, are just as true to ourselves as those who interpret the New York or Los Angeles scene as they see it in their abstract way. To us the "real" world is the natural world, and we cannot be other than realists in our interpretation of it.

There has been a burgeoning, almost explosive, interest in wildlife, especially birds, resulting in a breakthrough in environmental awareness on the part of the public. This has led to a greater understanding and acceptance of what the wildlife artist has been trying to say.

I hope the viewer of my paintings gains insight into the natural world. Basically, I am a teacher, as my mother was. I am a visual person, and that's why I enjoy painting. I like the form and the play of light. I enjoy the birds for what they are.

I am best known for birds, but I don't focus entirely on birds. I am an all-around naturalist, botanist, and mammalogist. Butterflies are also very important to me. But birds are so visible and so alive, they tend to attract more people than most other fields of study. A really good bird person usually becomes interested in the whole environment.

I act as editor of the field guides. We now have forty-one titles, everything from grasshoppers to stars. Someone has said my real contribution to the world of environmental awareness is putting millions of field guides into people's hands. True environmental ethics must be founded on a true understanding of natural history – after all, that's what ties this whole thing together. You first need to have a name for something before you can identify it. Why, even Rachel Carson learned her birds from my books.

A great naturalist will feel emotionally involved with nature. Humans are a part of nature; we cannot be separated from it. You cannot separate grasshoppers and leaves from birds or people. We are only part of nature, only one form of life. A great painting has to give the feeling that the artist knows the bird. It may be painted with great delineation or purely the fall of light. It should be accurate, but it does not have to be like bird in hand.

Today, there are literally thousands of men and women who paint or draw birds. Some are painterly illustrators inspired by Liljefors, playing with three-dimensional activity, mood, and light. Others are delineators following the tradition of Audubon or Fuertes.

The Leigh Yawkey Woodson Art Museum gives credibility to the best bird artists and to a wide spectrum of representational art. I feel a greater sense of friendliness, ease, and camaraderie when I am in the company of wildlife artists than I feel with any other group – and that includes the hotshot birders and professional ornithologists. Probably the greatest benefit of *Birds in Art* is that we get to know each other, exchange ideas, and raise the standards of bird art.

I recently heard someone say how extraordinary it is that this narrow focus of birds is so well represented. I got miffed. I thought, "Well, *Homo sapiens* is one species; the birds are at least 8,600." How can you call it narrow?

A friend of mine, who is a priest, said that watching birds can be a religious experience. I responded, "Well, of course, birds are God's messengers. The only other creatures with feathers in their wings are the angels." Birds are as much bound by natural laws as we are, but it doesn't seem so. They have wings. It seems as though they can fly wherever they want to, whenever they want to. Birds symbolize a kind of escape.

Free as a bird?. . . Ironically, the birds, which had symbolized freedom to me when I was a boy, seem to have enslaved me. Under the pressure of my publishers (and myself), I became a workaholic, averaging ten to twelve hours a day at my desk and drawing board – seven days a week, month after month, with time out only for the essential field work. . . . The paintings for most of these reference works were within the constraints of traditional ornithological illustration, several species on a page, rarely allowing for more inventive expression.

I look forward to returning to proper painting – juicier, more painterly canvases, with mood, three-dimensional activity, and movement in space. They will be a step beyond the Audubonesque portraiture for which I am best known, and some will be environmental. It may take me awhile to get into full stride and to experiment. We will see what happens. Perhaps finally I can really feel "free as a bird!"

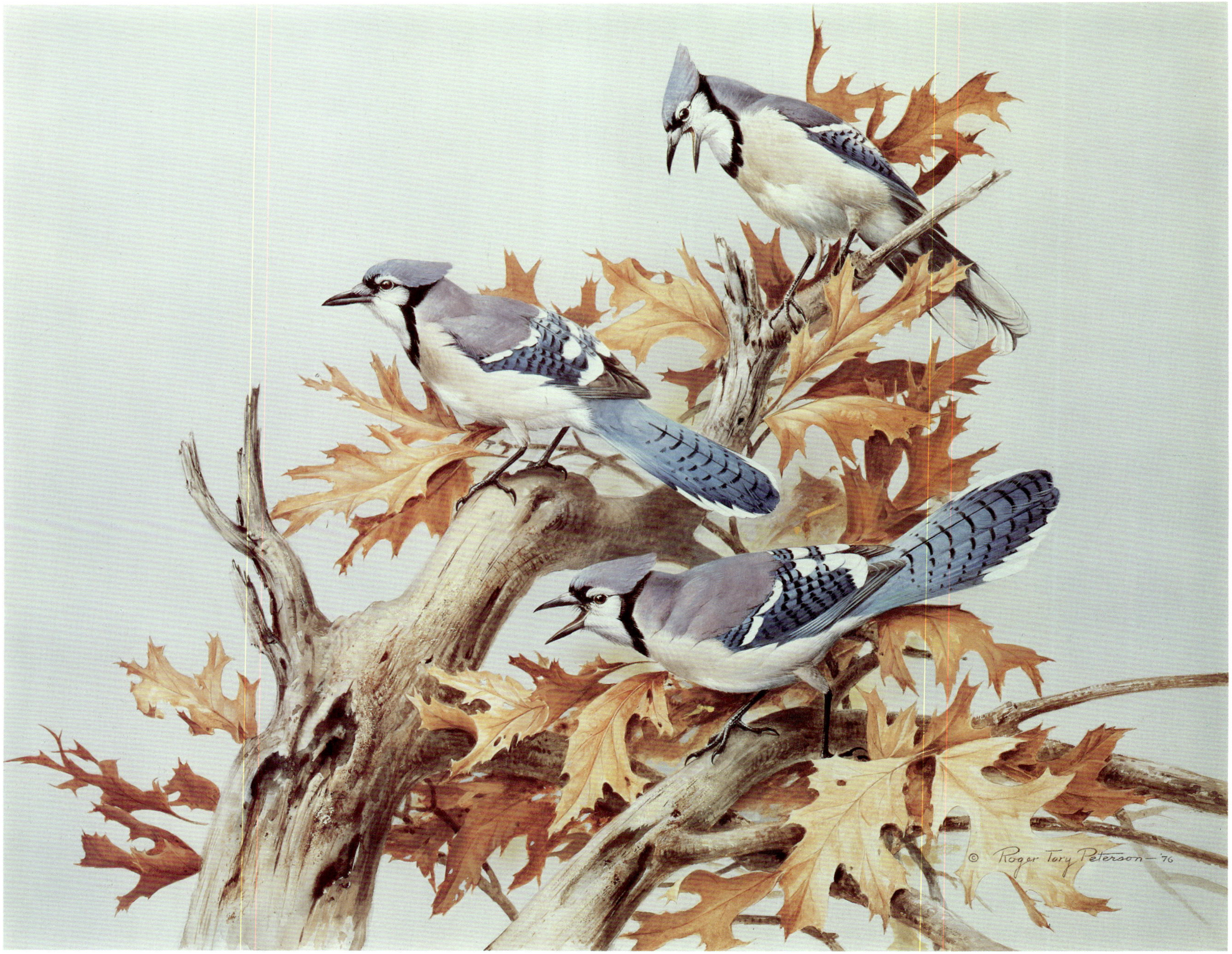

Blue Jays 1976, watercolor and gouache on board, private collection. *Birds in Art* 1985.

Our teacher also gave each of us a little box of watercolors, a brush, and a color plate from Fuertes' Birds of New York. *I was given the blue jay to copy, and I thought I'd done very well. . . . That was my first attempt to draw birds. . . . I've always rather liked blue jays.*

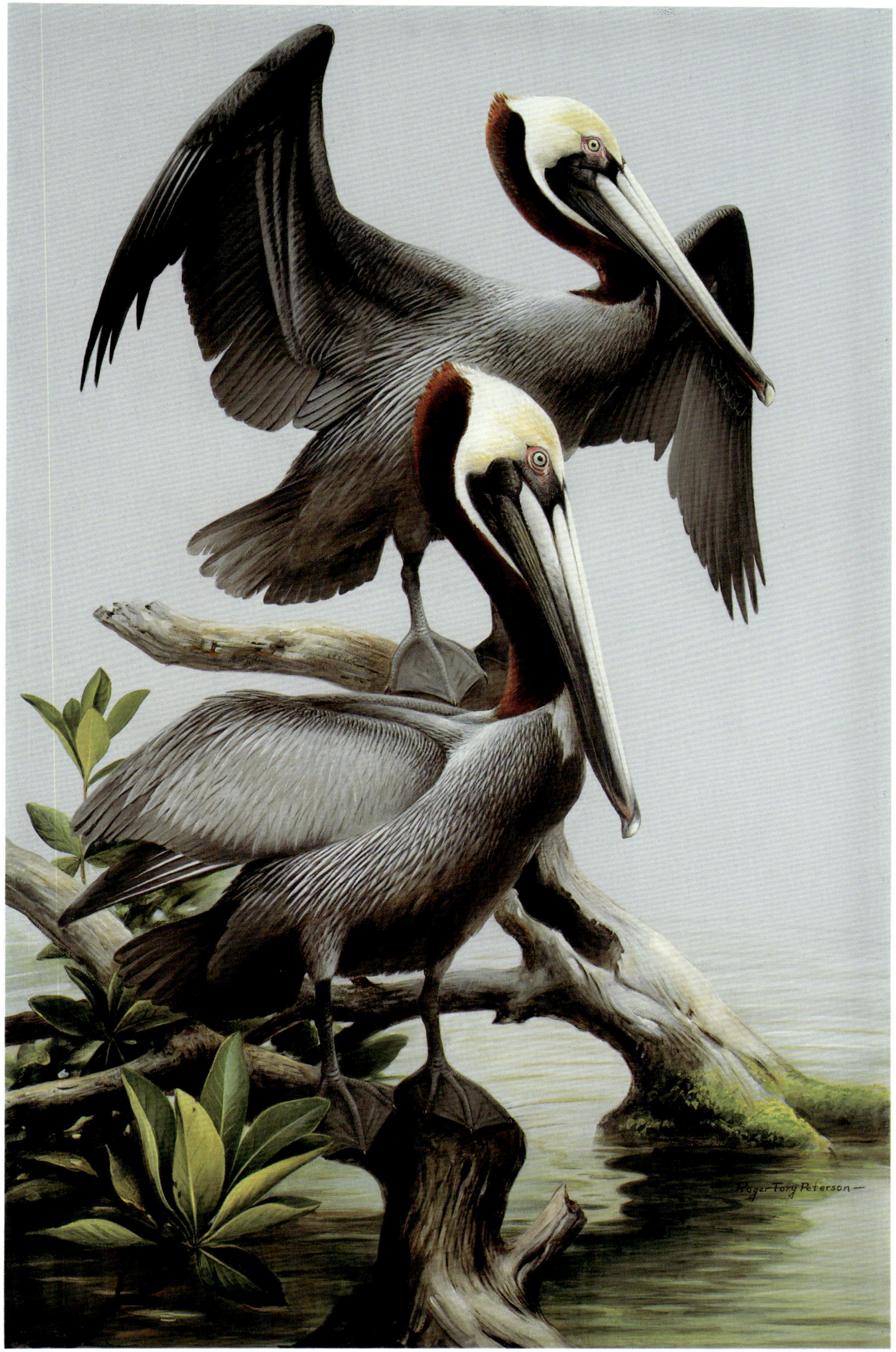

I met Fuertes in 1925. He was the first great one since Audubon, and he gave me one of his own paint brushes. I took it with me to a camp in Maine where I had a summer job. I kept the brush on a shelf, but somehow it rolled off and fell through a crack in the floor. The next year I ripped up the floorboards, but only the handle was there; mice had eaten off all the bristles. In a way, it returned to nature, to a mouse's nest. My own view of the world is that everything is so interlocked, you cannot separate one thing from another.

Brown Pelicans, watercolor, gouache, and acrylic on board, 36 x 24 inches, private collection. *Birds in Art* 1986.

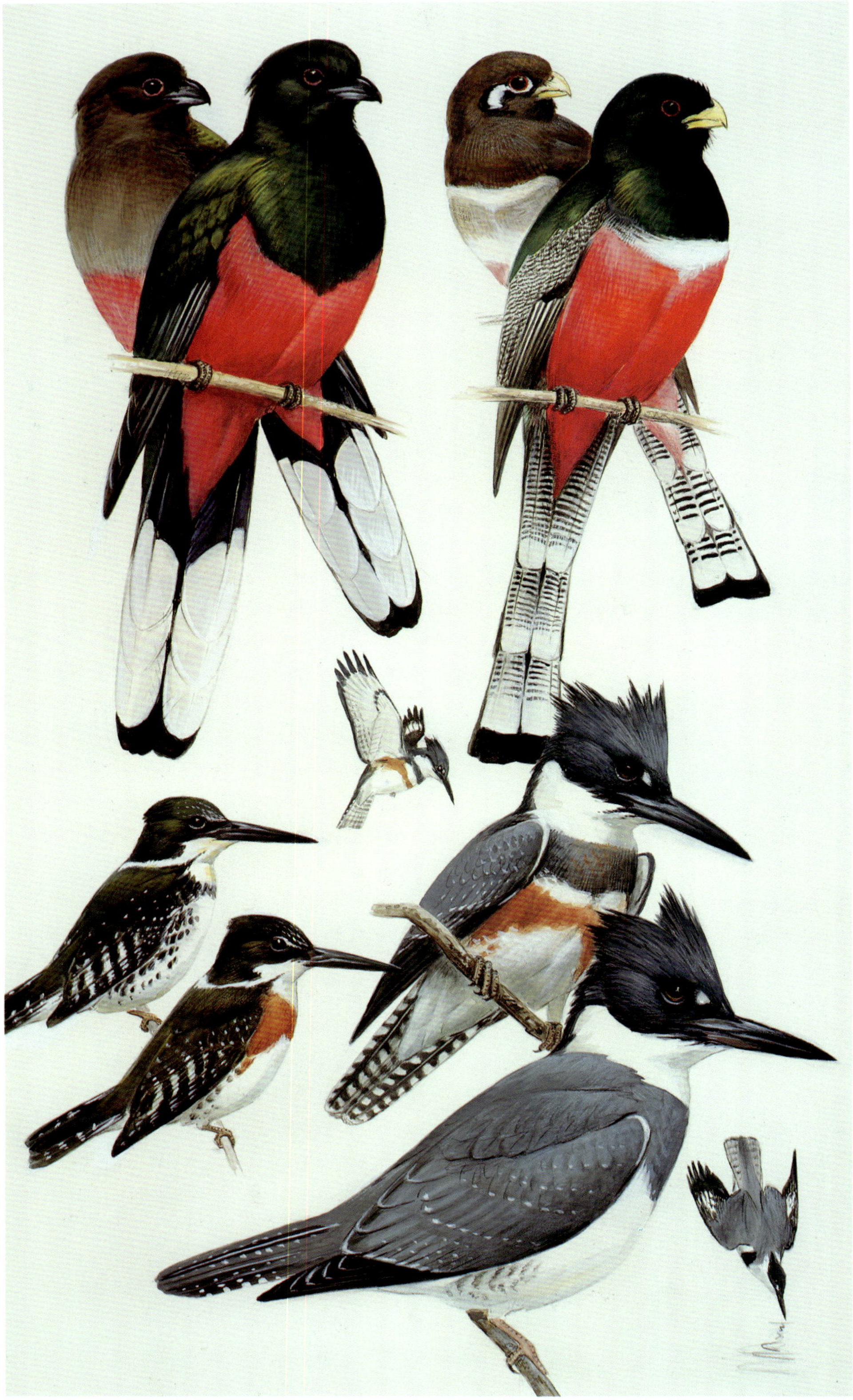

The many bird portraits I've done for guides were straight illustrations in which the main goal was to simplify each bird's feather patterns and highlight the easily identifiable features of coloring. There is little or no opportunity for personal expression in this type of work.

Trogons and Kingfishers (eared and elegant trogon; green and belted kingfisher) 1989, mixed media on board, 18¼ x 11¼ inches, collection of the artist. *Birds in Art* 1989.

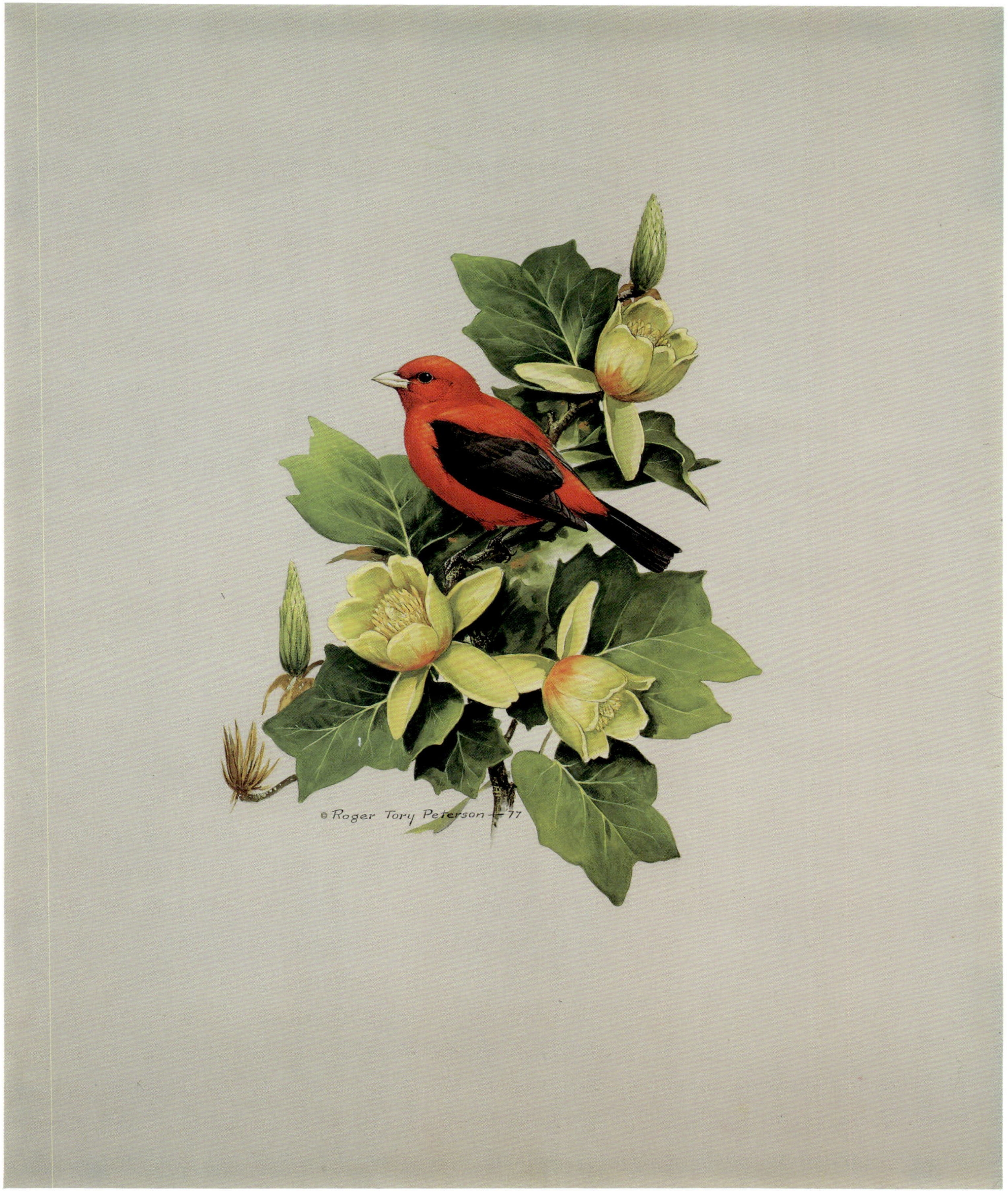

My fervent desire is to see the soils safe-guarded, the waters unpolluted, the forests and grasslands properly managed, and wildlife protected. To attain these ends means not only self-preservation but also a better future for the race. Conservation is plainly a moral issue.

Scarlet Tanager 1977, watercolor and gouache on board, 22 x 18 inches, private collection. *Birds in Art* 1977.

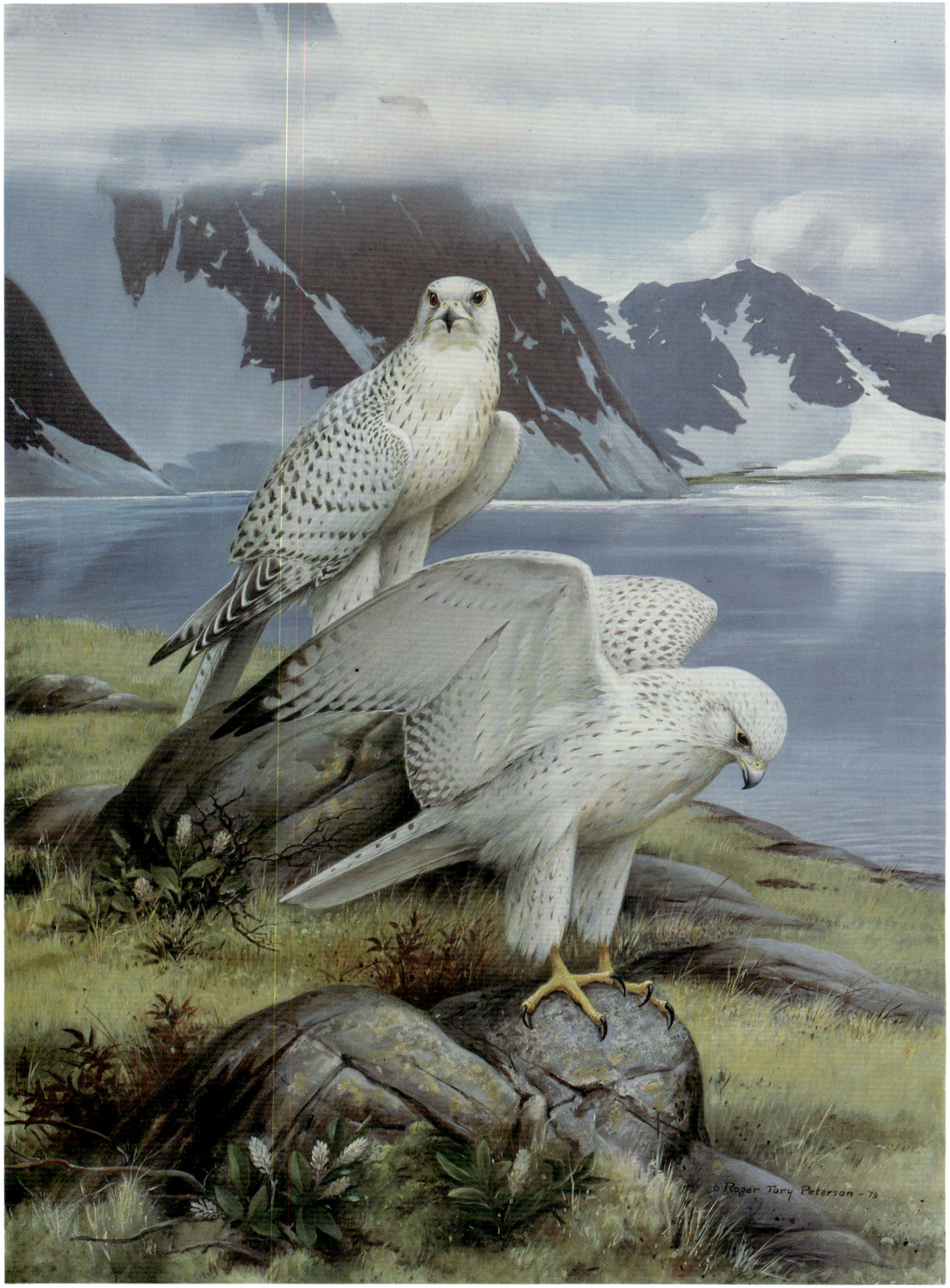

Many birds are camouflaged to blend with their surroundings, but when you paint a bird, you want it to stand out from the canvas. If you paint realistically, very often you cancel things out. It can be done, but it's a matter of arrangement and design.

Gyrfalcon 1979, acrylic and watercolor on board, 38 x 28 inches, collection of the Leigh Yawkey Woodson Art Museum. *Birds in Art* 1979.

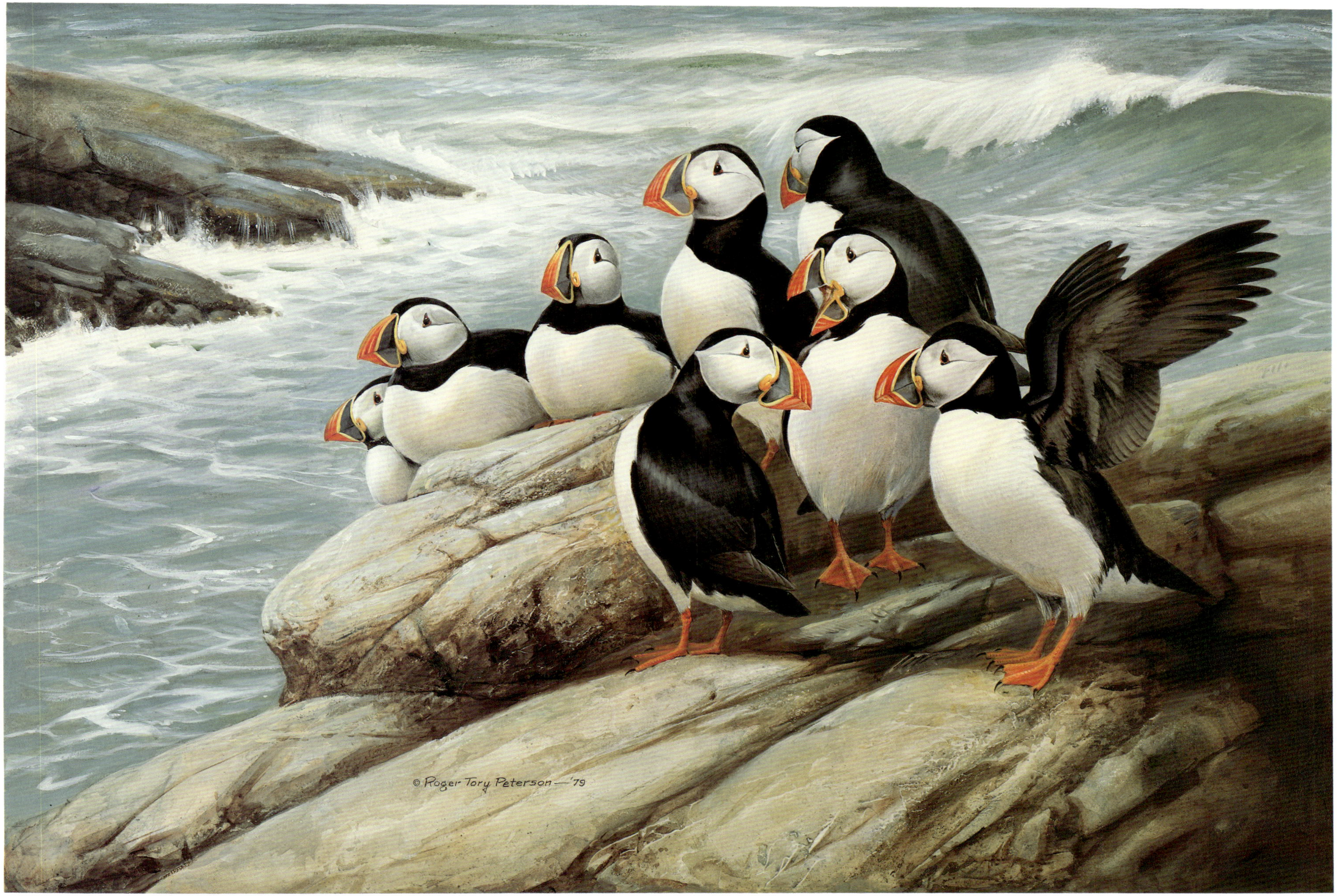

Puffins (Atlantic puffin) 1979, mixed media on board, private collection. *Birds in Art* 1979.

A great naturalist will feel emotionally involved with nature. Humans are a part of nature. You cannot separate grasshoppers and leaves from birds or people. We're only part of nature, only one form of life.

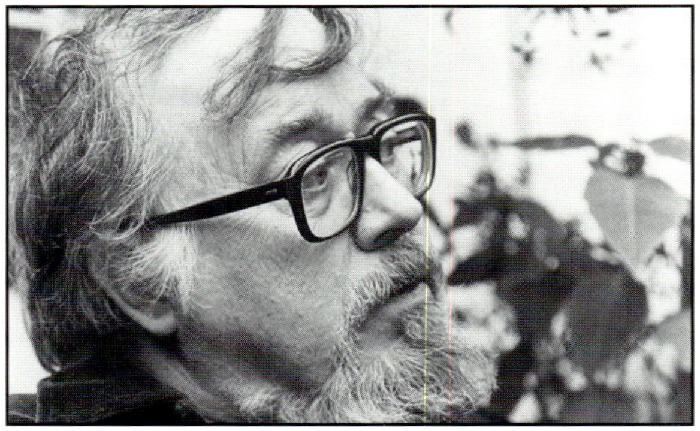

DON RICHARD ECKELBERRY

Master Wildlife Artist 1979
Born: 1921, Sebring, Ohio
Resides: Babylon, New York

What is art, any form of art? I have come to the conclusion that it is an equation, that art equals structure plus feeling, or architecture plus emotion. You have to have these two polarities. If it is art, it has to have both. But there is a wide range in between the highly architectural and the highly emotional.

Nature art has always lived in a sort of no man's land between art and science. A lot of people who understand art know that a lot of wildlife art is, in fact, not art. Art is a matter of intent. Hemingway knew when he was being a journalist and when he was being a novelist. I know damned well when I am illustrating and when I am painting. It may be the same material, it may still be birds, but in the one case, I am trying to inform people about, for instance, a black-throated green warbler, and, in the other case, I am trying to express a feeling about black-throated green warblers. Illustration is harder in one way because you have to know so much about your subject. But painting is harder in another way because you have to know your feelings so well.

Realism has been out of fashion since photography became a viable form of visual information. In part, the rejection of realism was to get around photography. In any case, the replication of an object cannot be considered art, otherwise all photography would be art, automatically. I am not putting illustration down, having spent about eighty percent of my time doing it and trying to do it well. It is just a different thing.

No one considers the chirp of a cricket, the roar of a lion, the song of a bird, or the rumble of a volcano to be music which the composer should carefully attempt to duplicate in his compositions. Why then do people persist in thinking that to reproduce accurately the visual appearances of these same things is to create graphic art? . . . I do not believe that art has anything to do with visual appearances. It is not what is seen but *what is felt* in what is seen that counts; in other words, not sight but insight.

Craftsmanship is that command over the mechanical difficulties of a medium which every artist needs to facilitate his expression. Oftentimes, this "means to an end" is taken for the end itself by the artist, by his audience, or both. Thus, virtuosity – or technical competence – is often confused with art. Craftsmanship is an accomplishment in its own right. . . . But it is the extent to which the artist goes beyond this in his expression and his design of the picture which determines its aesthetic value.

You paint out of your own experience, interest, and desires. I think artists have to be selfish. I paint in order to understand how I feel. I have the feelings I have about birds and other animals because I grew up in a little town with woods all around. I was a loner and I tramped the woods. When I was thirteen, I got an air rifle and, unfortunately, I started to shoot birds. I didn't know what they were, so I went to the five-and-ten-cent store and bought these little red, blue, and green bird books. Frankly, my intent was to shoot every bird in the book. Now that wasn't so much a life list as a death list! I got interested in birds and in nature around them. To me that was a great delight, and I've had a passionate interest in nature to this day.

I have always drawn. My earliest memory in life is drawing a streetcar. I don't know what age I was, but certainly under five. The child who draws, draws whatever interests him – conquistadors, sailing ships, or pictures from books. When I got interested in birds, I started to draw them and I really got hooked.

When I paint, I usually start out opposite from the way I start out illustrating. If I am illustrating, I have the bird skin in front of me, I have my preliminary drawing, absolutely exact, and I have it on the board exactly where I want it – the whole thing is prearranged before I wet a brush. If I am painting, I don't know what's going to happen. It's like having something nebulous or amorphous in my mind, which I am trying to bring into focus.

In one painting of a March scene, I wanted to express the feeling of a blowing, evening sky with just a line of trees where the sun had already set and a wet snow lay rotting on the ground. I started out with the general composition, an abstraction really, a blocking-in of the picture in the broad sense. I did not even know what bird to use until the picture was well along. A bird may be selected for its color, rather than species, or for its size in relation to the painting. Compositionally, I needed a light-colored bird against the dark woods rather than a dark bird low against the snow or high against the sky. What light-colored bird in March flies at twilight? A barn owl. I first painted

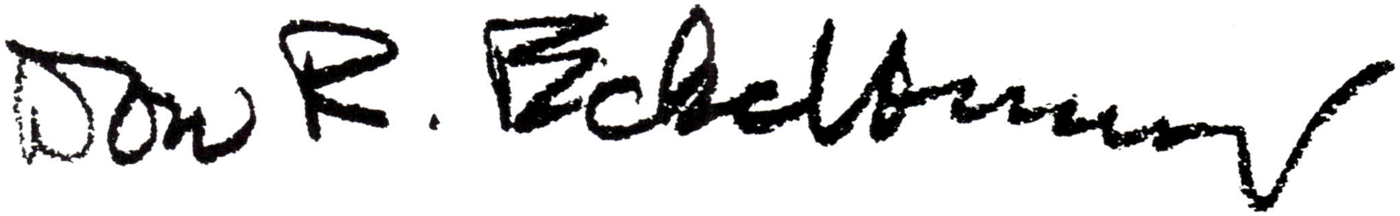

the owl rather roughly and wondered why it didn't work. Then I realized the background didn't move when the owl was rough. If the background is blurred, the owl had to be fixed to make the whole picture move. So I added detail to the owl, being careful not to add more than I needed, until it worked. The owl hung on the wind and the background moved past behind it. These considerations never arise in illustration.

To young painters I would say, look at everything as though you have never seen it before. If you are painting a robin, go look at a robin. You have seen robins so much you don't even see them anymore. Try to keep a fresh eye. Use anything that helps you, but don't depend just upon photography – it's so seductive, so much easier than drawing or seeing for yourself. Bird photographs can be misleading. If you don't know the bird, you won't know if the photograph shows it in an unusual pose.

Because I trust my eyes, none of my skimmers has eyes. The eyes on skimmers are black in a black area so you don't see any reflection. So I painted them without eyes. That's the difference between intellectual realism and objective realism. Intellectual realism is when you paint what is there, whether you see it or not. Objective realism is when you paint only what you see, even though you know what's there. I have worked both sides of the street, having been an illustrator and a painter.

I've made my living as an illustrator with only a little time on the side to paint. It's hard to be so near and yet so far. Sometimes I've thought I should have been a bag boy at the A & P instead of doing the drudgery of illustration while being so near to painting. The fun of illustration was always the fieldwork and the field experience. It was great living with all sorts of people in all sorts of places. But coming back home to the hard, plodding work of illustration was very tiresome to me because it didn't engage me enough. I would look longingly at that big canvas on the easel, knowing I couldn't paint on it for weeks or months to come. The happy part of illustration is in the research. The painting part of illustration is a bore, but the painting part of painting is a joy, especially when it is going well. It is as though you are in a trance, and afterwards you cannot say how you mixed that color or why, because you are so into it; you are so much a part of the painting.

Why do people paint? Why do people write books? Why do they need to express themselves? Why don't they just look and enjoy like millions of other people? Some say it is to make other people happy, but I don't think that's at all true. I think it is to make themselves understand what they are seeing and feeling. To explain themselves to themselves. My suspicion is that art is a form of neurosis that begins in childhood somewhere. For a "normal person," the lawn sprinkler goes back and forth and it sprays a nice even spray out over the lawn. For the artist, somebody kicked the lawn sprinkler and it got clogged up, except for two or three holes. But when the water comes out of those holes, you have a real gusher! So instead of dissipating feelings through all the aspects of life, the artist's mode of expressing feelings is concentrated and that's the reason one goes into art.

Art is powerful. If it doesn't come to you, if it doesn't grab you, if it doesn't have an arresting quality, it's not good art. I don't mean it must hit you like a sledgehammer – in nature, a spider's web has great tensile strength. Delicate can be strong. But art is never limp, it is never weak, it never just lies there like cooked vegetables on a plate. Art has to have impact. You've got to say, "Wow!" – whether you're looking at its delicacy or its magnificence.

I have done a few things that have the impact I wanted. But not always. I am usually disappointed. I think sometimes an artist is always painting the same picture and a writer is always writing the same book, over and over, hoping finally to get it right, to leave out all the non-essentials, so nothing stands in the way of the message. It's mostly disappointment, but on occasion, you get it right.

I view my own time period as a bridge to what I hope will become the real flowering of wildlife painting. There is still a lot of sorting out to do, but I think wildlife art is on its way. Time was maybe out of sync for me; there just wasn't the market for painting in those days. That's why I tried to help younger artists. I thought by the time they matured the time would be ripe for wildlife art, and it is ripening. I wish the times had been more in sync with the painting I wanted to do, but I have no regrets. I've had a great experience in both illustration and in painting, and I am very satisfied, very satisfied.

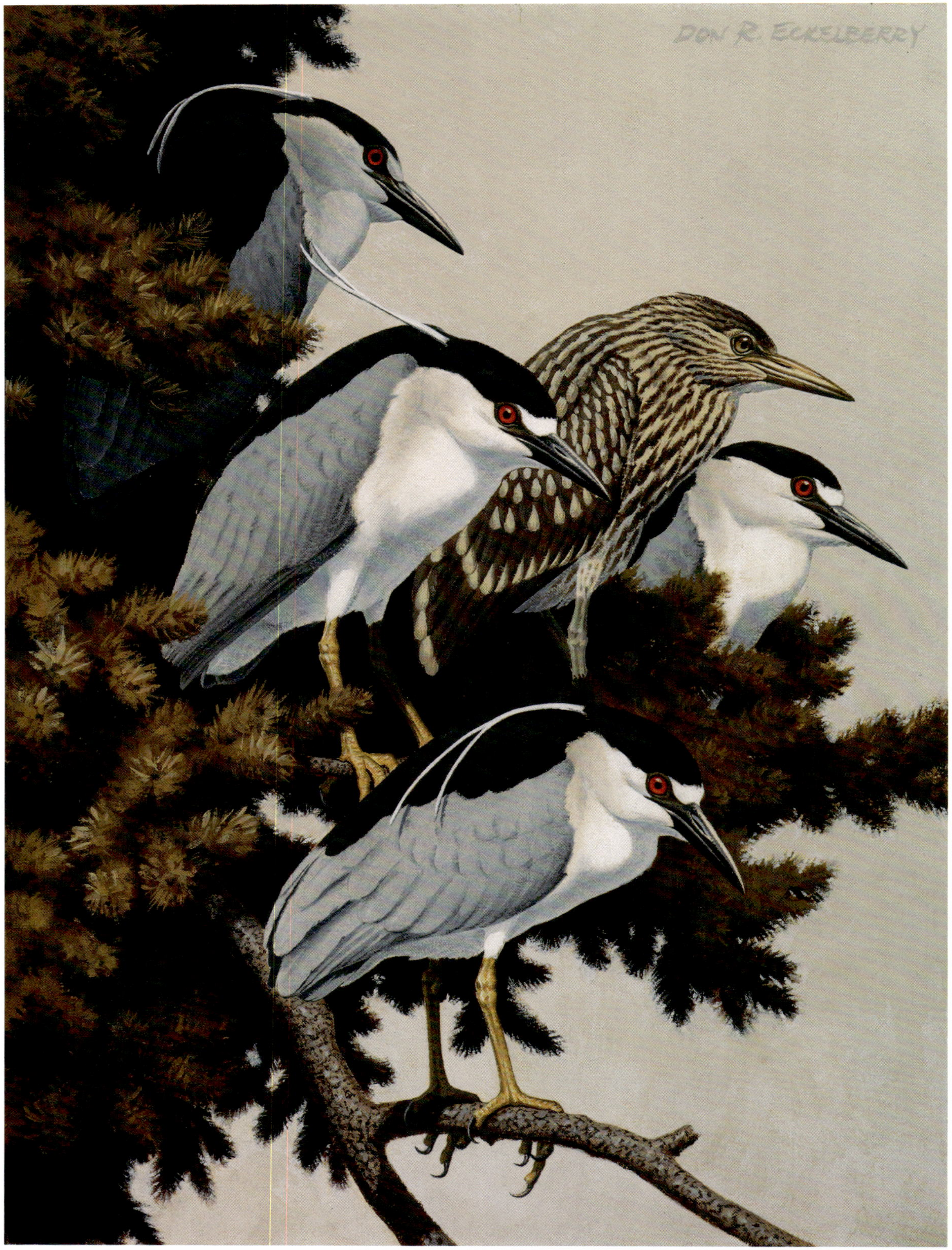

When a painter looks at nature, he is confronted with a confusion of colors, values, and shapes. . . . And from all this complexity, he chooses a few things. . . [to] convey. . . the feeling which impelled him to paint.

Black-crowns Roosting (black-crowned night heron), oil on board, 18½ x 14½ inches, private collection. *Birds in Art* 1980.

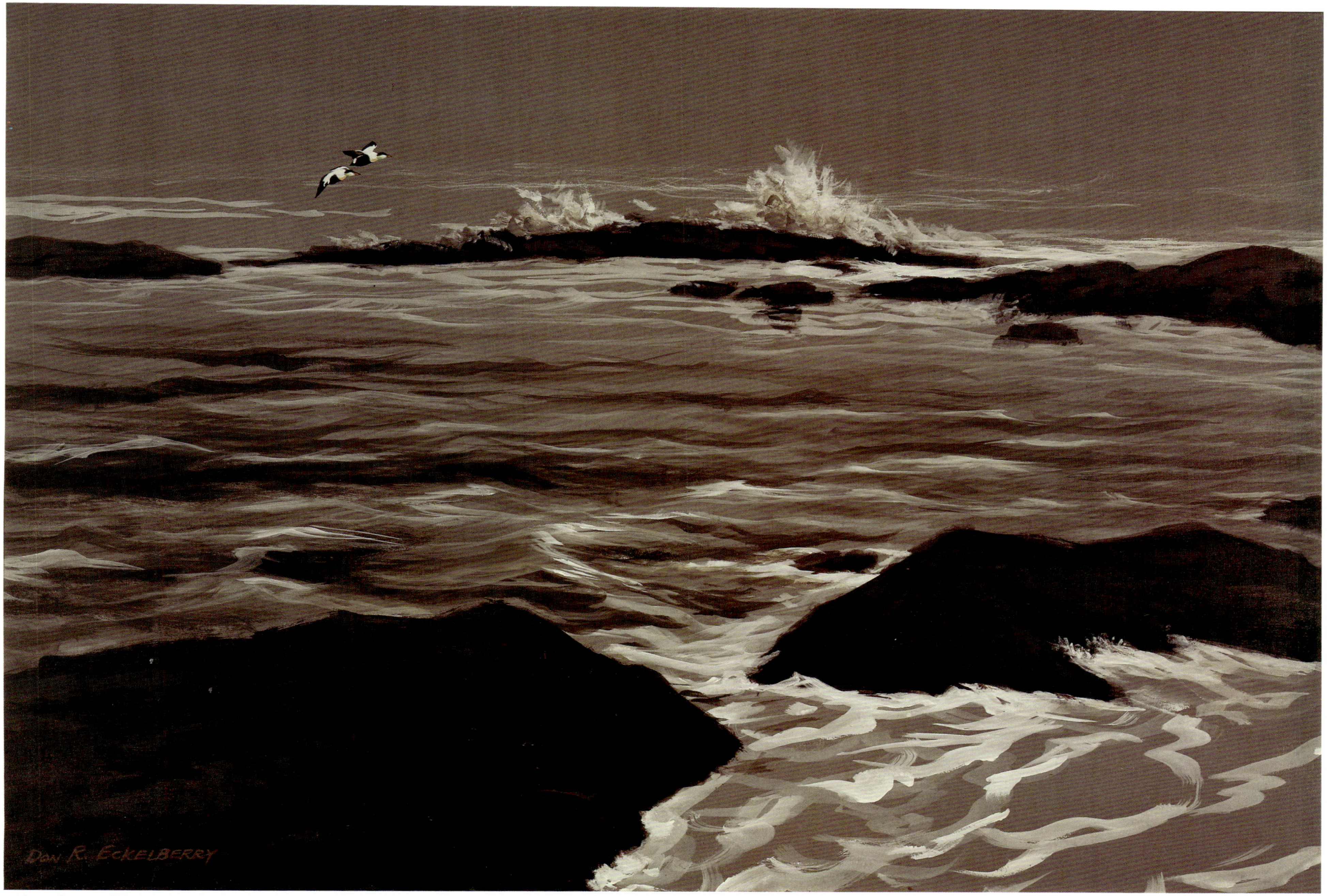

Eiders Flying Offshore (common eider), acrylic on board, 19½ x 29¼ inches, collection of the artist. *Birds in Art* 1978.

Wildlife painting. . . requires a particular knowledge of and interest in life-forms that often are difficult to observe, let alone pin down to a sitting.

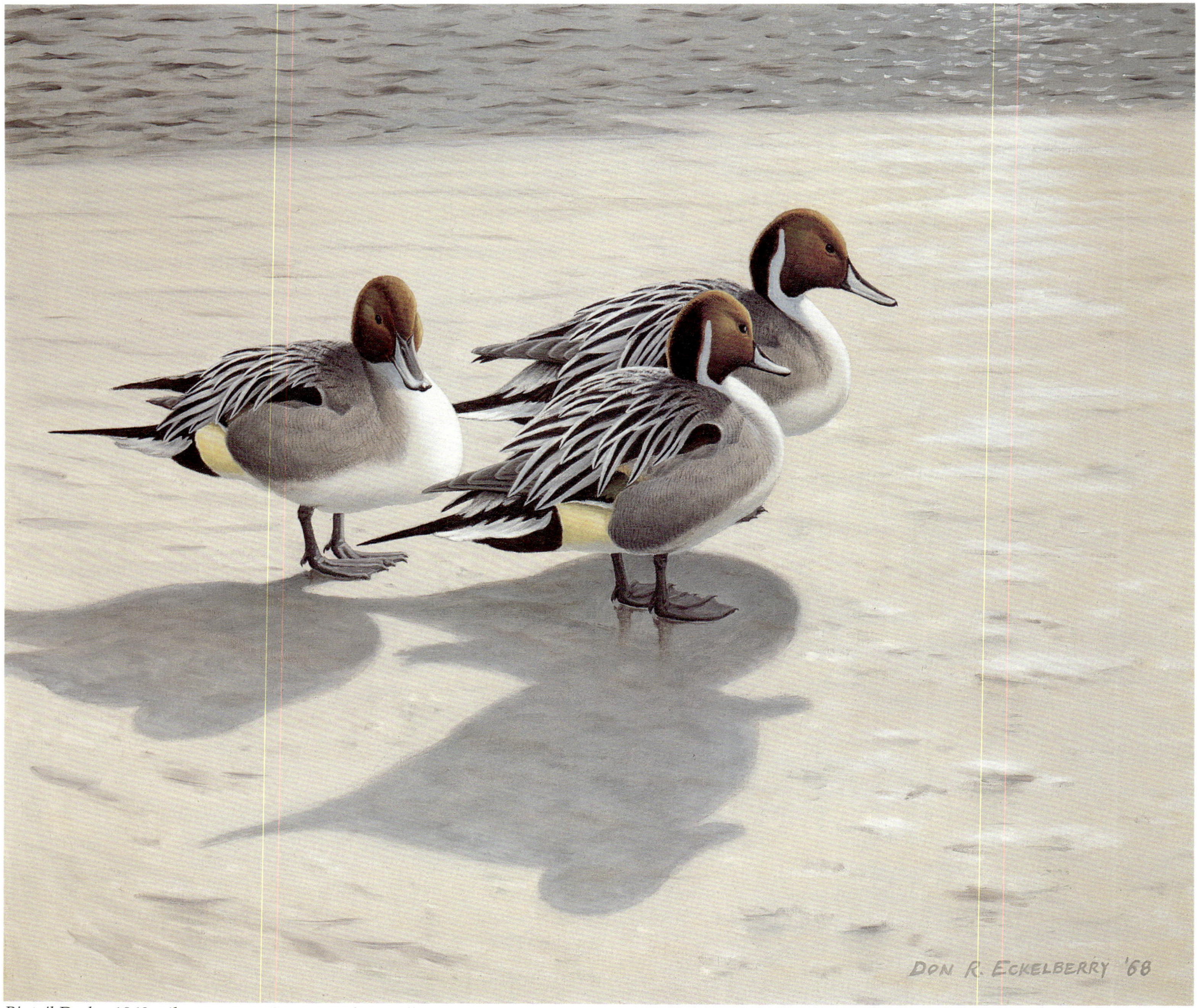

Pintail Drakes 1968, oil on canvas, 31 x 37 inches, collection of the National Wildlife Federation, Washington, D.C. *Birds in Art* 1981.

I do not believe that art has anything to do with visual appearances. It is not what is seen but what is felt *in what is seen that counts; in other words, not sight but insight.*

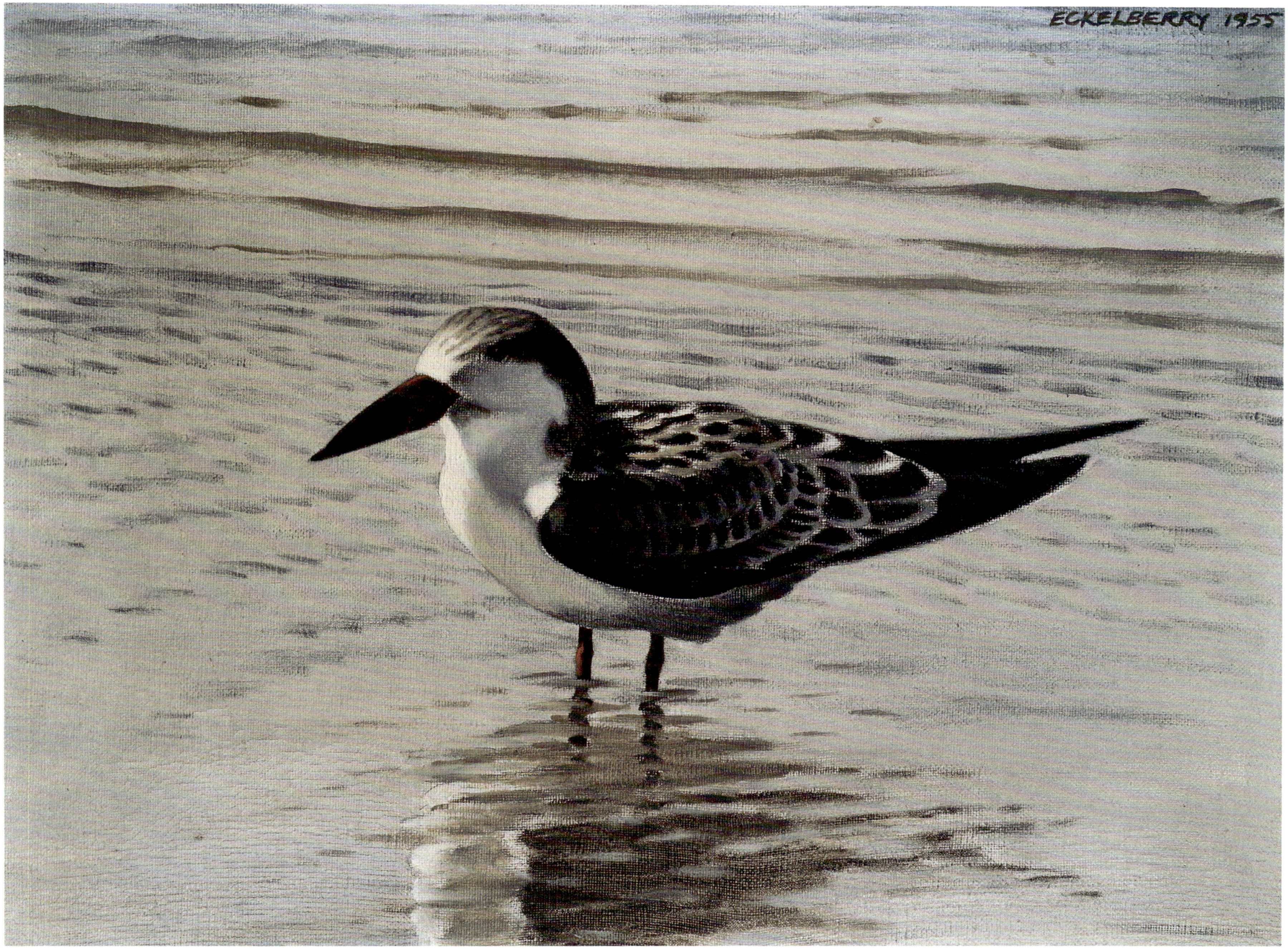

Young Skimmer (black skimmer) 1955, oil on canvas, 12 x 16 inches, collection of Virginia N. Eckelberry. *Birds in Art* 1979.

Art is powerful. If it doesn't come to you, if it doesn't grab you, if it doesn't have an arresting quality, it's not good art.

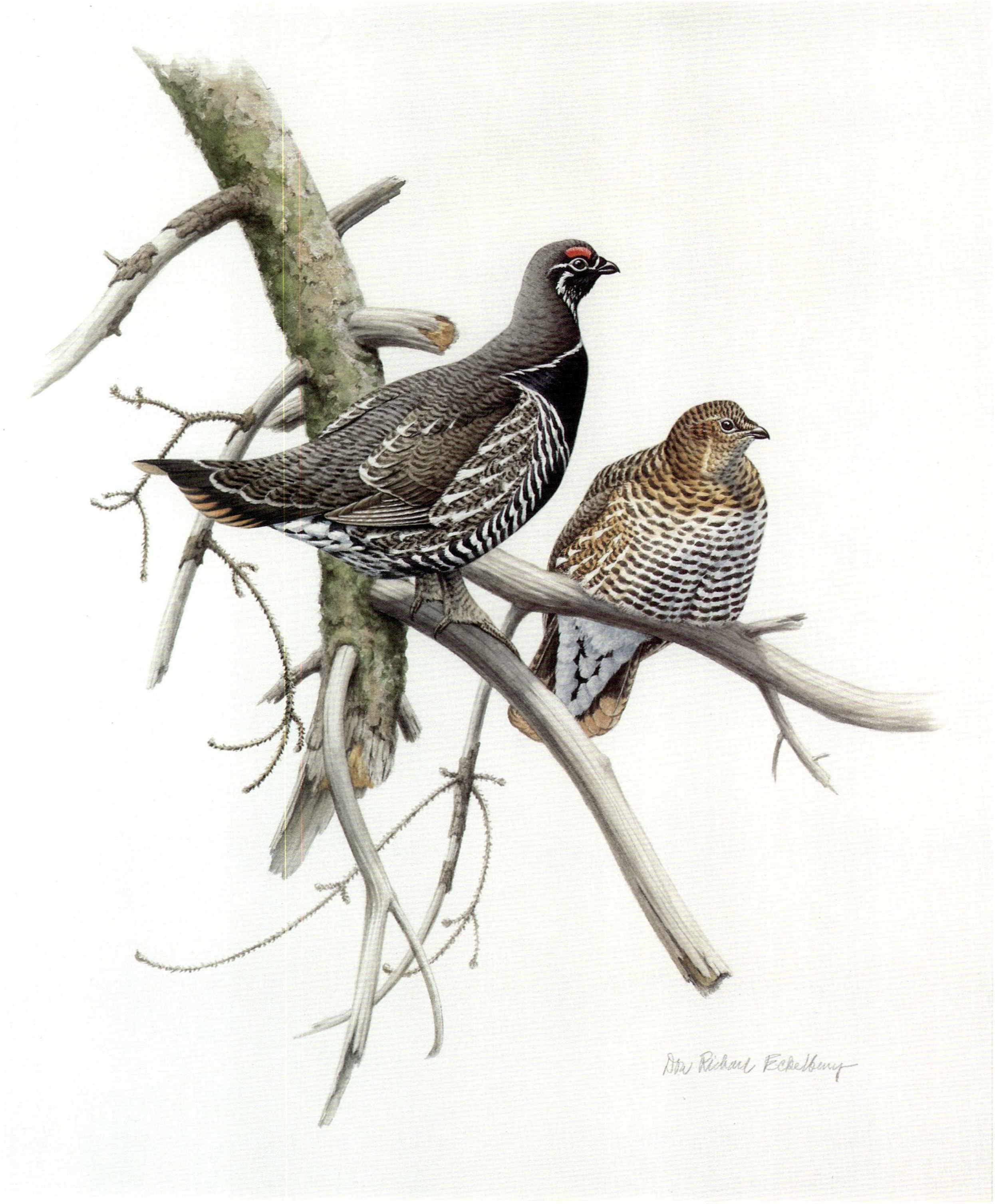

I view my own time period as a bridge to what I hope will become the real flowering of wildlife painting.

Spruce Grouse 1971, watercolor on paper, 30 x 26 inches, collection of the Leigh Yawkey Woodson Art Museum. *Birds in Art* 1979.

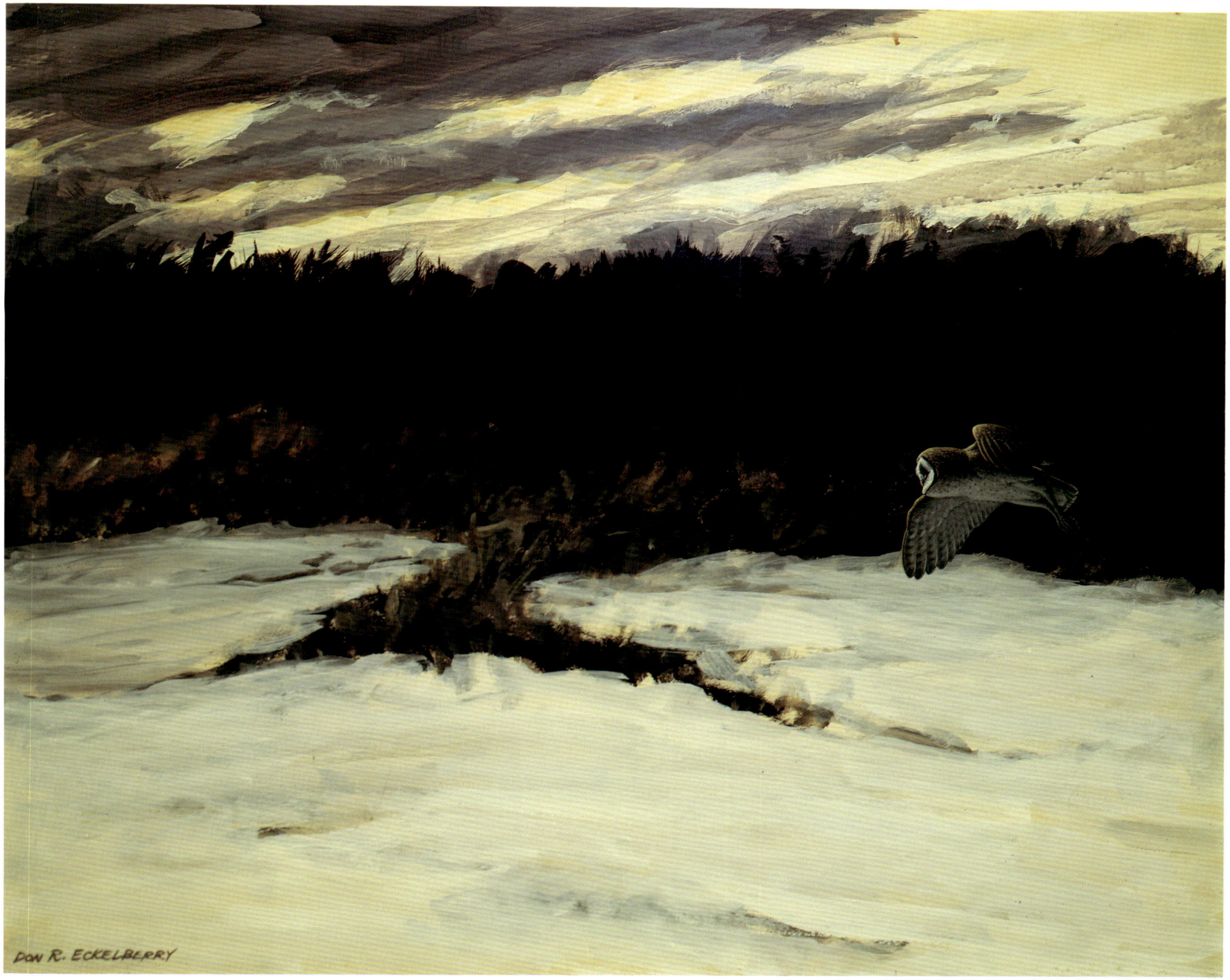

Evening Flight (barn owl), acrylic on board, 32 x 40 inches, collection of Virginia N. Eckelberry. *Birds in Art* 1977.

An artist perceives the aesthetic component of nature which can be expressed but not defined.

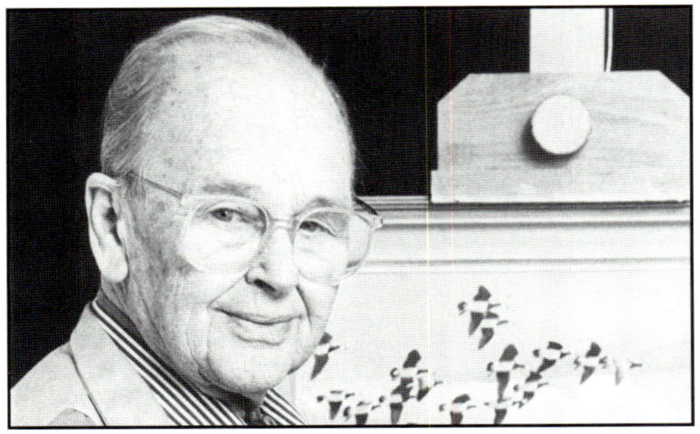

PETER SCOTT

Master Wildlife Artist 1980
Born: 1909, London, England
Died: 1989
"Make the boy interested in natural history. . . . They encourage it at some schools." Captain Robert Falcon Scott, Antarctica, 1912 (Last written message to his wife, Kathleen, before his death, regarding son, Peter.)

I have been a naturalist at heart ever since I can remember. And, I have always drawn or painted. I tried to be a biologist and abandoned that about halfway through my academic career to become a painter.

I was likely, I thought, to paint best those things which moved me most. That meant my wildfowl. They had never been painted in the way I saw them. . . . What I wanted to do was extraordinarily simple and easy. I had only to put on to canvas to the best of my oil painting capacity the birds as I had seen them at dawn or dusk or moonlight, or in storm or frost or snow, and I could not fail to be doing something original.

When I paint birds, I like them to be the right shapes and the whole effect to be as seen in nature. It is important to me to make an attractive composition which suggests the forward movement of their flight. Flocks have such beautiful composition. My style and technique are usually governed by my zoological training so that I try to avoid distorting what I know to be the correct shapes of the animals or plants that I am drawing or painting.

I draw quite a lot from nature. I also do a great deal of drawing from what I hold in my memory. [Sometimes] I go straight to the canvas and start putting paint on. Of course, an oil painting is the most wonderfully malleable thing.

But more often I set out to paint a commission, which means that the picture must have some preordained elements – some features which the commissioner required in the picture. This may involve a series of rough pencil drawings, usually smaller than a post card, to get a basic composition into my head before I start. It may call for aids of various kinds, field sketches and photographs to remind me of the place and the creatures I am going to paint, although most of my painting is done from memory.

My pictures have been sold in my own country largely to the shooting fraternity – wildfowlers in particular. They want to be reminded, in the comfort of their homes, of the excitement of their sport. Having been a hunter myself for many years, I can easily understand the appeal which leads to this steady demand. But the trouble with such a situation is that it dictates a limited number of subjects – the quarry species of waterfowl – and leads, in the end, to a type of picture in which the birds are not too large nor yet too small, the sky is "interesting" and the marshy landscape is attractive, while neither is allowed to detract from the quarry. There is room for some artistic creation in the sky and the landscape and in the positioning of the birds to suggest movement, but the upshot is a kind of formula which guarantees a sale but limits invention and innovation. It begets a degree of slavery to commissions.

I quickly discovered that if I worked too long on a painting, I was quite capable of ruining it. Working fast was the secret of quality as well as quantity. But I was also brimming over with new ideas. I could not wait until one picture was finished before starting the next, and I soon found that this was, in fact, a practical method; the first stage of one picture could be drying while the next was started. It also gave me the chance to adjust my work to my mood. If I was feeling creative, I could start on a blank canvas; if not, I could go quietly on with the chores – putting on a large area of blue sky, or laboriously painting up flocks of birds whose shapes and patterns I had already determined.

If beauty is truth and truth beauty, how much freedom is left for the imprint of the artist's individuality? When color photography was invented, what was left for the bird painter who believed, as I did, that nature had achieved a perfection that was sacrosanct? Who was I to distort the shapes, to exaggerate the colors, to try to improve on nature? Yet when an artist sets out to paint three-dimensional nature in two dimensions, the process of interpretation has begun, and consciously or subconsciously, some part of the artist's personality creeps in. There is composition – where and how the shapes and colors should be related to each other. There is economy – what to put in and what to leave out, what must be stated and what left unsaid, what should be underlined, and what merely suggested. And there is always the possibility that "caricature" can convey a basic truth more succinctly. These are the justifications for artistic license in the painter's continuing effort to make pictures that give pleasure to the people who look at them.

I am sometimes asked about my motives in painting. Why do I do it? What am I trying to do? What are my objectives? Well, I do it because I like doing it. I do it because I can't help doing it. I like to draw or paint something every day of my life, though

Peter Scott

I don't always manage to do it. And the first of my objectives is to give pleasure to people – as many people as possible, some possibly not yet born. I like to draw things that have excited me, to reflect my own enthusiasm for nature in general and especially for birds (and fishes and whales). I like to record, whenever possible, aspects of their behavior and their biology as well as their appearance. I like to help to educate others to enjoy them, thereby enriching their lives too, and at the same time advancing the cause of conservation. And finally, I have to earn money in my profession, and to have been able to do so for almost half a century has been another piece of good fortune.

Birds were a very early interest, from the age of four onward – especially the shorebirds to be seen from our cottage at Sandwich. I saw my first wild geese there, which led to a general interest in wildfowl, and ultimately to Slimbridge and the Wildfowl Trust.

Art and science, or perhaps science and art (for that was the order in which I was trained in the two activities), have been twin preoccupations all my life; and the furtherance of scientific research has always been one of the Wildfowl Trust's prime objectives. However, research was not the only consideration I had in mind for Slimbridge. There was also education, and I had for long been concerned about conservation – concerned for the prospects of survival of many of the wildfowl species in a hostile world. I was anxious not only about the wildfowl, for it was clear that all over the world a great number of other animal species – and plant species too – were threatened with extinction. These species were the current end products of forty million centuries of evolution – four billion years. This is how long it has taken for all the diversity of living creatures on our earth to evolve into what we know today; and, of course, the process is continuing.

My biological training told me that an environmental crisis was on its way. It was becoming abundantly clear that all was not well with planet Earth. It was not necessary to be an environmental expert to realize this. . . . [So] we persuaded the world's leading conservationists to sign a solemn declaration called the Morges Manifesto, and soon thereafter we formed the World Wildlife Fund.

Conserving what is left of the world's wildlife and wild places belongs to the mainstream of civilized human progress. . . . I do not believe that man could survive without the rest of nature; but most important, what good will it be if we live to inherit a barren world devoid of the natural things, the wild things, that make life worth living?

Being able to put a name to an animal or a plant has a special appeal, and if the differences are small and require careful observation to determine them, the activity is all the more appealing, taking on a kind of "crossword puzzle" fascination which can easily become compulsive. With luck it can, and often does, lead to a lifelong enthusiasm for the subject, making Roger Peterson's [field guide] a major contribution to the relationship between man and the rest of nature. . . . I am not sure whether he realized the extraordinary revolution that he was about to create by publishing this book. . . . In my view, this invention was a major step in human progress.

The science of ecology had not been invented when I was learning biology; yet the instant its principles were enumerated, I immediately realized the essential truth that all nature is interrelated, that we are a part of it and need contact with it. Furthermore, because we are, as a species, the direct cause of so much of the environmental damage, we have a clear responsibility.

In my opinion, this puts conservation as a philosophical imperative – not merely as a device for saving our own skins – out in the mainstream of human progress. How much of it we can achieve, on the ground and in the oceans, is, of course, another story. As the American conservationist Aldo Leopold once wrote: "Conservation is a state of harmony with a friend; you cannot cherish his right hand and chop off his left."

One thing is certain: Conservation is only meaningful in the long term. I once rather sententiously dreamed up a "100-years rule." It said that for work you should seriously consider whether your activity was likely to make life better for someone in a hundred years' time. Any time spent doing anything else was play or spare time stuff, of no real significance.

I hope the viewer derives as much pleasure out of seeing my art as I, as an artist, have derived out of seeing my subjects.

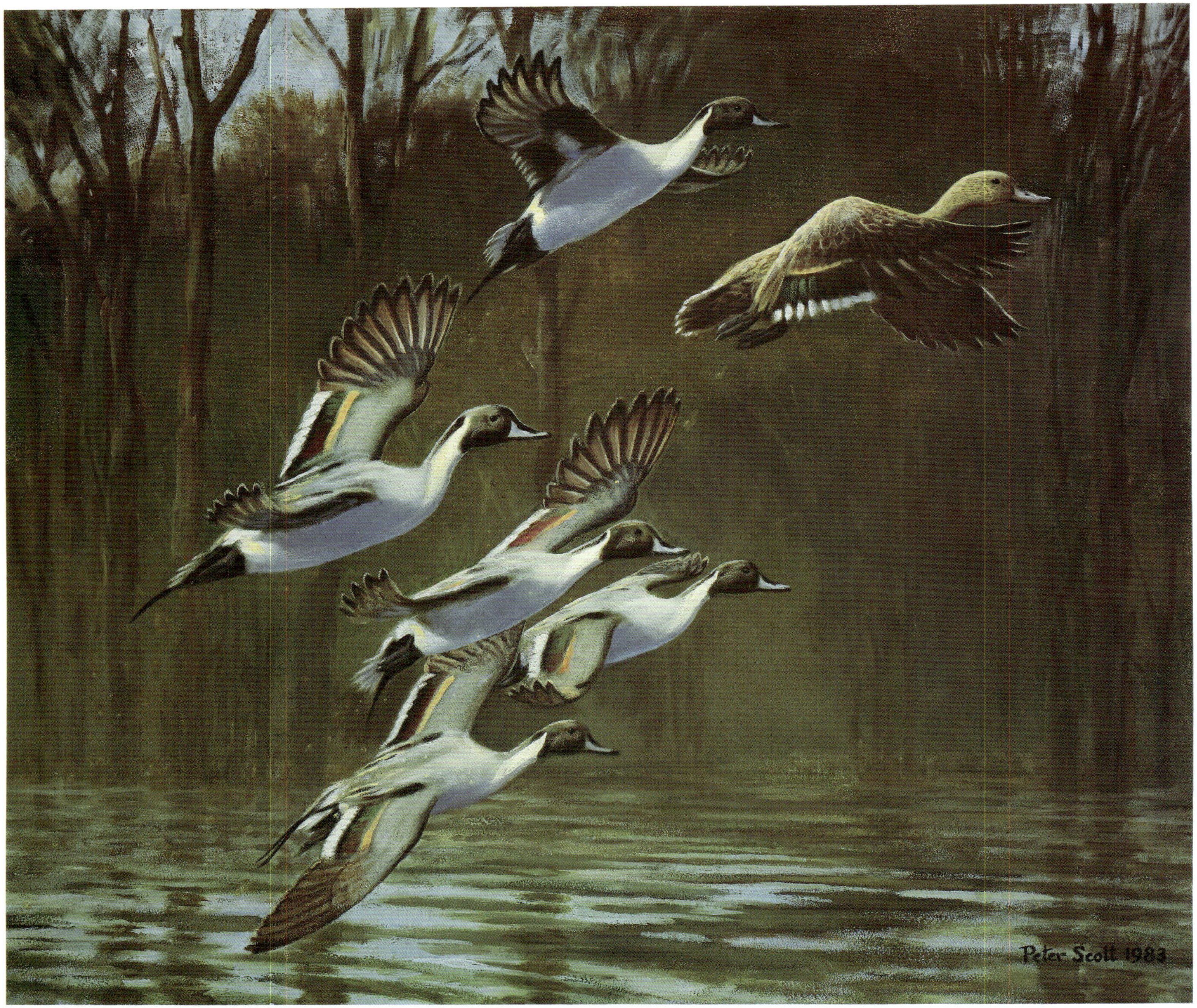

Courtship Pursuit (pintail) 1983, oil on canvas, 25 x 30 inches, private collection. *Birds in Art* 1984.

I painted from memory, which is to say that I did not find it necessary to have what I was painting in front of me as I worked. In the case of flying birds, this would scarcely have been practicable.

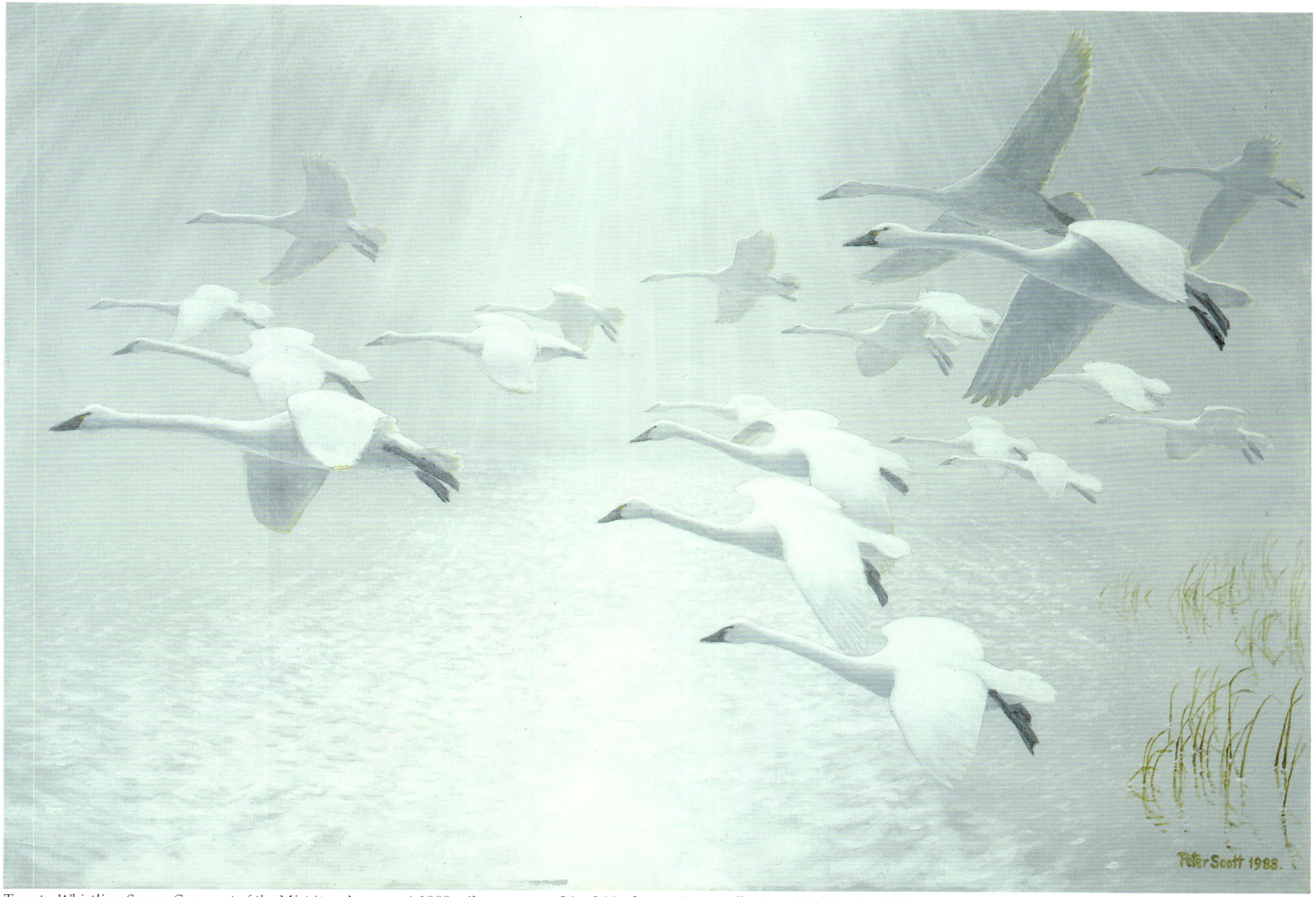

Twenty Whistling Swans Came out of the Mist (tundra swan) 1988, oil on canvas, 24 x 36 inches, private collection. *Birds in Art* 1988.

The idea of a white bird seen against the light in a thick mist has always appealed to me, and I have painted a number of pictures depicting swans flying over water, backlit by a misty sun, with very little color – a silvery symphony.

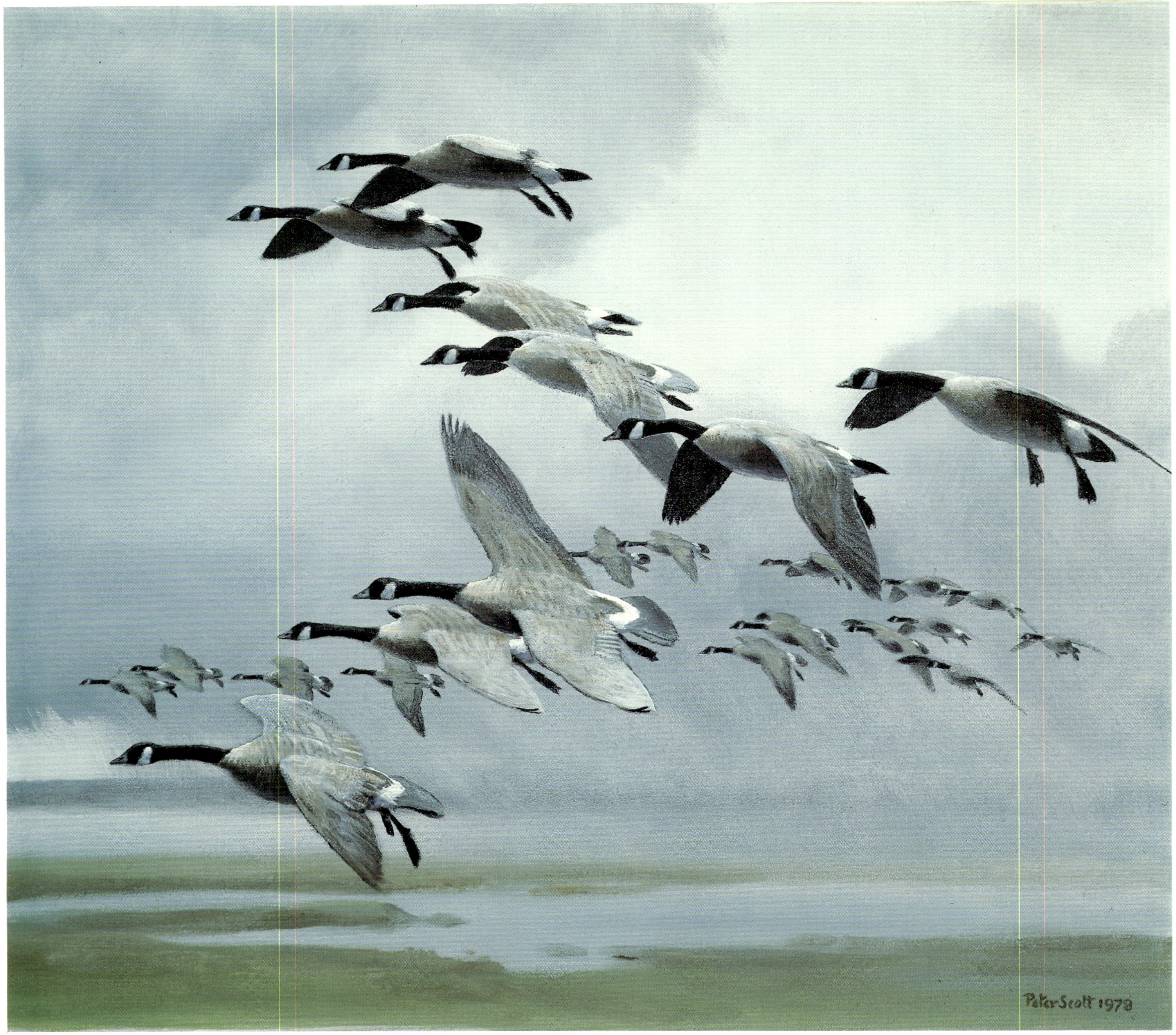

Canada Geese Out of a Rain Squall 1978, oil on canvas, 20 x 24 inches, private collection. *Birds in Art* 1980.

I passionately believe in man's individual and collective responsibility for all life on earth.

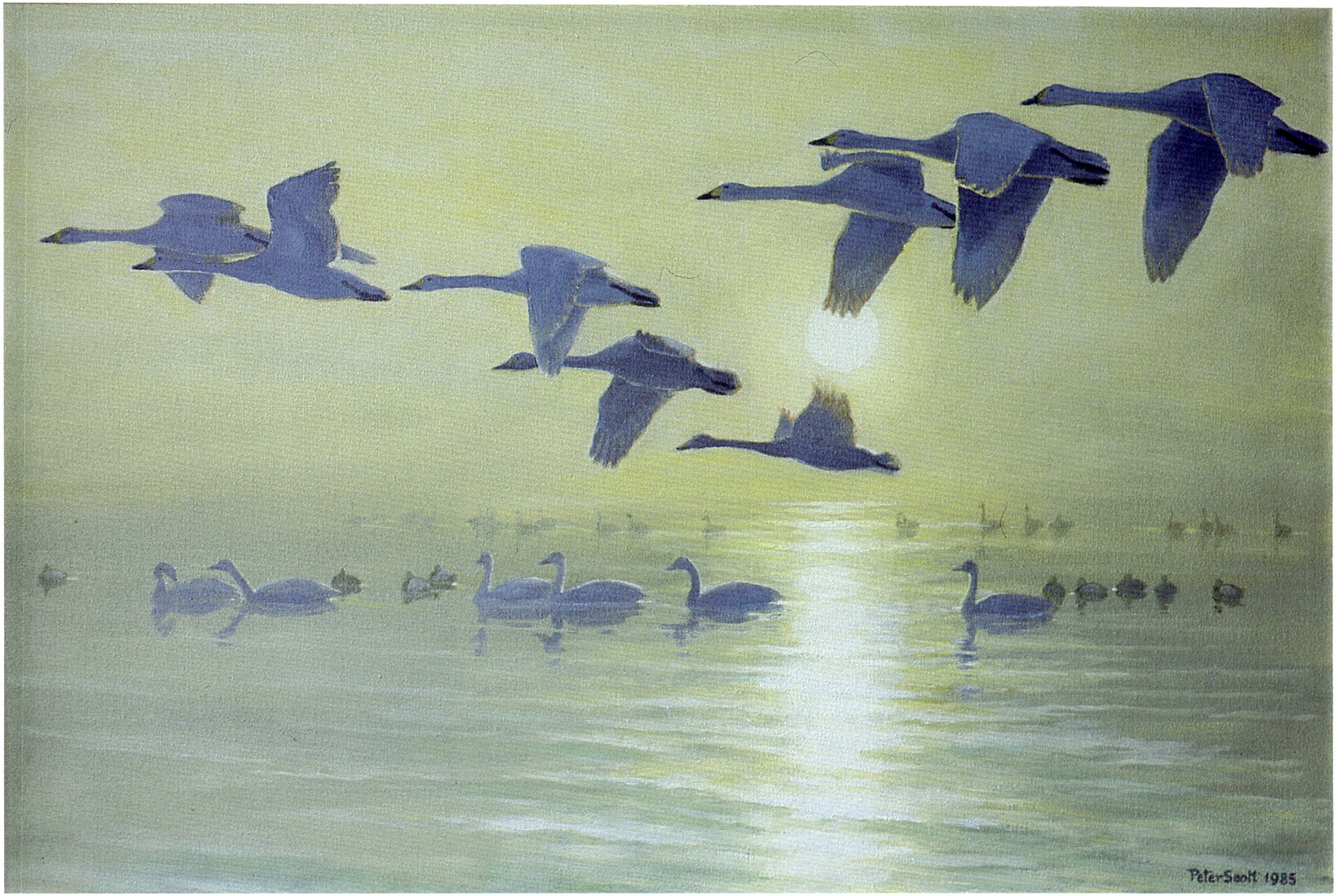

Blue Swans Against a Misty Yellow Sunrise (tundra swan) 1985, oil on canvas, 20 x 30 inches, private collection. *Birds in Art* 1985.

Who am I to try to improve on the beauty of the wild swan in flight?

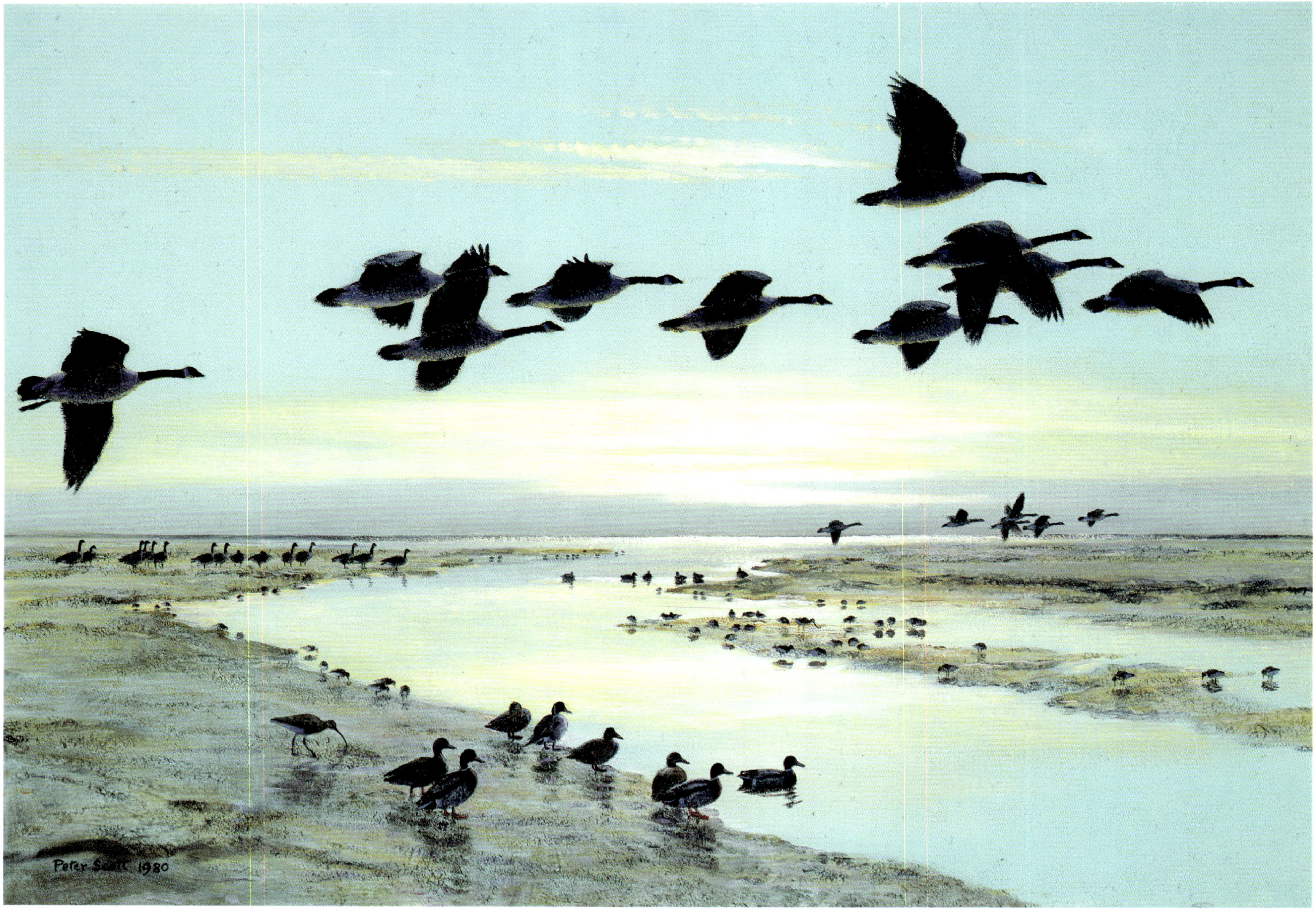

Low Tide at Dawn (Canada goose, mallard, curlew, shorebirds) 1980, oil on canvas, 20 x 30 inches, private collection. *Birds in Art* 1980.

For me, one of the greatest fascinations in nature is the way that evolution has produced this diversity of species molded by the particular environment they live in. Their study leads me. . . to look upon species extinction at the hands of unthinking man – sometimes even by his deliberate choice – as wicked irresponsibility.

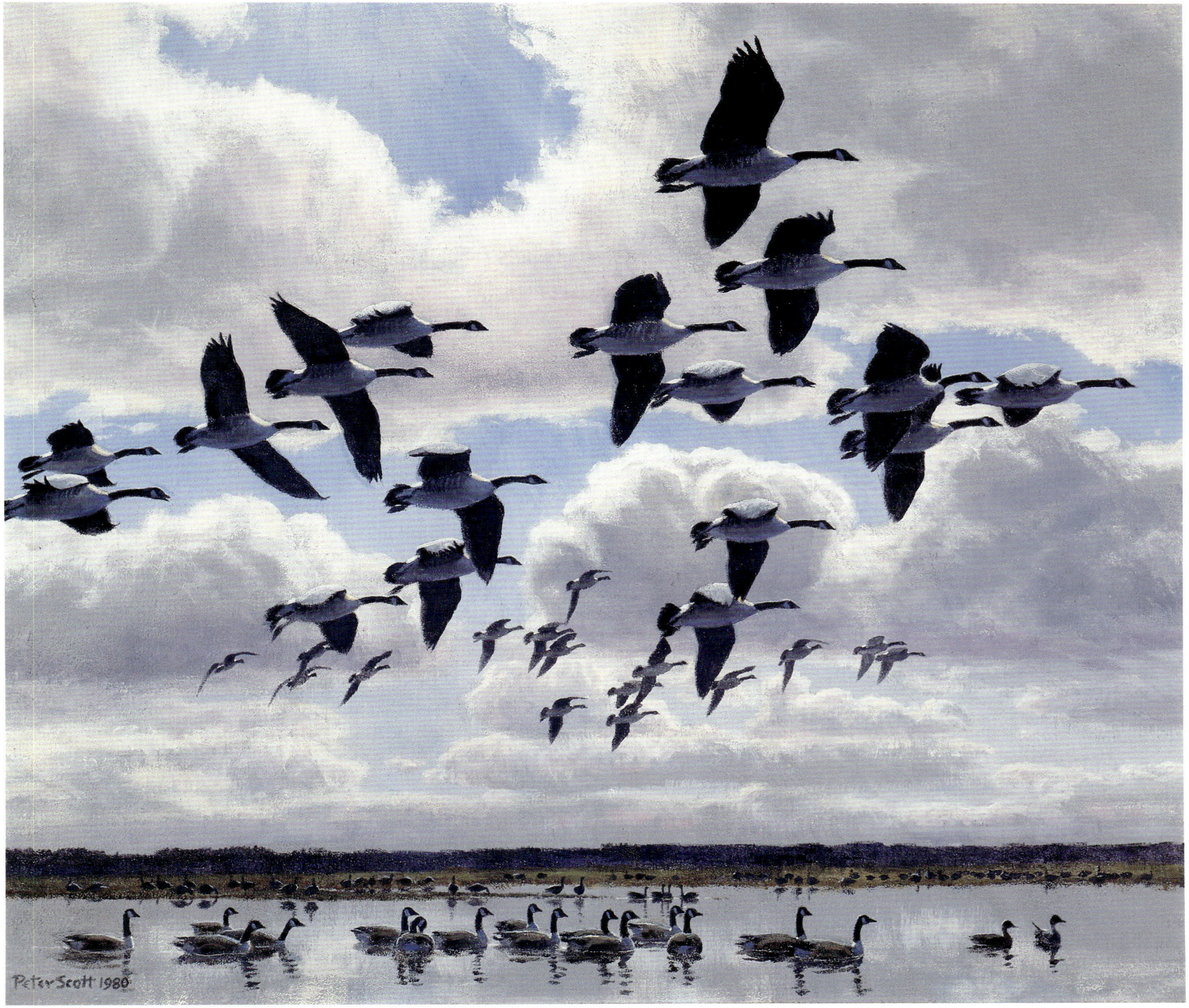

Honkers Against a Cumulus Sky (Canada goose) 1980, oil on board, 20 x 24 inches, collection of the Leigh Yawkey Woodson Art Museum. *Birds in Art* 1983.

I do not believe that man could survive without the rest of nature; but most important, what good will it be if we live to inherit a barren world devoid of the natural things, the wild things, that make life worth living?

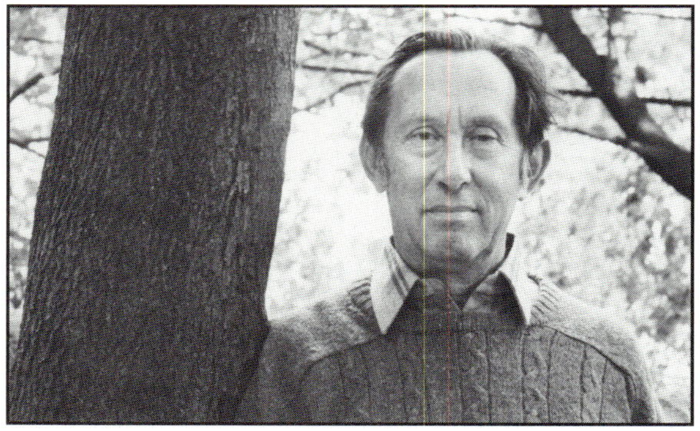

ARTHUR B. SINGER

Master Wildlife Artist 1981
Born: 1917, New York, New York
Died: 1990

I started drawing as soon as I could hold a pencil. Growing up in the city of New York, all I ever saw of field and forest were on vacations during summer months. My awareness of wild mammals and birds came from frequent visits to the great New York Zoological Society in the Bronx. My parents knew that I loved visiting the zoo so they took me there frequently.

Reading excited my interest in wildlife and art. I liked stories written by naturalists, particularly Ernest Thompson Seton, who was also an artist. I was emotionally moved by his stories of animals that took on personalities. I loved to read about far-off places, especially books on Africa with descriptions of a "paradise of animals" and illustrations of big game animals. I was inspired to collect all the pictures I could find. In the depths of the Depression, I could buy secondhand magazines – *National Geographic, Natural History,* and other nature magazines – for a nickel apiece. I kept separate files on each category of animals, like birds and mammals. Until then, I had drawn and painted all kinds of subjects. I decided I'd like to draw animals so I began by copying paintings and later attempted my own compositions.

I often visited the American Museum of Natural History. This was especially exciting because the great African and North American Halls were just being created. I was allowed into the exhibits to see how the backgrounds were painted. The artists painted in a very impressionistic way, yet when I backed up thirty feet the scenes looked extremely realistic.

This coincided with the Depression. Men were selling apples on street corners and the song of the day was "Brother Can You Spare a Dime," so I didn't think seriously about making a living as an artist. I treated my interest as a hobby – a hobby that occupied much of my time.

But after high school, I took the competitive exam and got into Cooper Union Art School. With my interest in painting wildlife realistically, I probably should have applied to the National Academy. I could see I was headed for conflict with the movement in art toward expressionism and abstractionism and away from the more conservative realism. I decided to keep my mind and eyes open, to absorb what I could, and to try to understand what was good in each artistic style.

Sometimes I spent days off at the Bronx Zoo drawing from life, because at Cooper Union we generally painted scenics. I was a little afraid to draw living things, and I was self-conscious about drawing at the zoo. I soon learned to harden myself to the comments of crowds that would gather around. I spent most of my time drawing mammals, and I highly recommend working from living animals.

Several teachers learned of my interest in natural history and directed me to the work of Oriental artists. Oriental painting was quite different from Western painting, and I admired its delicacy and subtlety and dramatic composition. My teachers also made me aware of man's earliest attempts to depict animals on cave walls. Even today, these images retain the great vitality of primitive art and capture the very essence of the animals that were their subjects.

One of my instructors showed me Audubon's double elephant folio *Birds of America* – all five enormous volumes. It was an overwhelming experience that had great impact on me. When I asked myself why I responded to Audubon's work so strongly, I realized it was for a reason other than the painting of the bird itself. In their design and composition, many of Audubon's plates hold up as fine art. Of the Western bird artists, he comes closest to being as great a designer as the Oriental artists. One need only compare his work with the art of his older contemporary, Alexander Wilson, to understand the contribution Audubon made to bird painting. I studied Audubon's prints whenever I had the chance, and I think they were one of my best teachers of design.

I also studied Louis Agassiz Fuertes' marvelous watercolor portraits. In the portrayal of birds without background, Fuertes reached a perfection that no one has surpassed. But his full background paintings fall short. His principal difficulty was in the way he interpreted light. I remember a book on North American mammals published by the National Geographic Society. The contrast of a Fuertes painting with one by Carl Rungius was startling! Rungius captured the light so well you could tell the approximate time of day pictured. Fuertes' paintings looked quite flat, but he could create magic with the portrait of a bird. His untimely death cut short a great talent.

Arthur Singer

In my opinion, the greatest of all wildlife artists was Bruno Liljefors. Liljefors painted from life. He was not a tight, detail painter, but gave the impression of the living bird with his expert handling of paint. Some of his paintings I consider the best wildlife art ever done. They are masterpieces that rank with the great stormy ocean paintings of Winslow Homer. I just can't understand why he has never been better known outside of Sweden.

Shortly after I graduated from art school, van Gogh's paintings were exhibited in New York City for the first time in many years. He wasn't held in the high esteem he is now. I was very much impressed with van Gogh's use of color, and I feel his work has influenced mine. Just out of art school, I wondered how I would combine what I had learned from studying the masters.

In the old days, museums sponsored expeditions to far-off places to gather material for exhibits. The expedition party always included an artist who went along to record the scene. This was before the days of color photography, which didn't become popular until after World War II. Color photography brought the demise of most expedition painters and illustrators. It ended a career opportunity. I figured the only chance I had as a wildlife artist was to do something the camera could not.

In the years following World War II, opportunities and interest in wildlife art were at a low point. Most of the assignments were for hunting magazines, and I didn't feel my work was appropriate for these magazines. Consequently, I got a job as an art director for an advertising agency in New York, and I spent evening hours doing the work I enjoyed. Gradually, I started to get commissions. I did a series of vignettes of state birds and flowers for *American Home Magazine* that was highly successful. Many millions were printed and distributed all over the United States.

The next project was like a dream come true. I had always wanted to do a beautiful book on birds. In the late fifties, I was commissioned to do *Birds of the World*. I thoroughly enjoyed the work even though it took almost four years to complete. *Birds of the World* was the first serious book on the subject to be handled with such freedom of design. I had a golden opportunity to do what could not be done with a camera. For example, in my egret painting, you find egrets from different parts of the world in one composition, a feat that could not be accomplished photographically outside of a zoo.

For the next ten years, I worked on one book after another. By no stretch of the imagination could I say that the Golden field guide, *Birds of North America*, was fun to do. Unlike *Birds of the World*, the field guide gave me little creative freedom. As it turned out, however, it is probably the most important job I ever did.

At last, in the 1970s, as a wildlife artist, I had the opportunity to paint for limited edition prints, not just for books. Selling prints is a business and sometimes you compromise to paint what the public wants. Consequently, you see few subjects from far-off places, with the exception of African big game animals with a preference for the great cats. The cardinal tops the list of bird subjects for prints.

There will always be room for artists in designing educational materials. A wonderful example is the state bird and flower postal stamps that I painted. To do them photographically would have been impossible. An artist can play with scale, but a photographer would have a difficult time. For example, Louisiana has a brown pelican and a magnolia blossom as state symbols. The two are so out of scale from one another that it would be impossible to photograph them together and to show each of them well.

My basic philosophy about wildlife painting is that it should not be a slavish imitation of photography. Design and composition should play the major role in the painting. A realistic portrayal of the bird in its native habitat is necessary, but design and selectivity are also very important. In creating the initial composition of a painting, I spend a great deal of time on preparatory sketches before I decide on the one that most successfully combines these aspects of realism and design.

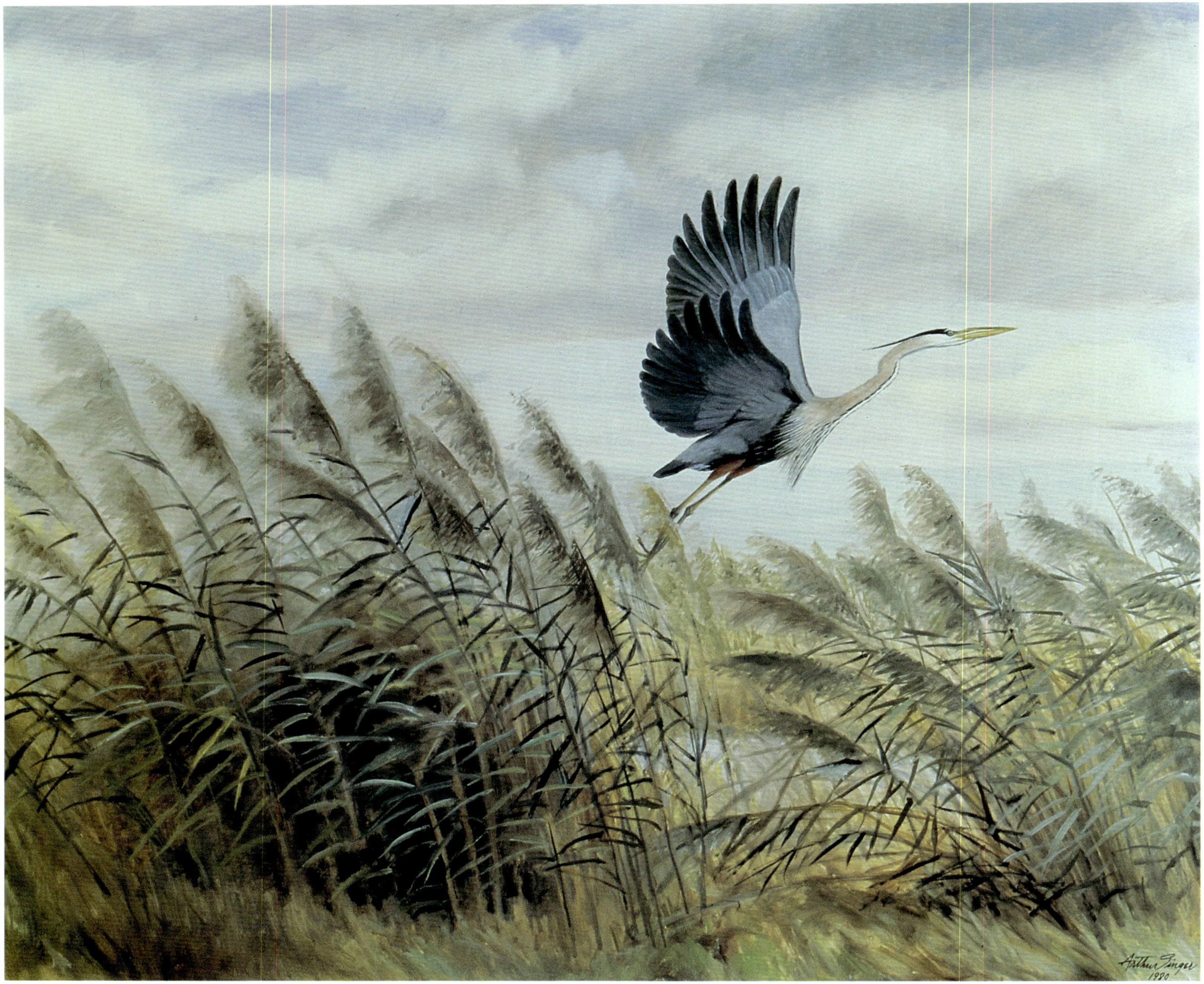

Takeoff Before Storm (great blue heron) 1980, oil on canvas, 24 x 30 inches, private collection. *Birds in Art* 1983.

Bird art should be more than an accurate portrayal. It should stand up creatively as a work of art.

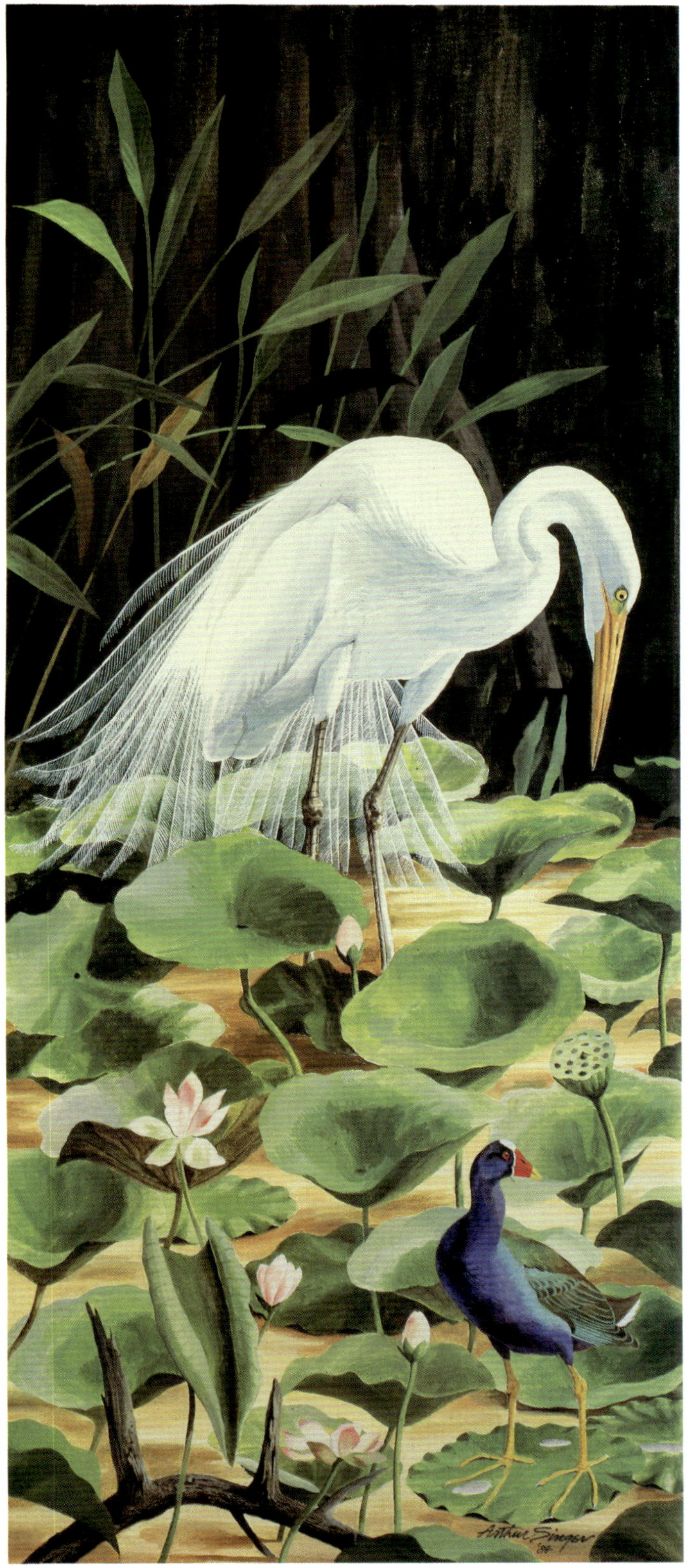

I have tried to achieve an Oriental simplicity that reveals the grace of the egret and the rich color of the most spectacular member of the rail family.

Great Egret and Purple Gallinule 1984, gouache, 30 x 13¼ inches, private collection. *Birds in Art* 1987.

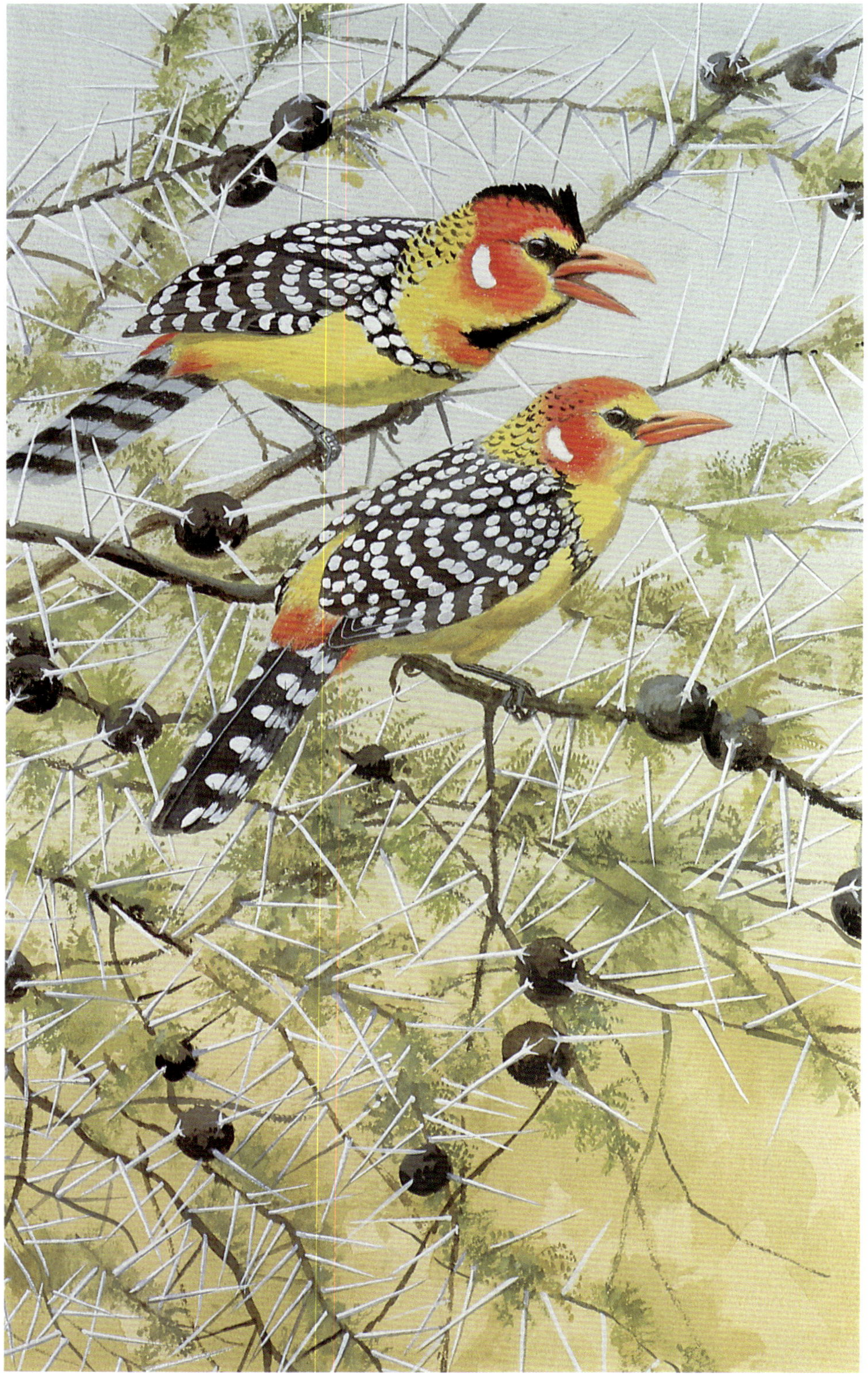

I studied Audubon's prints whenever I had the chance, and I think they were one of my best teachers of design.

East African Barbets (red and yellow barbet) 1980, watercolor and gouache on paper, 17½ x 11 inches, private collection. *Birds in Art* 1984.

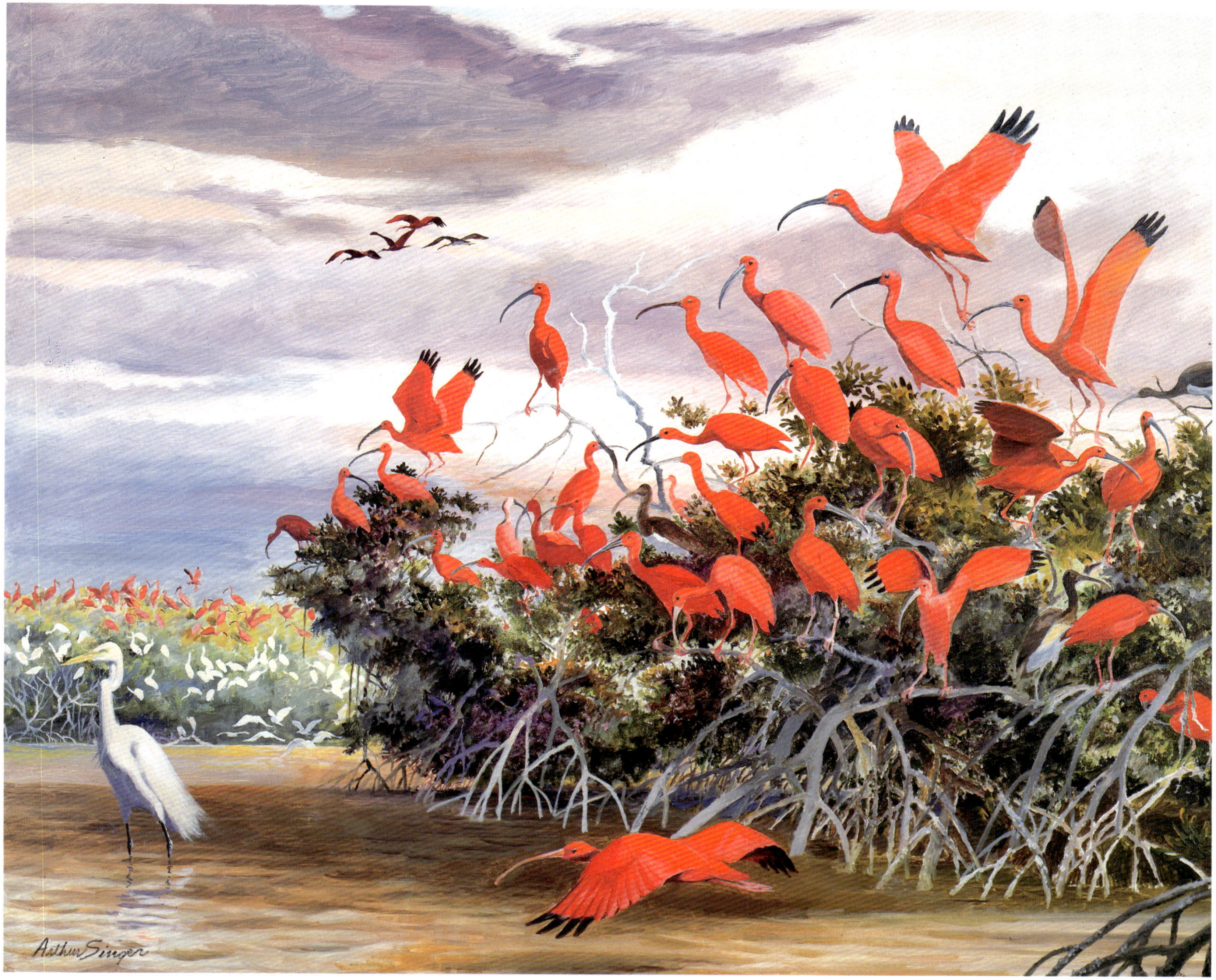

Caroni Swamp at Sundown (scarlet ibis) 1981, oil on canvas, 24½ x 30½ inches, collection of the Leigh Yawkey Woodson Art Museum. *Birds in Art* 1981.

Aside from accuracy, the most important elements in painting birds are design, beauty, and color.

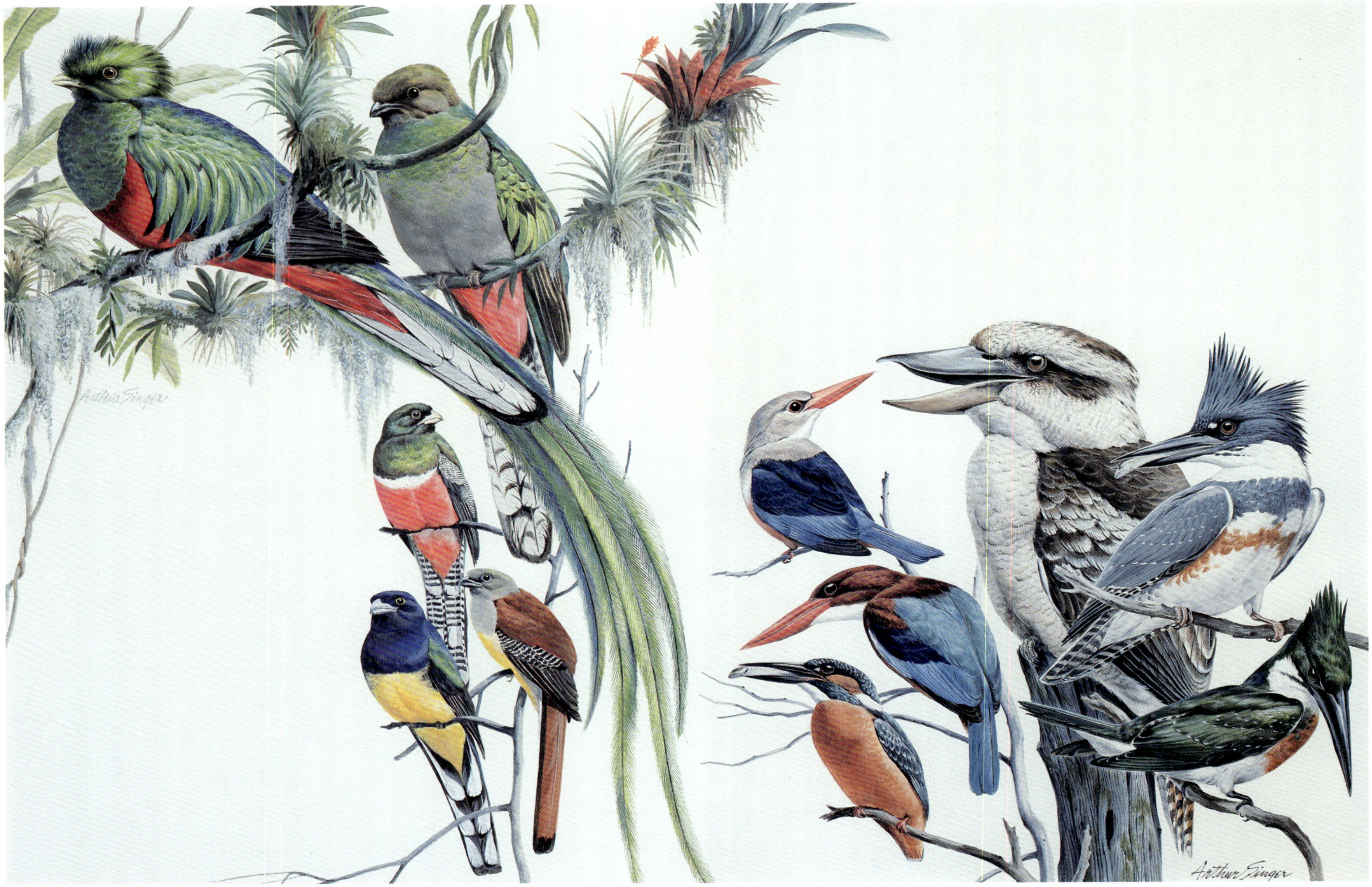

Quetzals, Trogons, Kingfishers 1959, gouache, 19 x 25½ inches, private collection. *Birds in Art* 1981.

Birds of the World *was a dream come true. I had always wanted to do a beautiful book on birds. I painted the birds in great detail and very realistically, and I tried to vary every spread in the book so no two were alike.*

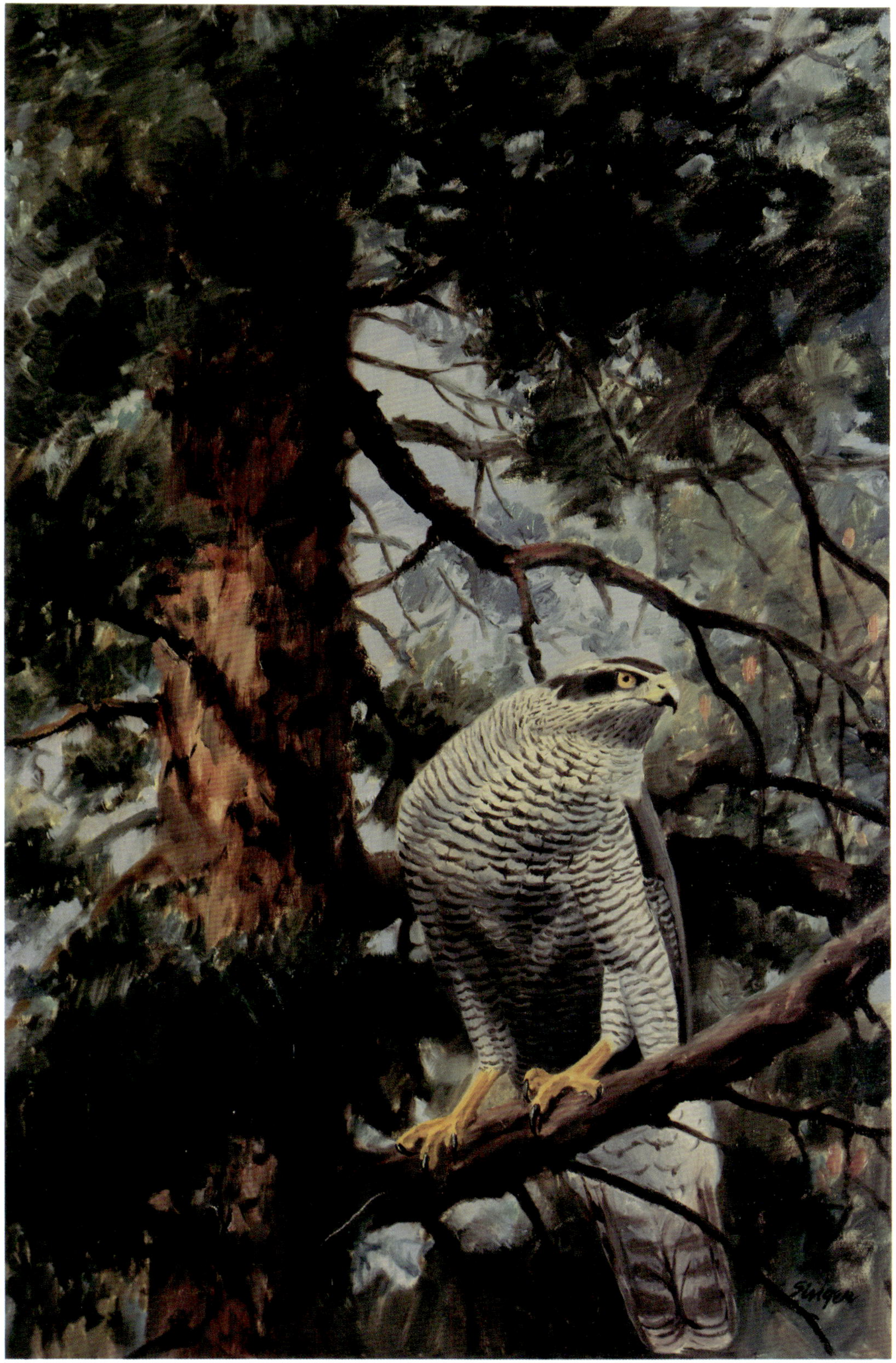

When I began my career, wildlife painting was an offbeat way to make a living. But over the years, more and more people have recognized the value of saving wildlife and wild lands.

European Goshawk in Swedish Forest 1968, oil on canvas, 30½ x 20½ inches, collection of Dale C. Singer. *Birds in Art* 1979.

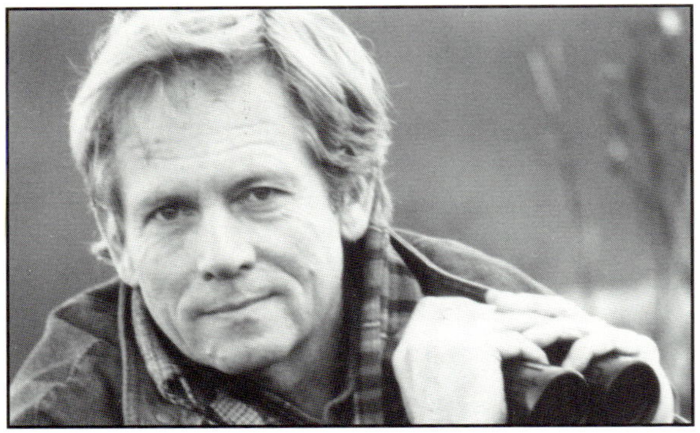

Robert Bateman

Master Wildlife Artist 1982
Born: 1930, Toronto, Ontario, Canada
Resides: Fulford Harbor, British Columbia, Canada

I can't conceive of anything being more varied and rich and handsome than the planet Earth. And its crowning beauty is the natural world. . . . I want to soak it up, to understand it as well as I can, and to absorb it. And then I'd like to put it together and express it in my paintings. This is the way I want to dedicate my work.

I wouldn't say I try to reveal something about myself in my paintings. If I'm painting a screech owl being mobbed by two chickadees, I try to get into the skin of the chickadees, into their nervous irritation, and their flap and flutter. I try to immerse myself rather than to display myself. Painting is as full of surprise and complexity for me as is the world of nature.

The most exciting wildlife is always on the move. You're lucky if something stays still for two seconds, let alone for twenty seconds. . . . I can capture an image of something I've only seen for two seconds, such as a bird flying by, and I may work on that sketch for two minutes while it's still fresh in my memory, filling it out, using my knowledge of birds, their proportions, and their feathers to help me finish it off.

When people look at one of my paintings, I want them to feel they are seeing something wild that just happened. Oriental art tends to have things in a dynamic state of transformation. It sort of leaves you with one foot in the air; something is about to happen. I don't want my paintings to look like a frozen moment for immortality. I want them to be a kind of fleeting glimpse. The impressionists did the same thing. My paintings often look a bit off-balanced.

Composition is dividing positive and negative spaces into shapes. The abstract design of a painting comes through the power of contrasting shapes and colors, light and dark. Ideas often come to me as shapes which take on the form of birds and animals later when I paint.

If you take a piece of the natural world, whether it's a big landscape or a little piece of bark, and look at it in abstract terms of curves and tones and contrasts and color and shape, it opens up a tremendous new range of possibilities. Just learning to look at things from an abstract point of view had a big impact on me.

In many of my paintings, a pattern or a shape that I discover in the feathers or anatomy or structure of the subject becomes a repeated theme throughout the picture.

Art is like music. You orchestrate the painting, giving it a theme which is echoed over and over.

Some art critics say wildlife artists are not interested in art, they're interested in wildlife. My background is art. I noticed in the *Birds in Art* catalogue that most of the artists are in the same boat as I am. We're concerned about art – color, design, form, rhythm, texture – all those elements of art are important to us. It shouldn't matter to us at all whether our paintings are exhibited in art galleries or in natural history museums. The problem is, I do care personally.

An art curator in Sweden told me, "If you paint natural history, you show in the museum of natural history. If you paint boats, you show in the maritime museum." I guess if you paint nudes, you show in the nude museum, or if you paint wine bottles and guitars, you show in the wine bottle and guitar museum.

I'm a bit puzzled and a bit amused by it. There seems to be some kind of a wall among art museum curators regarding wildlife art. They'll accept realism if it's a person, a motel, or a motorcycle. But they won't accept it if it's a bird or a wolf.

When I was about twenty, I gave up doing wildlife art because, according to my friends at art college, wildlife art – especially bird art – was "mere illustration." I kind of went along with it. I said to myself, "Well, Fuertes did it, Allan Brooks did it, and Francis Lee Jaques did it, so it's been done." That was the great banner of modernism – if it's been done, then don't do it. I merrily went on my way to loftier things, to impressionism, post-impressionism, and cubism. I only occasionally tried a wildlife painting, just to see if I still had it in me. I hadn't seen any realist artists who were accepted by the art establishment and there certainly was no wildlife art hung on museum walls.

At the same time, there were strong naturalist stirrings in my life. The difference in the leaf of a sugar maple and a black maple, or the difference in the bark of a slippery elm and an American elm, became extremely important to me. All this time I was painting wilderness, but I was painting abstract stuff with big gobs of yummy paint and concentrating on how exciting the paint looked. Then I saw an Andrew Wyeth show and I was immediately excited. He really cared about the surface of the earth, not just the surface of his paint. No one was calling Wyeth's paintings "sentimental art." It was like the "*Good Housekeeping* Seal of Approval" that realism was okay. Suddenly, the ecologist in me saw a way of coming together with the art snob in me. I could paint a leaf to look like a leaf and bark to look like bark.

It's understandable and almost natural that wildlife art is not accepted by the art establishment – I prefer the word "priesthood." They believe the public is ignorant and needs to be educated into fresh adventures in vision. To the priesthood, art must be avant-garde, it cannot have been done before. If art, specifi-

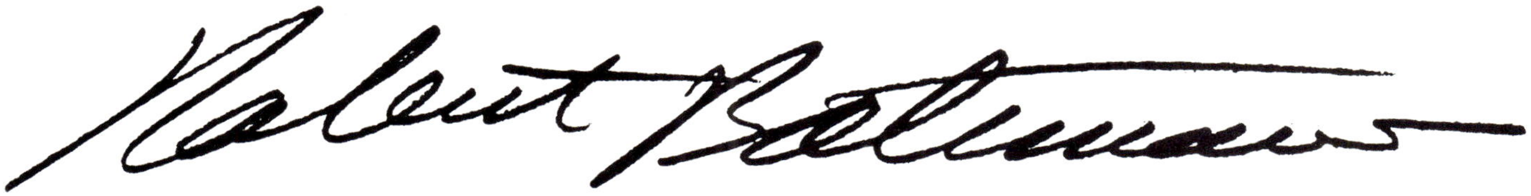

cally wildlife art, is easily understood by the public, the priesthood considers it pandering to the lowest common denominator. To the priesthood, it's like comparing Pepsi-Cola with a very dry Burgundy. They assume the very dry Burgundy is far superior *because* it's an acquired taste and not everybody likes it. A lot of wildlife art is easily digested and tastes sweet at first glance.

A *Washington Post* art critic panned my 1987 Smithsonian exhibition because the paintings were too beautiful, too glorious, too overblown. He thought the work looked like beautifully groomed taxidermy, and he asked, "Where is the dark underbelly of nature? Nature is out there suffering; it's struggling; it's dying." That element is all too rare in wildlife art, even in my art. So I thought his criticism was valid for wildlife art in general and for that show in particular. What interests me most about nature is what's wonderful about it, not what's bad and sick and struggling. But this other part is certainly not to be ignored at this time in the twentieth century.

There are many artists who target their paintings to the market. Cardinals, eagles, wolves – this short list is just an awful trap to creativity. It's something I consciously think of as I select subject matter and I hope I don't let myself fall into it. I enjoy taking sharp turns. I take pleasure in knowing you cannot predict what I am going to paint. If you come to one of my shows and try to imagine what will be on the walls before you enter the gallery, you wouldn't have any idea. This is the opposite of targeting paintings for the market. However, I am frequently asked to donate paintings and limited edition prints to charity art auctions. When I donate a piece, I know it has to have appeal, so I'm actually doing more bald eagles, chickadees, and owls than I would like to. I'm concerned that my interest in helping charities is bending my creativity in the direction of the market.

My art may be popular because I was an abstract artist and something subliminal may be coming through my paintings. Perhaps there is something inherently good and strong about the whole abstract movement, some artistic merit, that comes through as structure, drama, composition, or whatever. If there is, it's intuitive, just something that feels right to me as an artist.

If I ever have a conflict between art and science, I let art win. But I always want to capture the personality or the particular quality of the creature I'm portraying. A peregrine has a characteristic expression that is totally different from a red-tailed hawk's; a bald eagle's face is nothing like a golden eagle's. I'm after the personality of the species, but I take great liberties.

If somebody says to me, "I love your work, it's so detailed," it is not a compliment and it is not an insult. It has nothing to do with quality. It's like saying, "Oh, I love your sweater, it has so many stitches in it." It implies that a cableknit Irish sweater is much inferior to a lamb's wool sweater because of the bulkier knit. By the same token, I hear people say the new wonderful way of wildlife art is no detail. A lack of detail won't necessarily make a painting great either. It's totally irrelevant. It's up to the artist how best to express what he wants to say. To me, details, textures, and colors enrich my vision of the earth, and these may be rendered with loose *or* fine brush strokes.

I consider it a principle of life itself that the more finely you are tuned into its details, the more fully you can appreciate it. . . . What I am interested in is the complexity of the world, and what I find so exciting are the differences and distinctions between things. I could represent a group of trees with a gray mass that I could put on with a roller in twenty-five seconds, but for me that's not enough. I want to pay homage to these trees, and I want you to know what kind of trees they are.

I've done very radical things toward the end of a painting. I've wiped out an entire week's work, scraped it off with a razor blade, painted over it, and started again. . . . For me, it either has to be exactly the way I want it or I'd rather not have it at all.

More than half the time I'm working on a piece, I'm in a state of despair, not knowing where to turn. I may have fifty photographs in front of me, but from an abstract point of view, they can't help me. Thank goodness, in ninety-nine percent of the cases, given enough time, something will come out of left field, some sudden little thought to open up a possible thrust or rhythm. It starts me going again. Usually, I just avoid the problem by starting a new painting or working on one that doesn't look as discouraging. My muse is more workmanlike and problem-solving than inspirational.

I paint for myself, for my own satisfaction. While it is not my goal to leave a legacy, I hope I have helped a little bit in raising people's awareness about the planet. My paintings are one person's view of the world he has seen, a celebration of what's wonderful and beautiful about nature.

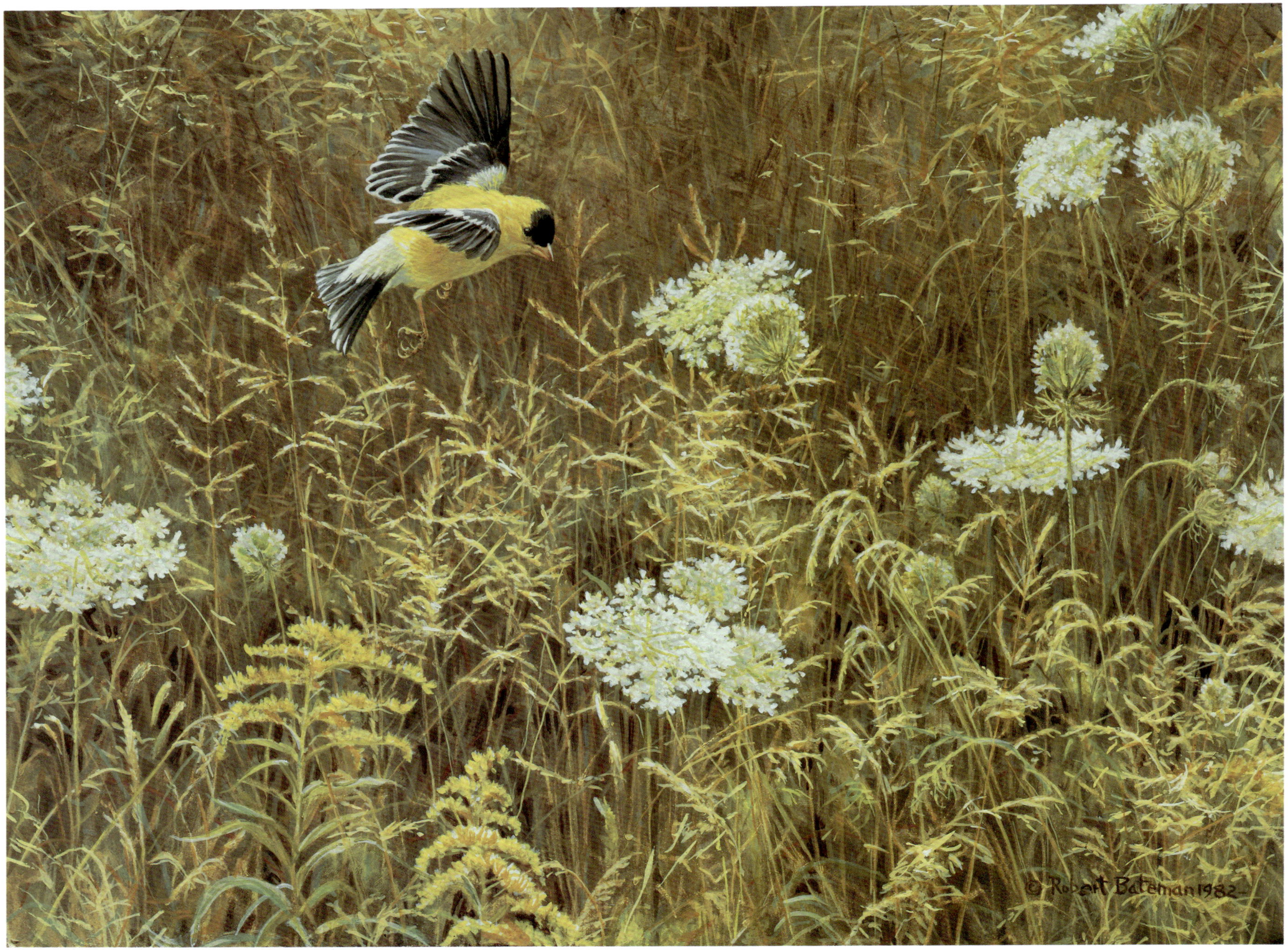

Queen Anne's Lace and American Goldfinch 1982, acrylic on board, 11 x 15 inches, private collection. *Birds in Art* 1985.

My paintings are contrived to look natural. I see a strong parallel to Japanese gardens, where the finished gardens are very carefully contrived to look as if they just happened.

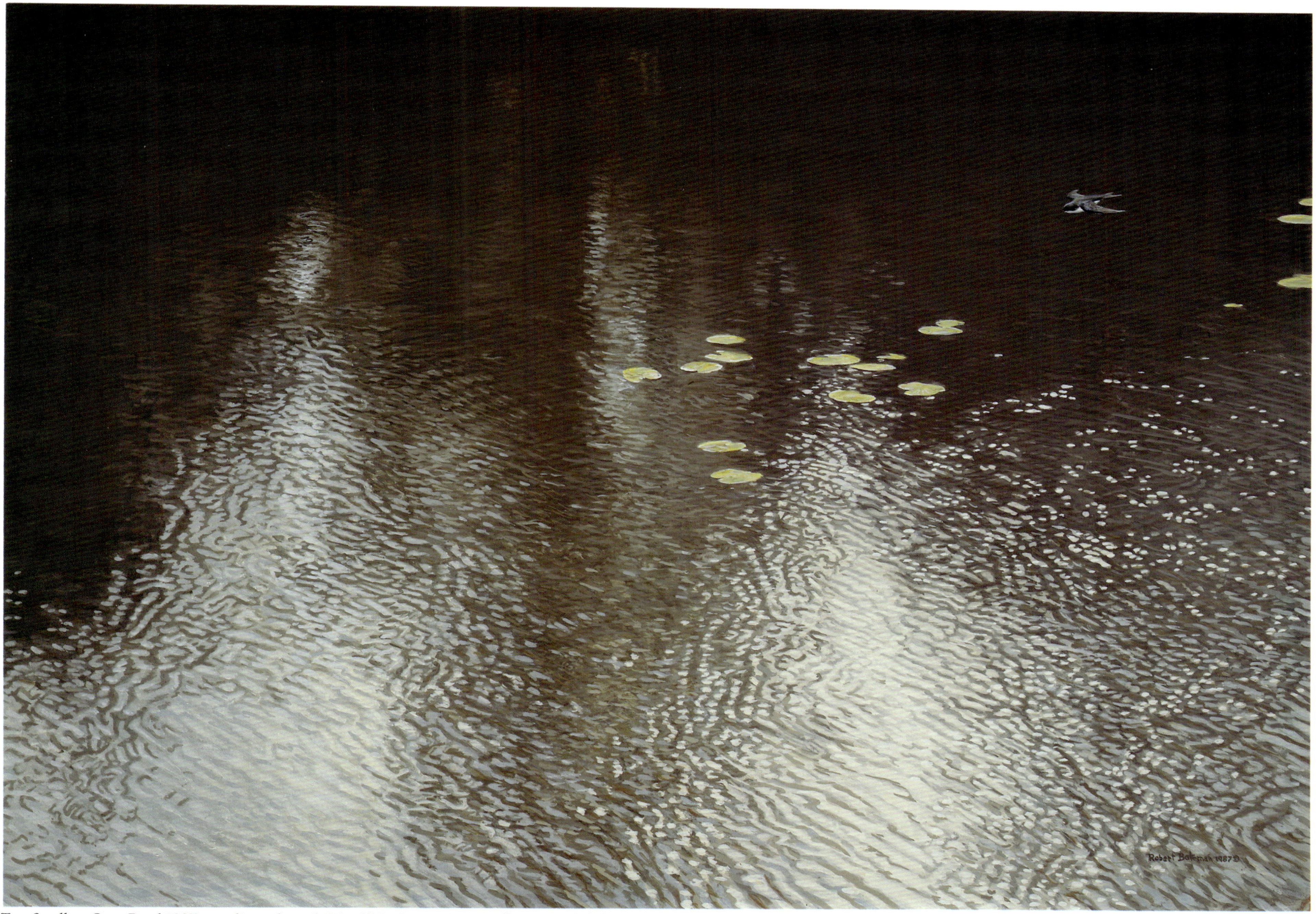

Tree Swallow Over Pond 1987, acrylic on board, 24 x 35 inches, private collection. *Birds in Art* 1988.

I intended this painting to be empty of any center of interest – simply looking down into a pond in a Zen-like way – the kind of thing we have all done hundreds of times, our mind wandering in peace about nothing in particular. Suddenly, a tight little flash catches the eye – the metallic glitter of a tree swallow which will, in a moment, be gone.

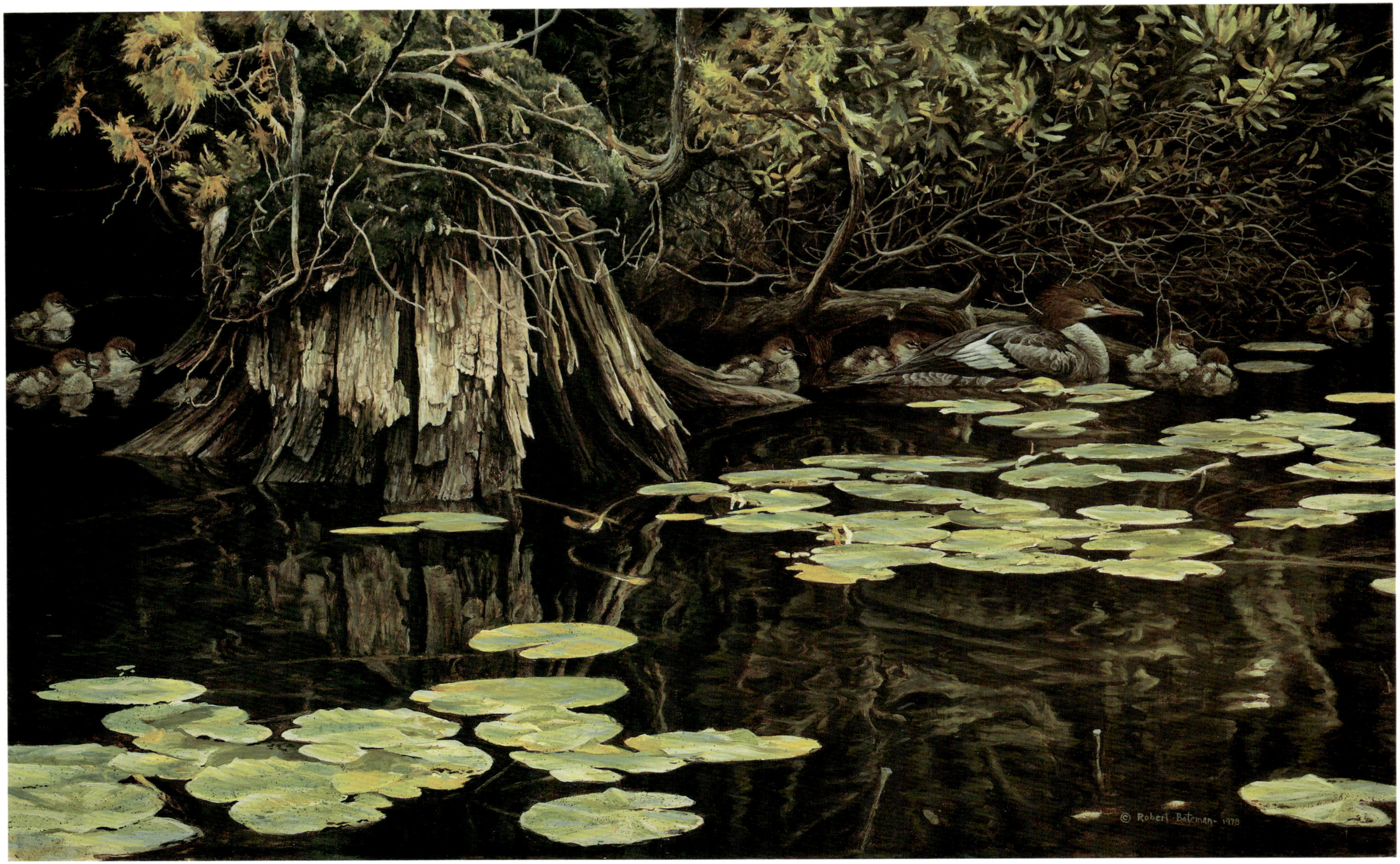

Merganser Family in Hiding (common merganser) 1978, oil on board, 22 x 36 inches, private collection. *Birds in Art* 1982.

I care about the surface of the earth – not just about the surface of my paint.

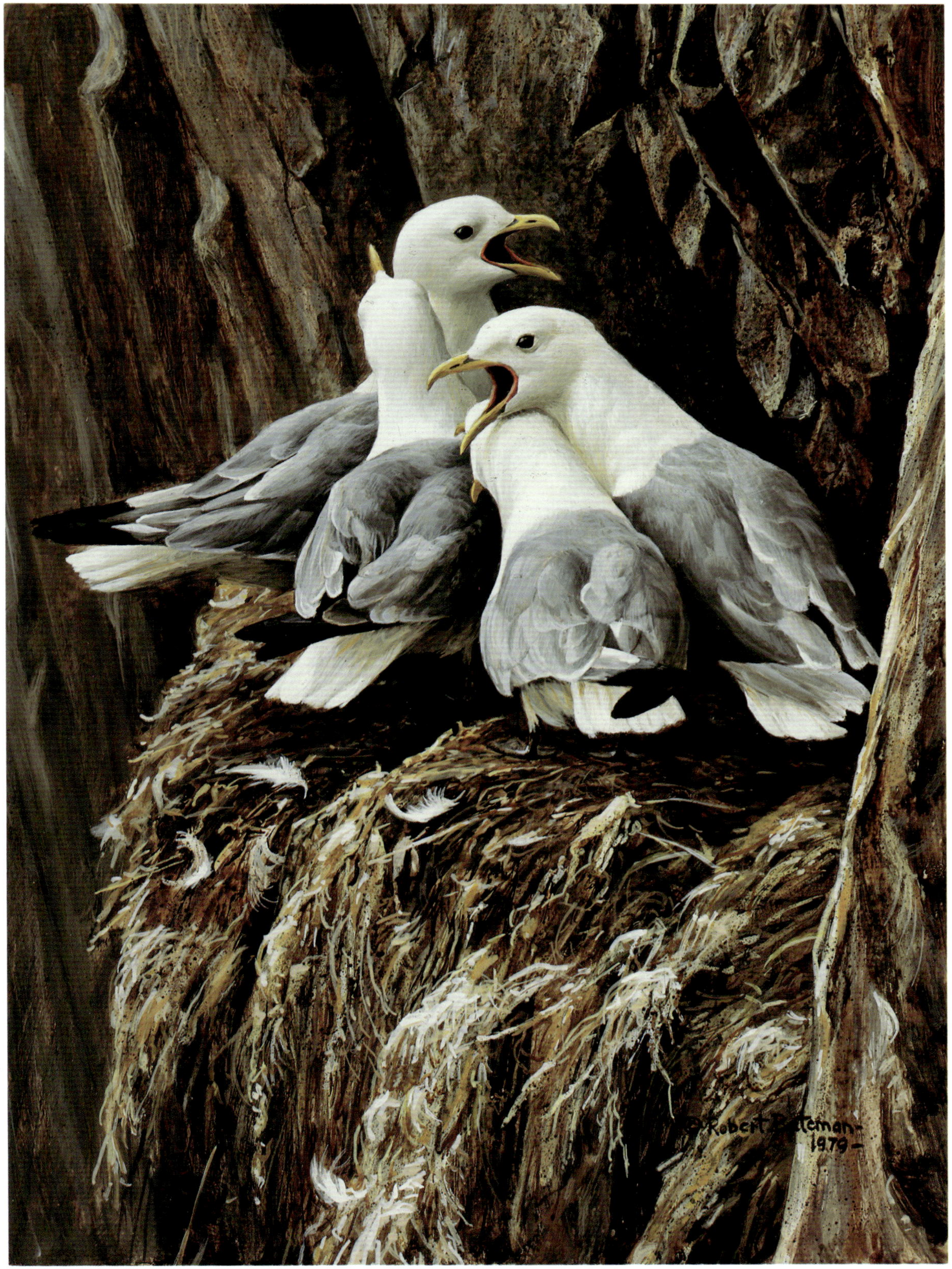

If I ever have a conflict between art and science, I let art win. But I always want to capture the personality or the particular quality of the creature I'm portraying.

Kittiwake Greeting (black-legged kittiwake) 1979, oil on board, 16 x 12 inches, private collection. *Birds in Art* 1984.

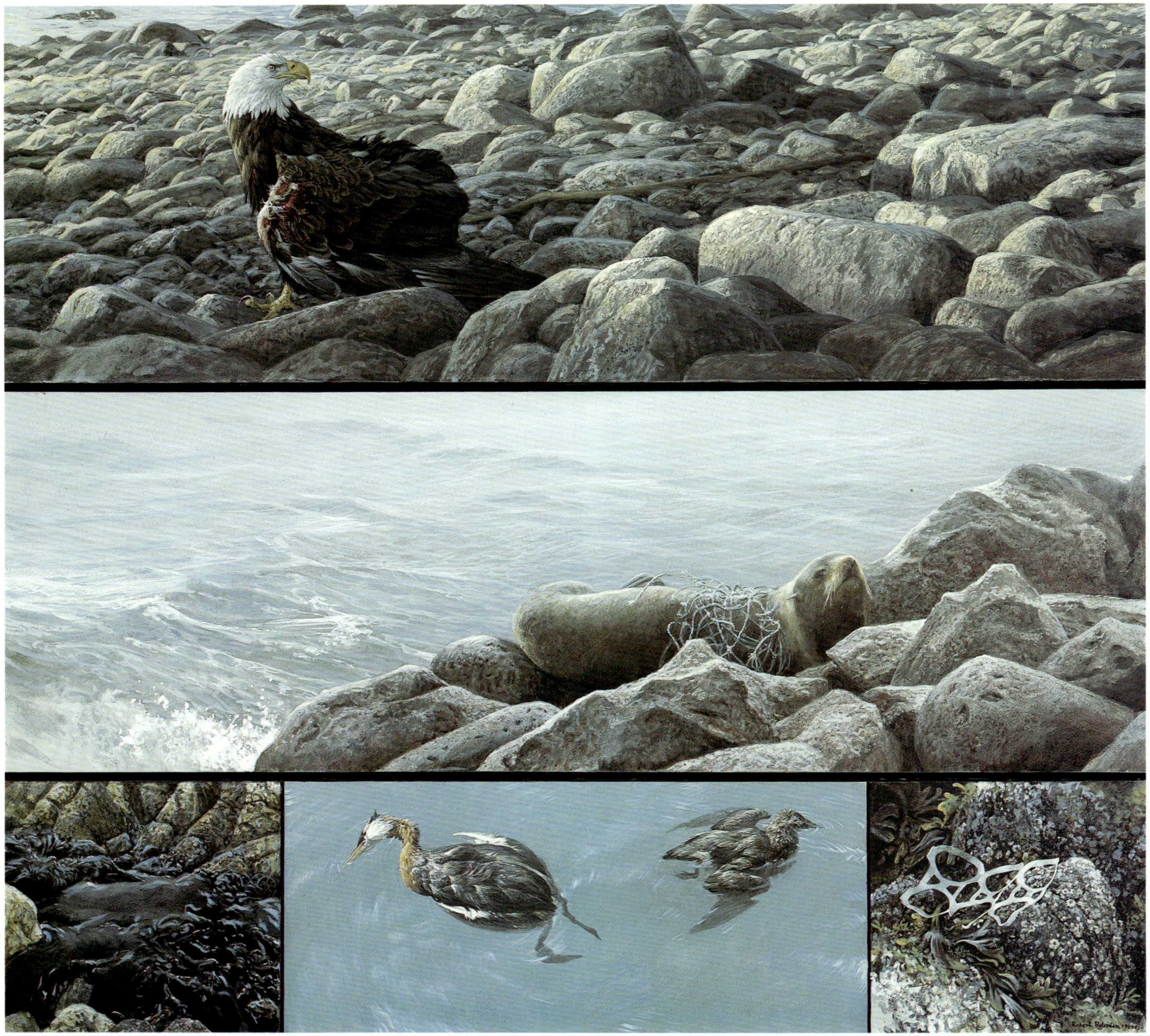

Wildlife Images – Environmental (bald eagle, fur seal, red-necked grebe, immature rhinoceros auklet) 1989, acrylic on canvas, 40 x 45 inches, private collection. *Birds in Art* 1990.

What interests me most about nature is what's wonderful about it, not what's bad and sick and struggling. But this dark underbelly is not to be ignored at this time in the twentieth century.

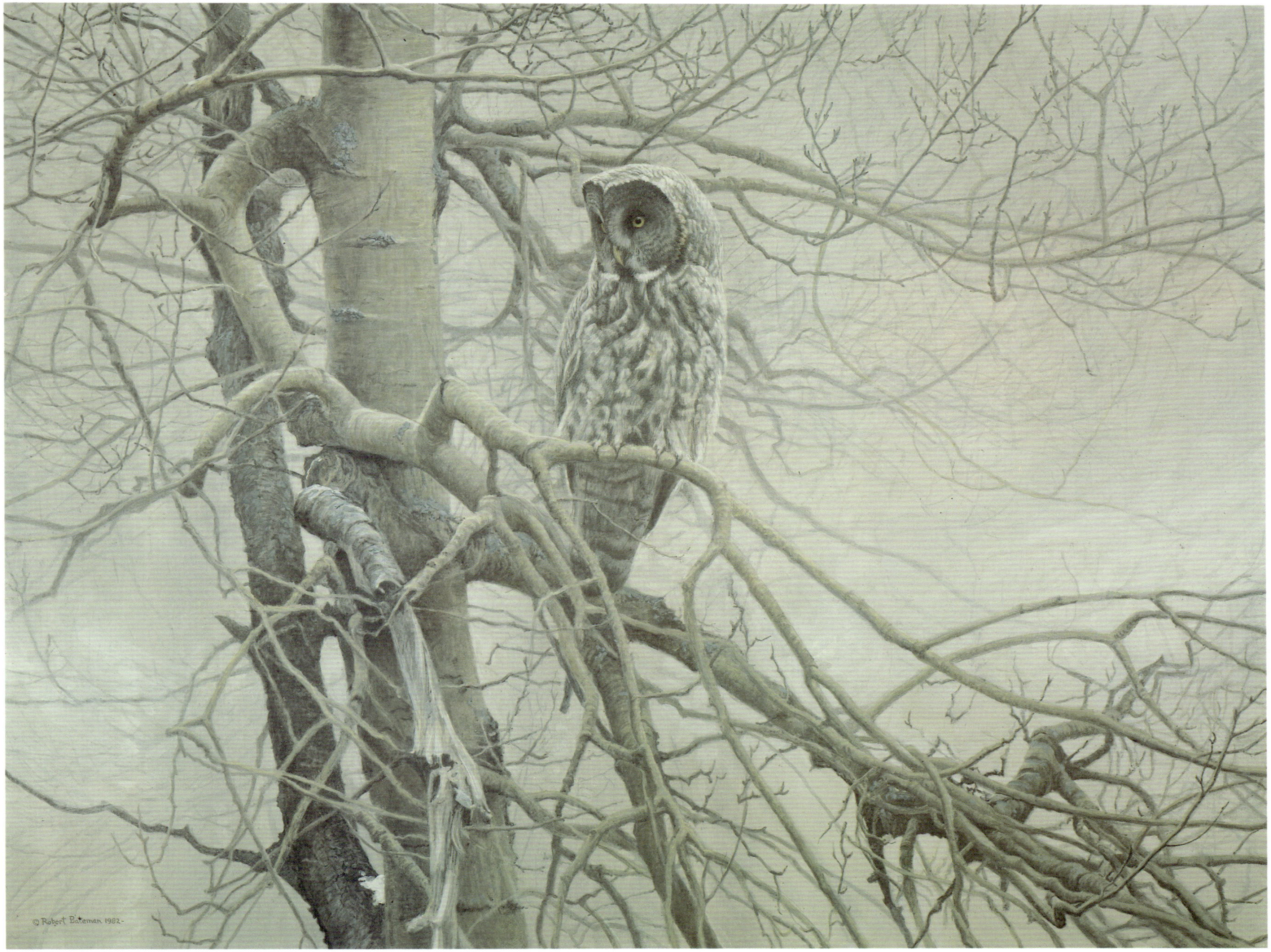

Ghost of the North (great gray owl) 1982, acrylic on board, 36 x 48 inches, collection of the Leigh Yawkey Woodson Art Museum. *Birds in Art* 1982.

Art is like music. You orchestrate the painting, giving it a theme which is echoed over and over.

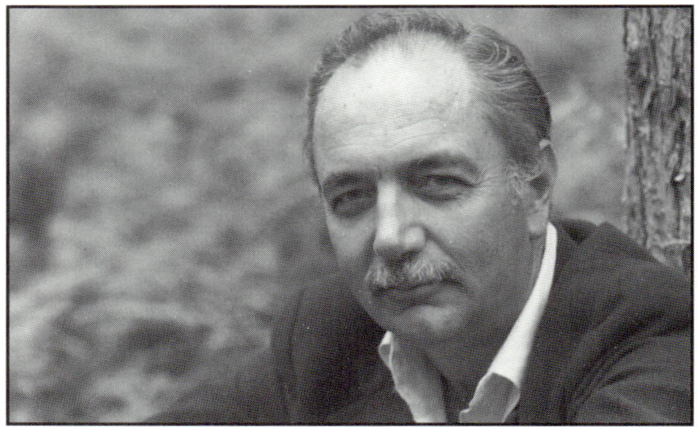

GUY COHELEACH

Master Wildlife Artist 1983
Born: 1933, New York, New York
Resides: Bernardsville, New Jersey

I grew up in Baldwin, Long Island, when there were woodlands, farms, and wildlife all around. Ten years later, the whole area had turned from potato fields and woods into Levittowns.

Our forefathers didn't want paintings of wildlife because grizzlies were knocking down their front doors. They wanted pastoral scenes of their homelands in Europe. Now, of course, all we've got is asphalt and concrete and glass, and when I do a painting of a great blue heron, people say, "Well, that's an exotic African bird," and I say, "No, it's the bird in the catch basin, right down the street." People who grow up in the suburbs have a big thirst for wildlife.

Interest in nature art flourished after the Peterson field guide was published. It became very easy to identify birds in the backyard. And when a bird from the woods came and ate the bird in the backyard, people would go into the woods to learn what the predator was. All of a sudden, bird clubs flourished all over the country. More and more people became birders and raised their children that way. Today, these children are buying homes, cars, and artwork.

When I picked up my first Peterson field guide, I was fascinated with it. Within two weeks I knew the Latin name of every bird of prey in North America. My mother liked to feed the birds. She would ask, "What's that bird in the yard?" and I'd look it up.

I was caught drawing in the first grade. The nuns sent home a note saying I should be punished for defacing a school book, but they also thought my parents should know I had a talent. For Christmas I got a drawing table and for my birthday I got an oil paint set. Although these are inexpensive gifts nowadays, it was a big nut to crack during the Depression for a family with nine children.

We had a drawing teacher who came into grade school fifteen minutes a week. . . . She taught professionally, but she offered to teach me for nothing. I was about ten years old [when] she taught me to use oil paints. My first was a copy of a picture of a parrot from a postcard, and it showed me how to mix paints. My first original painting was of a wood duck.

In high school I didn't know what I wanted to do with my life. I heard Cooper Union Art School was a scholarship school, so I took tests for engineering and art. I figured whichever one I passed, that's what I would do. I passed both tests, but I became an artist because back then an engineer had four years and an artist had only three. I'd like to think I made a better artist than engineer. Maybe there was more intuition running the show than I wanted to admit. I am a firm believer that our subconscious should be listened to and not just our conscious mind – but I am still trying to get in touch with it.

My instructors at Cooper Union taught non-objective art with abstract design. I ran into an awful lot of bigotry toward realism in those days. But I had a marvelous sculpture teacher who really knew art and taught me a lot. He suggested I do everything half-way and try not to identify the subject until after the piece was graded. So I blocked in the shapes and colors and showed them that way. Later, I took them home to finish. I got straight A's after that because apparently I had a good sense of design.

I met Don [Eckelberry] in 1962 at an Explorers Club meeting in New York. He convinced me that I could become a successful wildlife artist. Months later, he even backed me up for my first job in bird illustration by telling the publisher that if I couldn't do the job, he'd do it for nothing. Fortunately for both of us, he never had to do it. We've been good friends ever since.

Bird painting for me can range from a very detailed portrait meticulously worked out to a broad impression of bold, gloppy brush strokes with a lot of mood and atmosphere. Both, however, should be accurate, aesthetically appealing, and alive. I see birds two ways: first, as an emotional experience – a fleeting moment in time; second, as two-dimensional detail – a map of feathers and patterns. While I would rather paint something looser, I still get a kick out of doing a really tight painting that looks like you could stick your fingers into the feathers – but that's craftsmanship, not art.

I don't know who I am, artistically, and I don't know if I'm trying to find out. I can sit down and do impressionistic work and then do something really tight. I want to do the impressionistic work first, but I still have to make a living, and tight painting wins the popularity contest hands down. I admire people who do more impressionistic work, because I know they are doing it against great odds. They have guts enough to stick to it even if it means forgoing a comfortable living.

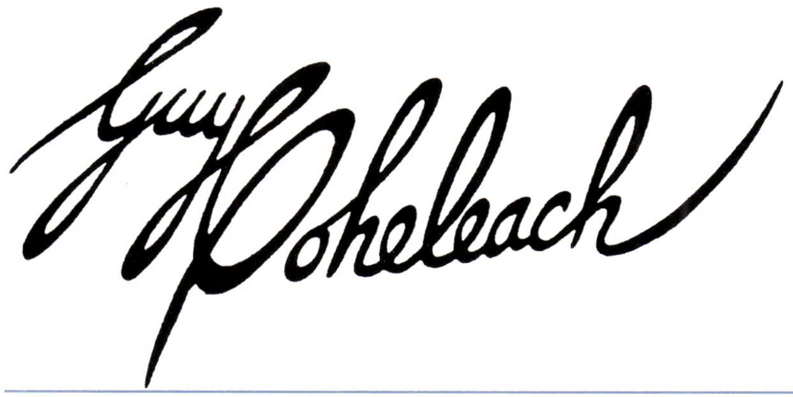

The print market drives wildlife art toward realism. The publishing houses are not afraid to print loose or even abstract work, but it's not going to sell. You can sell the original painting, but not the prints. If you are in a sold-out position, you can paint less realistically. There are some dealers who buy only the more impressionistic paintings, so I think the print-buying market is going to become more sophisticated. But the new print buyer will nearly always go for hair and feathers. Like when you first go to the opera, *Carmen* is almost always the favorite because you recognize the music.

The process I go through to take an idea to a finished painting is almost as varied as the paintings themselves. In my paintings, ninety-five percent of the work is in pencil. That is where I get the anatomy correct. It is a lot easier to make a correction with an eraser and one pencil line than it is to go over something in paint. On the other hand, in *Great Horned Owl* (1990), both the background and the owl are worked over. I painted the owl on a pure white background and then filled it in. I drew the background on the canvas and changed it half a dozen times, not in pencil but in paint. It takes longer to change the painting itself, but it keeps the painting spontaneous.

I approach every painting like it's going to be the best I've ever done. It's not always going to work out because taking risks can mean wasting time on a worthless painting.

The biggest mistake beginners make is not learning to draw. They need to practice and they need to draw from life. Drawing teaches you to see the difference between this horned owl and that horned owl. You don't want to paint a horned owl that has freak ears four inches longer than every other horned owl. It may exist on that particular owl, but you're going to look foolish painting it. Anyone can learn to draw; it takes hard work, but you have got to do it.

Some artists are slaves to whatever is in a photograph. They'll paint a photograph of a bird with the light coming in from one side, and paint the background from a photograph with the light coming from the other side. That's just stupid; and it's not art. When somebody is an artist, he's supposed to create an original thought of his own. If he copies a photograph in paint, he is a renderer. To me, art implies creativity. I use a ton of photographs for reference. However, there are too many copied photographs being paraded as art today. If the photograph is that good, frame the photograph.

If you paint well and paint a landscape, or a figure, or a portrait, or a still life, you can be a fine artist. Paint an animal, and you are an illustrator. There is a base of prejudice there, but a lot of us deserve it because we're slaves to this literal translation from photography. I think the two go hand in hand.

I believe that if I am painting wildlife, my painting must look wild; it should look alive. You need the experience of being in the field to see the extra hustle of the shorebird when the peregrine is after it. The chase is a predominant theme in my paintings. It is exciting to me.

I don't know about other artists, but I know I can paint a gazelle running from a cheetah a lot better having been at the business end of a dangerous animal and having tried to get an animal for my next meal. I know what it is like to be afraid of something that wants to kill you, and what it is like to see something afraid of you because you want to kill it. I try to catch the terror in the eyes of the antelope and the intentions in the eyes of the cheetah. I either capture the look or I don't, but I feel it when I paint. I really think that gives me the energy to get it right. I enjoy getting the blood going through my veins. I do not love fear, but I love the feeling I get when I get by it.

I spend a lot of time in the field because I enjoy being in the field. If I were a good enough photographer, I'd make my living as a photographer. Then I could do all my work in the field rather than in the studio, which to me is a cage. I love doing a good painting that is meaningful to me, but I dread the time I must spend in the studio.

I work hard, and there are very few paintings where somewhere in the middle of it I haven't said, "I am a fraud. I don't know what I am doing." At four in the morning, you get depressed and you just want to paint over it. But you plod along and put in your time and, if you put in enough time and make enough mistakes, some of them will be happy accidents.

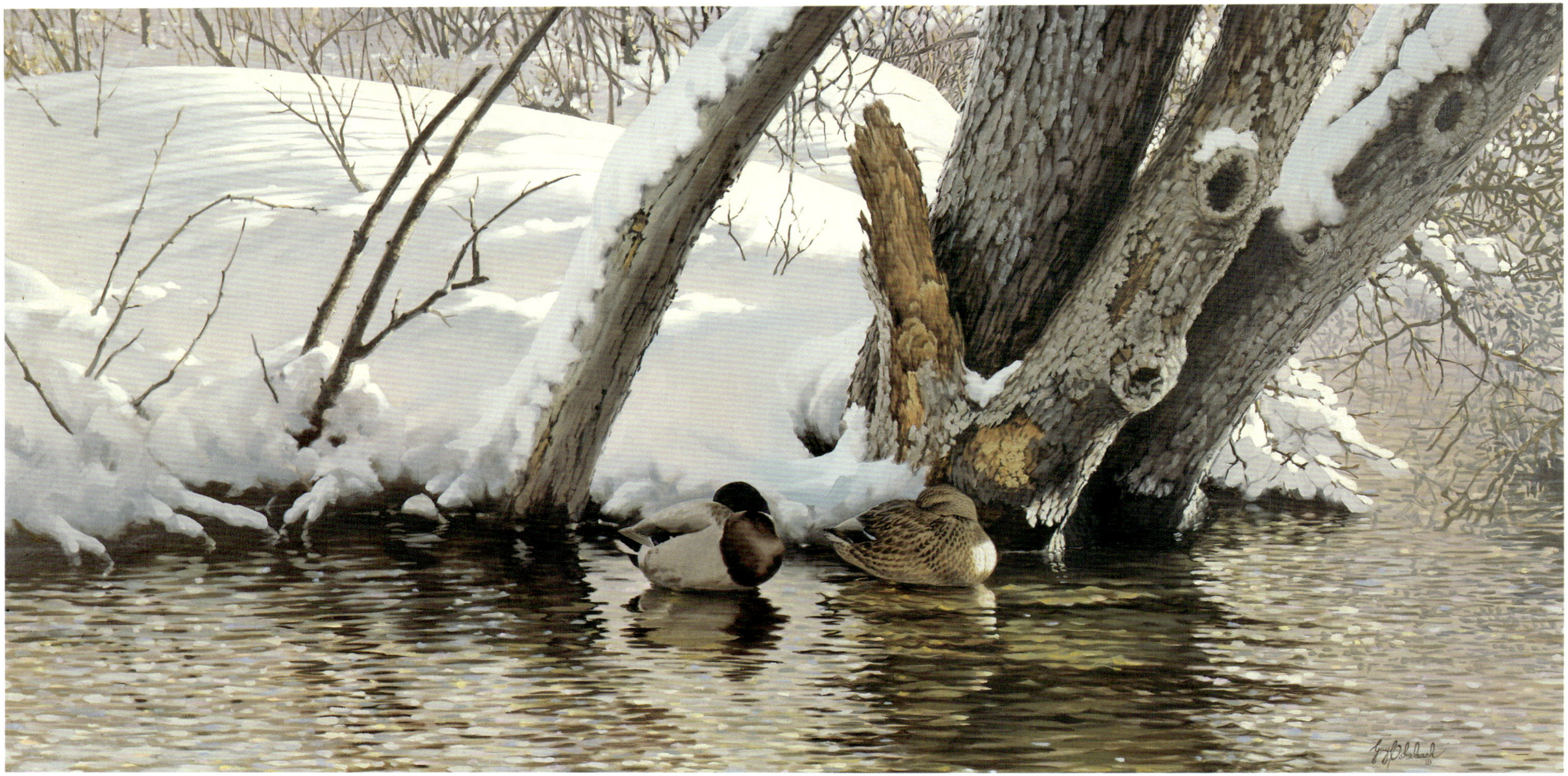

Brightwaters Creek (mallard) 1983, oil on canvas, 36 x 72 inches, collection of the Leigh Yawkey Woodson Art Museum. *Birds in Art* 1983.

If the mood is overpowering, the rest will come together.

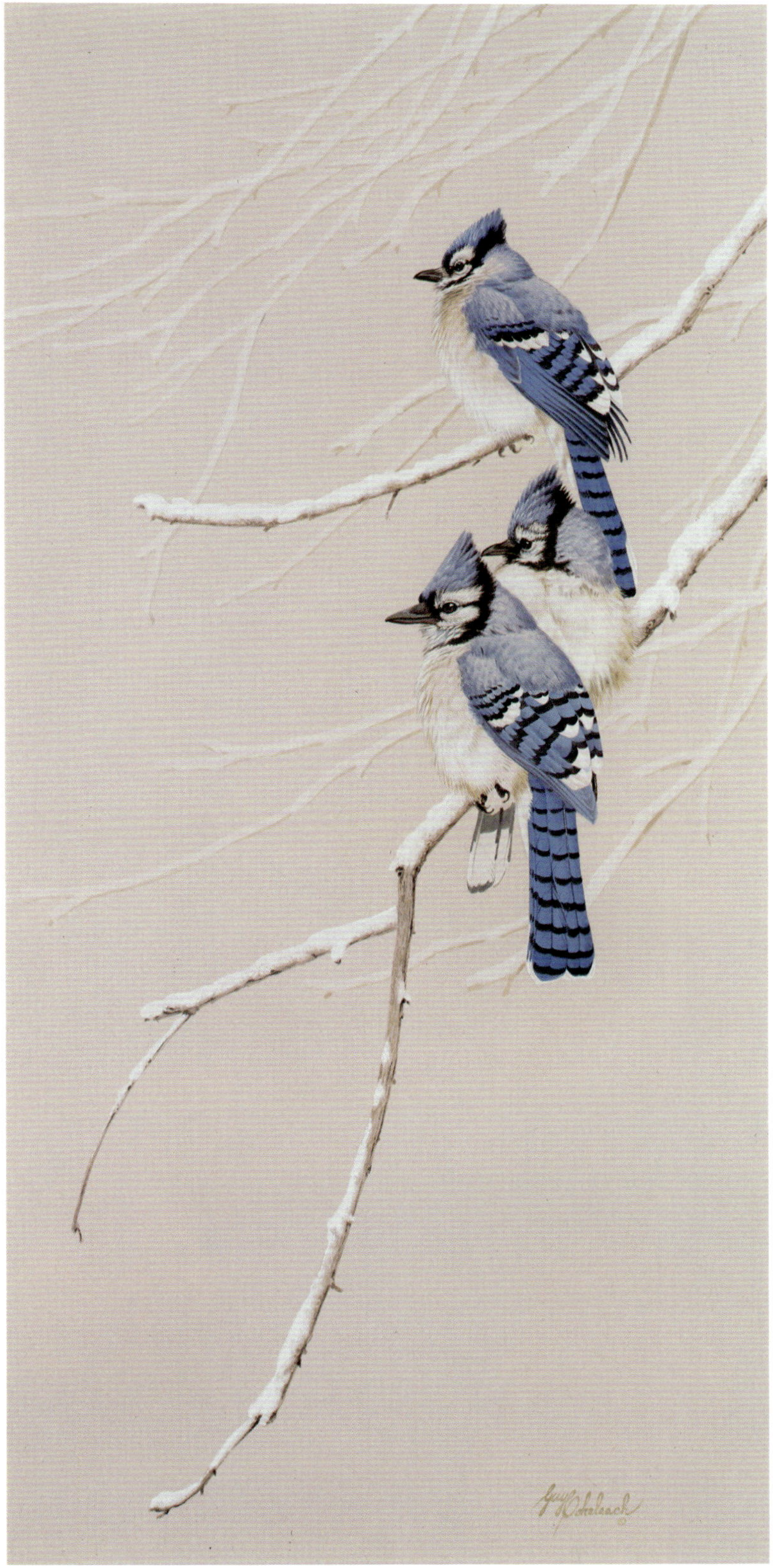

I try to paint the soul and the character of an animal.

Blue-gray (blue jay) 1982, gouache on illustration board, 30 x 15 inches, private collection.
Birds in Art 1983.

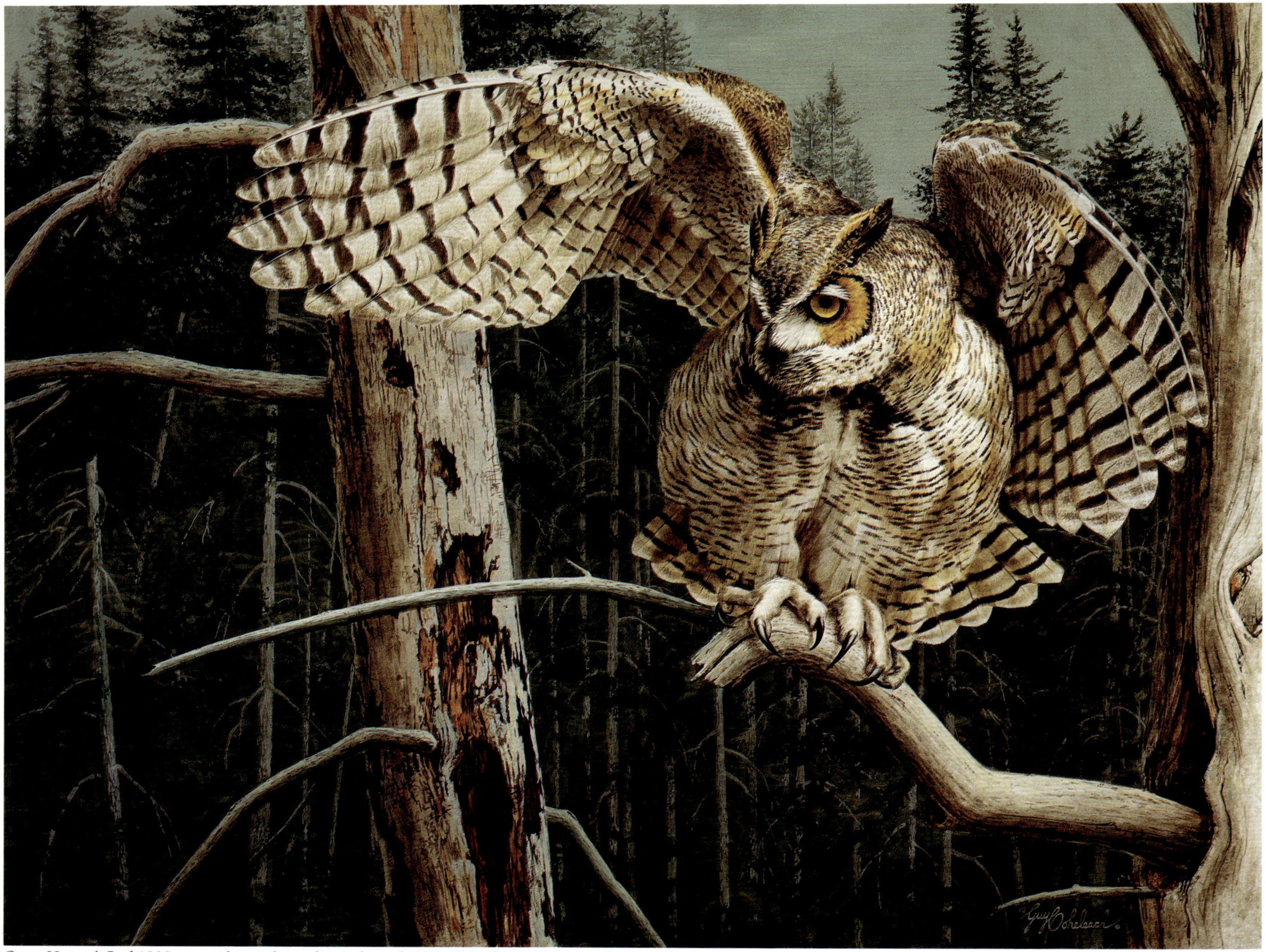

Great Horned Owl 1990, gouache and acrylic on board, 30 x 40 inches, private collection. *Birds in Art* 1990.

If you're observant, you can see a lot. There is an alert, fierce look when owls are hungry; they don't miss a thing.

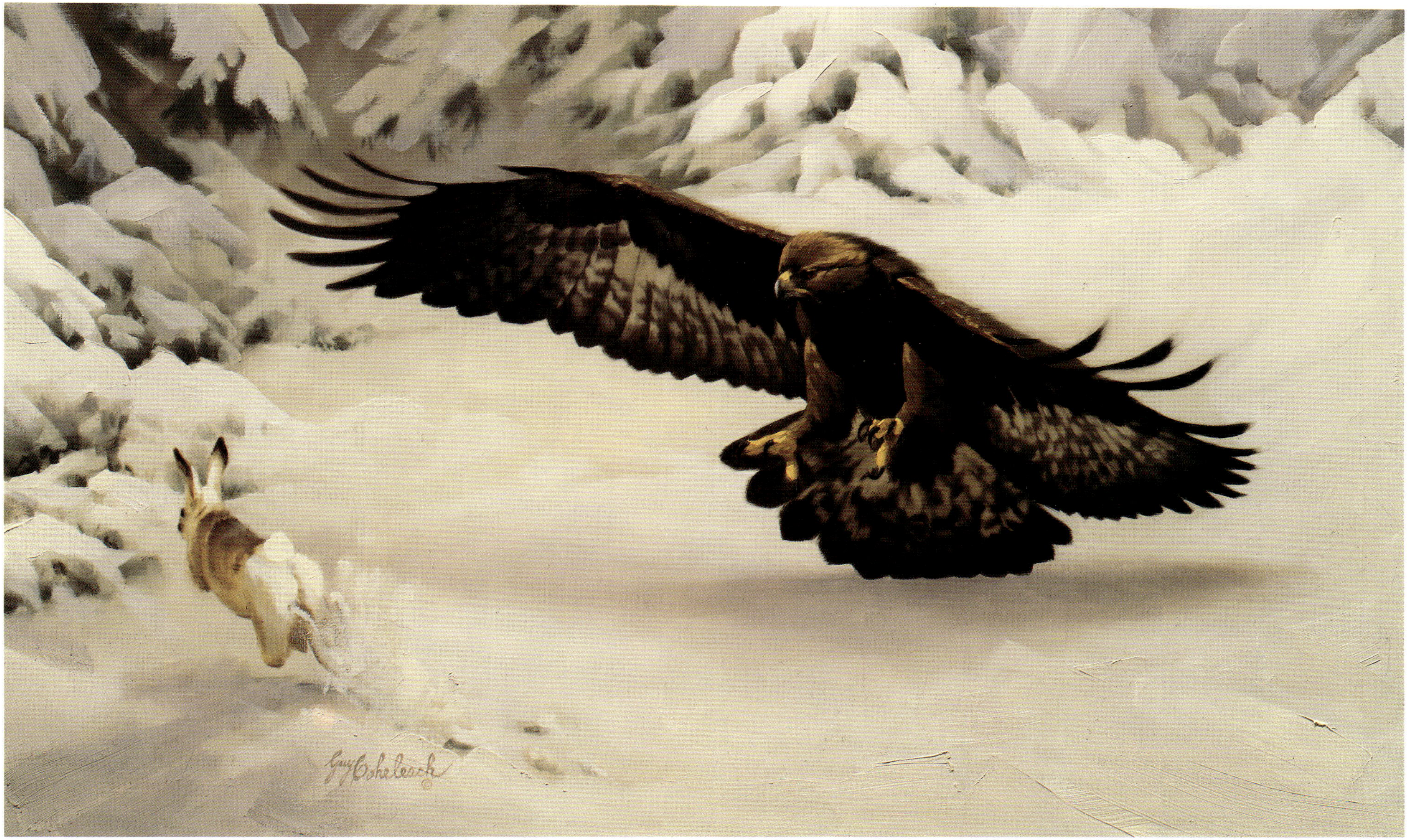

Haree Moment (golden eagle) 1978, oil on canvas, 36 x 72 inches, collection of Joe and Annett Bishop. *Birds in Art* 1979.

Painting wildlife isn't like painting anything else. A wild animal doesn't look or act the same when it is tamed. Wildlife has got to look alive – yes – but it's got to be wild on the canvas.

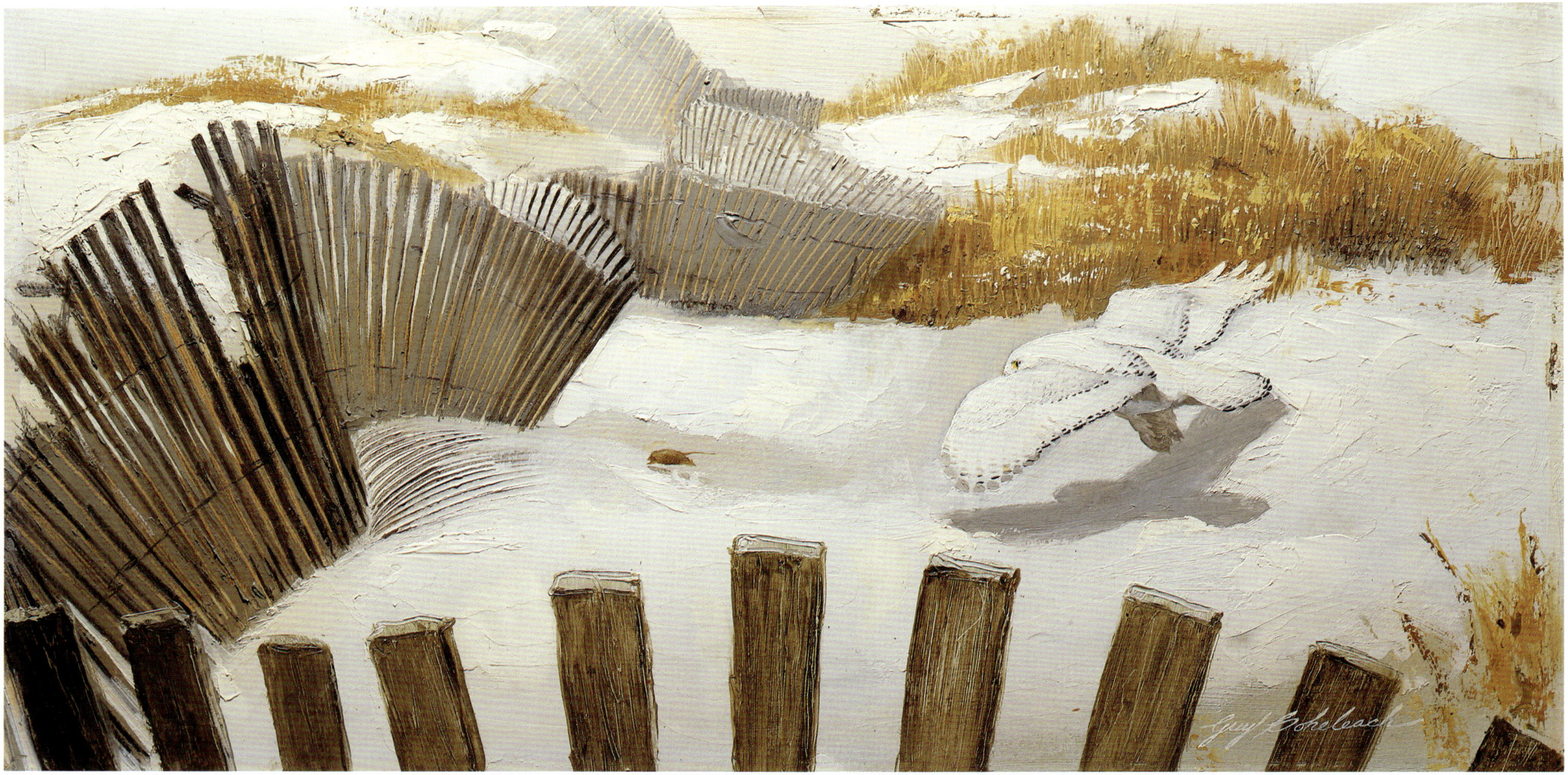

To the Fence (snowy owl) 1962, oil on illustration board, 12 x 24 inches, collection of Don Richard Eckelberry. *Birds in Art* 1983.

Whether it be a tight rendering or an impressionistic piece, it must smack of life. The subject, design, and colors, no matter how subtle, should live!

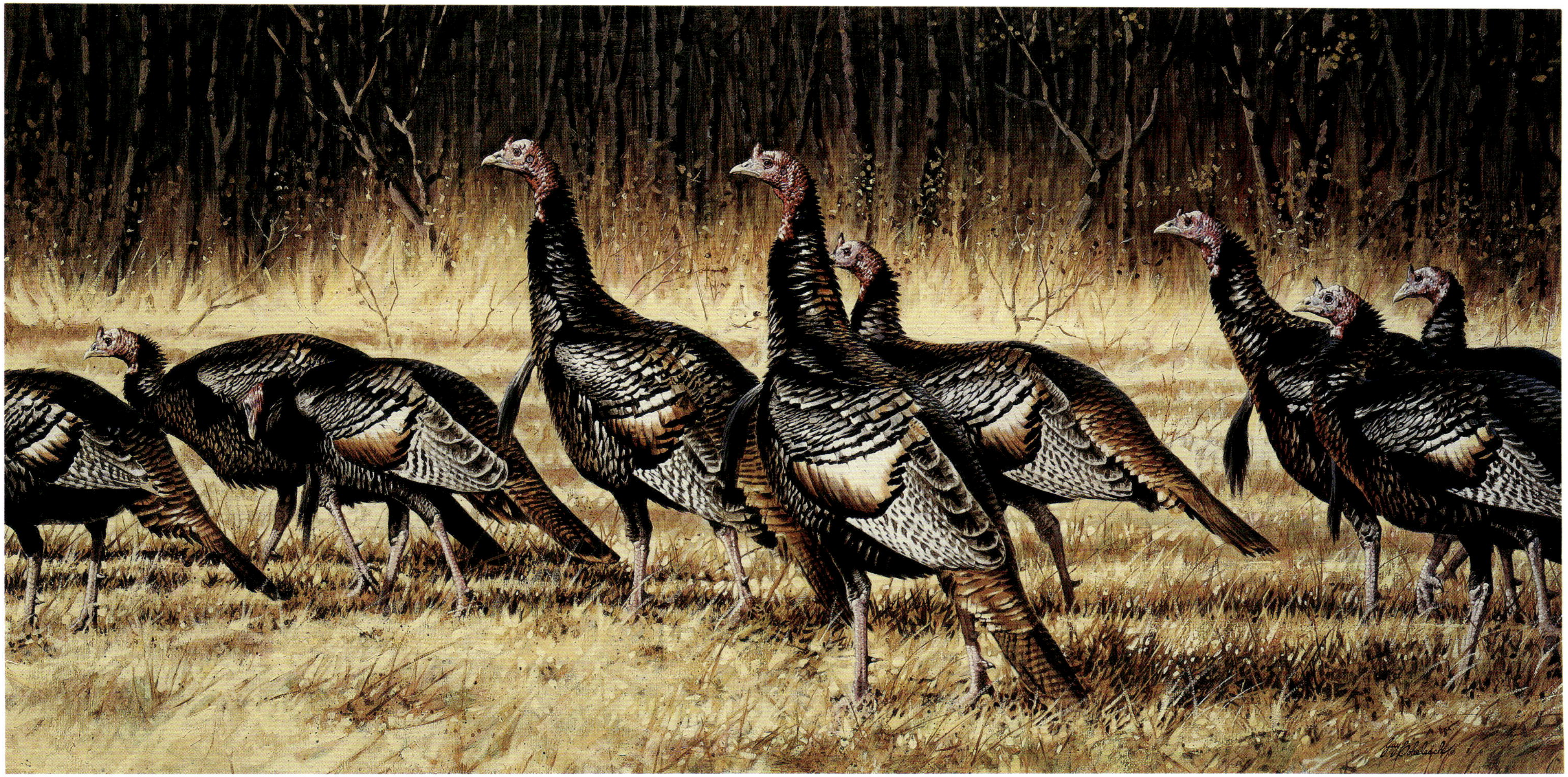

Gobblers (turkey) 1985, oil on canvas, 36 x 72 inches, private collection. *Birds in Art* 1986.

Saving wildlife is very important. . . . Wildlife is like a canary in a mine; it's a bellwether, a warning sign of what's going to happen to mankind.

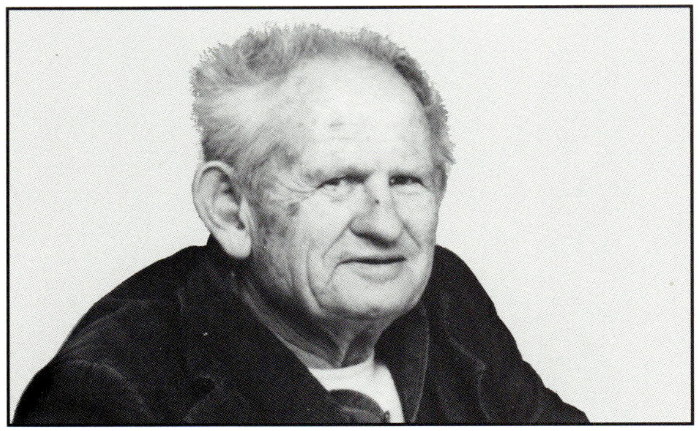

CHARLES GREENOUGH CHASE

Master Wildlife Artist 1984
Born: 1908, Boston, Massachusetts
Resides: Brunswick, Maine

My first carvings were baseball players, little ones about the size of lead soldiers cut from one piece of wood. I painted them with uniforms of the Boston Red Sox and the Boston Braves – which really dates me. This was way back in the early 1920s, when I was studying mathematics at Harvard. I didn't have that much interest in art, I just liked to whittle. It wasn't until much later, when I became interested in bird hunting, that I started to carve birds. I didn't begin sculpting full time until around 1952. I had done about a hundred birds by then, but they were all little. Now the only math I do is scaling down a sculpture.

My first bird carving was a partridge in 1934. I modeled it after a ruffed grouse I had on my mantle. I cut it out on a band saw and cut in around it with a penknife. It was in pine and, of course, the legs went right across the grain, which made them likely to break off. Then I took the partridge to a woman in Wiscasset who knew about art, and I said, "How do I paint this?" She said, "Don't paint it. It's good as sculpture." And my reaction was, "Thank God, I don't have to paint it." Then I began to think that pine looks awful for a partridge – it's too light-colored. The next one I did was in mahogany which is a better color for a partridge. From then on I started choosing wood only with regard to color.

Since I don't paint, I want to choose a wood more or less the color of the bird I am doing. Almost half my birds are black walnut – geese, ducks, eagles, and vultures. One of the best birds to do in black walnut is the glossy ibis. Bubinga wood, which polishes up to a beautiful red, is perfect for the scarlet ibis. Honduran mahogany is another good red wood. Maple, birch, beech, ash, elm, or persimmon are all good for light-colored birds like white ibises and egrets. I did a whooping crane in maple. I have done gulls, terns, and a snowy owl in elm. Ebony is great for cormorants, anhingas, crows, storm petrels, and black oystercatchers. I use jacaranda, which goes by the awful name rosewood, for pheasants and spoonbills. So most of the time I can match the color of the bird.

I am somewhat limited in the birds I sculpt since I don't paint them. I choose bigger birds with forms you can recognize. I wouldn't do warblers, since the only good thing about warblers would be painting them. I try to choose a typical pose and include something from the bird's habitat that will help you recognize the bird.

If you are going to paint the feathers, you might as well go into taxidermy. But I do admire the beautiful job done by assemblers. I call what I do pure sculpture or subtractive sculpture. The other style is assembly, because they actually disassemble the sculptures to ship them to competitions.

Their art is as good as what I do. But I like the wood to show just as it is. I like to see the great surface of polished wood. It's almost like a stone sculpture, and you wouldn't paint a stone sculpture.

The word sculpture is so loosely used that it can mean anything now. If a guy welds a few things together and calls it *Why Girls Leave Home*, they call it sculpture. If somebody paints an old box blue and calls it *Opus 13*, that's sculpture, but it's not. I think sculpture is when you cut stuff away – that's what the word means. So I thought of the name subtractive sculpture. I think that sort of defines it, because all you do is take away. In subtractive sculpture, everything has to be planned ahead of time because you are cutting away, and once you cut away, it's gone.

First, I get an idea and draw it up. Then I see if I can get a stuffed bird or the measurements of a bird. Next, I get a piece of wood that's big enough to take care of what I want. If it won't quite fit, I scale the bird down. I don't go below seven-tenths the actual size of the bird, because the sculpture gets too little and it won't have the feeling of an eagle or a vulture. For instance, at half scale, a sculpture has only one-eighth the volume or mass of the full-size bird, and it would not give you a feeling for the bird's bigness.

Then I draw a planned view of the bird and mark the wood. I draw a side view, and the top view, and maybe the front view. When I do that, I can see great big blocks of wood that can be cut away. If the bird is leaning forward, there is a big cut that can come off the back. I figure out which blocks of wood I don't want, and I cut out the big blocks with a gasoline chainsaw. I also use an electric chainsaw for finer cuts. After that, I chop away at the rest of the stuff with hammer and chisels and power grinders.

Charles Greenough Chase

Blocking out takes awhile. As soon as I can, I do the head. Once the head of the bird is shaped up, it starts to look like something. I can look at it and know what I'm doing. I see the eagle instead of just a shapeless mass. When I get the head done and the body shaped up, I get going faster and faster. It's fun then because I see it coming out. I sand down the parts I want smooth and leave other parts roughed up for contrast, like the bald head on a vulture. To get a shiny look, like the shimmery effect of water, I take something really hard and mash down the grain. You can use a bone or a smooth piece of steel; I use a whale's tooth. This gives the wood a hard, reflective surface, and when I polish it, I get a nice reflection of the reed and the bird in the water. I do the beaks of birds the same way. You can see the contrast in the condor's beak with the rest of its head, which is roughed up. To finish a sculpture, I spray it with a clear lacquer, sand it again, and wax it.

I don't worry about the grain of the wood. Grain is always beautiful. I usually have the grain running with the legs, and I always get a nice pattern on the cross grain of the body. I don't worry about the wood checking. Checking is going to be radial from the center or concentric around the rings. I don't worry about seasoning the wood. I save all the little scraps of wood so I can make a chip with the right grain spacing to fit any crack. I fill the crack with glue, tap in the chip, cut it off, and I can match the grain line for line. I can take care of all checks that way. Five minutes of epoxy glue and you can hardly see any repair.

I try to have the bird touch the base in three places. The bird's body is one big mass, the base is another big mass, and with only two spindly legs to connect them, the sculpture can rock a bit or break under its own weight. If there are three connections, it's not going to rock. I always try to include a reed or branch or something to have three points, not in a line, touching the base. Then I've got a stable sculpture.

It's so important in sculpture to plan everything out. You've got to know ahead of time exactly what you're doing, what you're going to cut.

That's the trouble with subtractive sculpture; I mean if you take it off, it's gone. For the first two or three days, you lay out your plans and from then on you carry them out.

California Condor was one of the most difficult sculptures I ever did – he's so huge. The log was lying down, and it took me a long time working on it before I could even move it to an upright position. *Scarlet Ibises* was also quite a challenge. It involved three birds and a mammoth piece of bubinga wood. I had to plan all that from the side, the front, and the top to see what areas could be cut out.

I think the best way to record birds if you want to sculpt them is to take movies. Take all the footage you can if you get a good scene. I came upon the scene of a vulture feast in Africa and took about 200 feet of film. Just at the end, the vultures moved away and there was the winner, standing on top of this skull. Well, I've used that subject more than any other – a vulture on a skull. I love doing vultures on skulls. They are not only sculpturesque, but dramatic. I recently finished a sculpture of a marabou stork, which is the ugliest stork in Africa, hovering over a topi skull. African antelopes have the most beautiful horns. I just think of what is dramatic; I don't have any spiritual feelings about it.

The only way you can learn to sculpt is to use a tool and see what happens, see how a chisel works and how a gouge works. You have to get the feel of a tool to see what it can do. I taught myself how to sculpt; I've never been to art school. I was influenced by painters because when I started out not many people were carving birds. Of course, there were the people who did little ducks and painted them, but they didn't inspire me at all. Roger Peterson's paintings were great and I liked the work of Fuertes. Many of the paintings of that era inspired me.

I don't have any trouble getting orders. I don't want too many. Four or five a year is fine; that's about all I can do.

At a local art show, there was a piano on the stage and an eagle of mine on top of the piano. Everything else looked very imposing so I thought, "Maybe I'll get a sale." When I saw a couple who kept coming back to look at the eagle I said to myself, "I've got a sale." I went up and pretended to look at the next piece of sculpture and listened. The woman said, "That's a nice eagle; how much does it cost, dear?" He looked at the catalogue and said, "Five thousand dollars." She looked kind of stunned and asked, "Wow, does the piano go with it?"

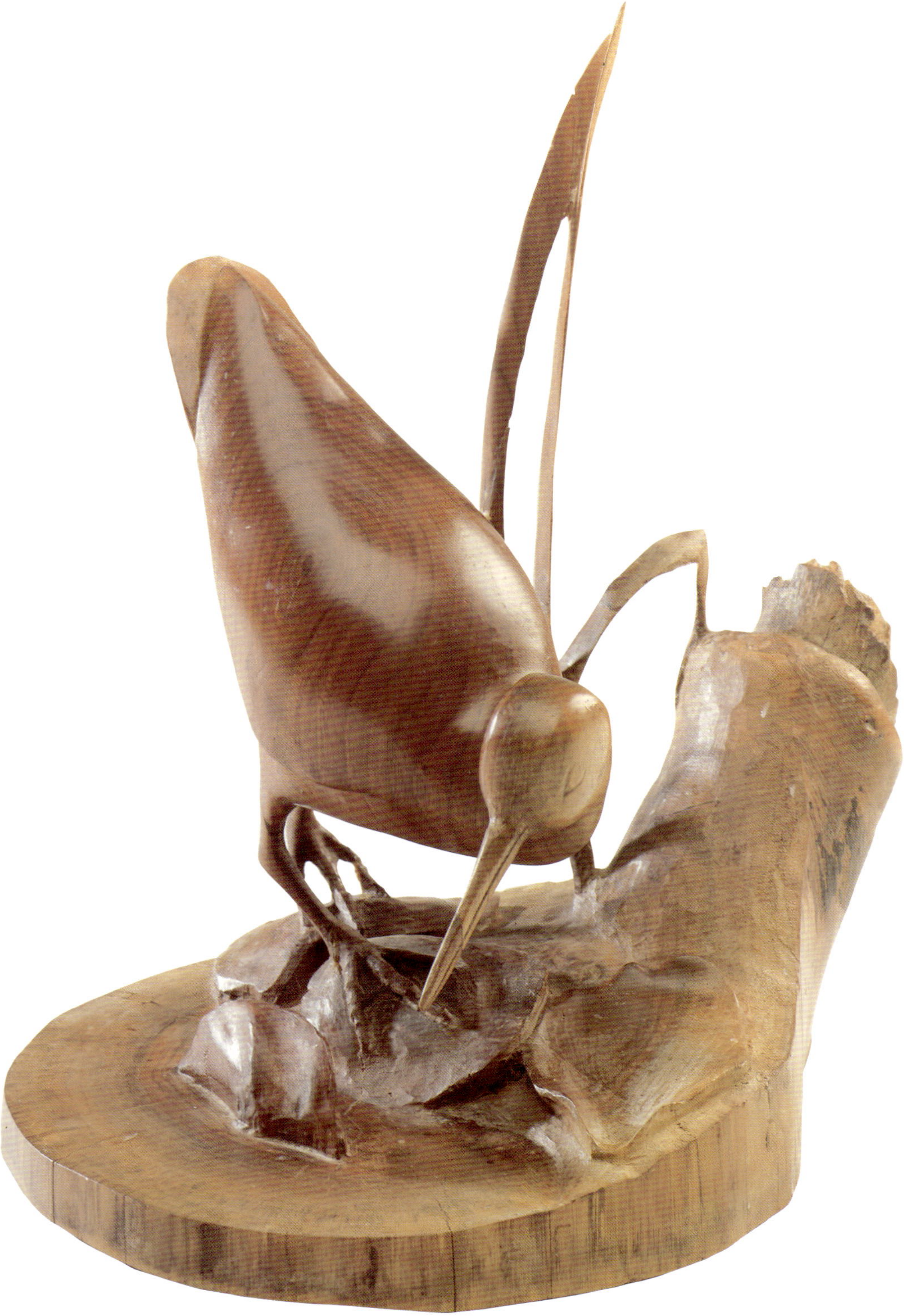

I was influenced by painters because when I started out not many people were carving birds.

American Oystercatcher 1975, black walnut, 13 x 9 x 10½ inches, collection of the Leigh Yawkey Woodson Art Museum. *Birds in Art* 1980.

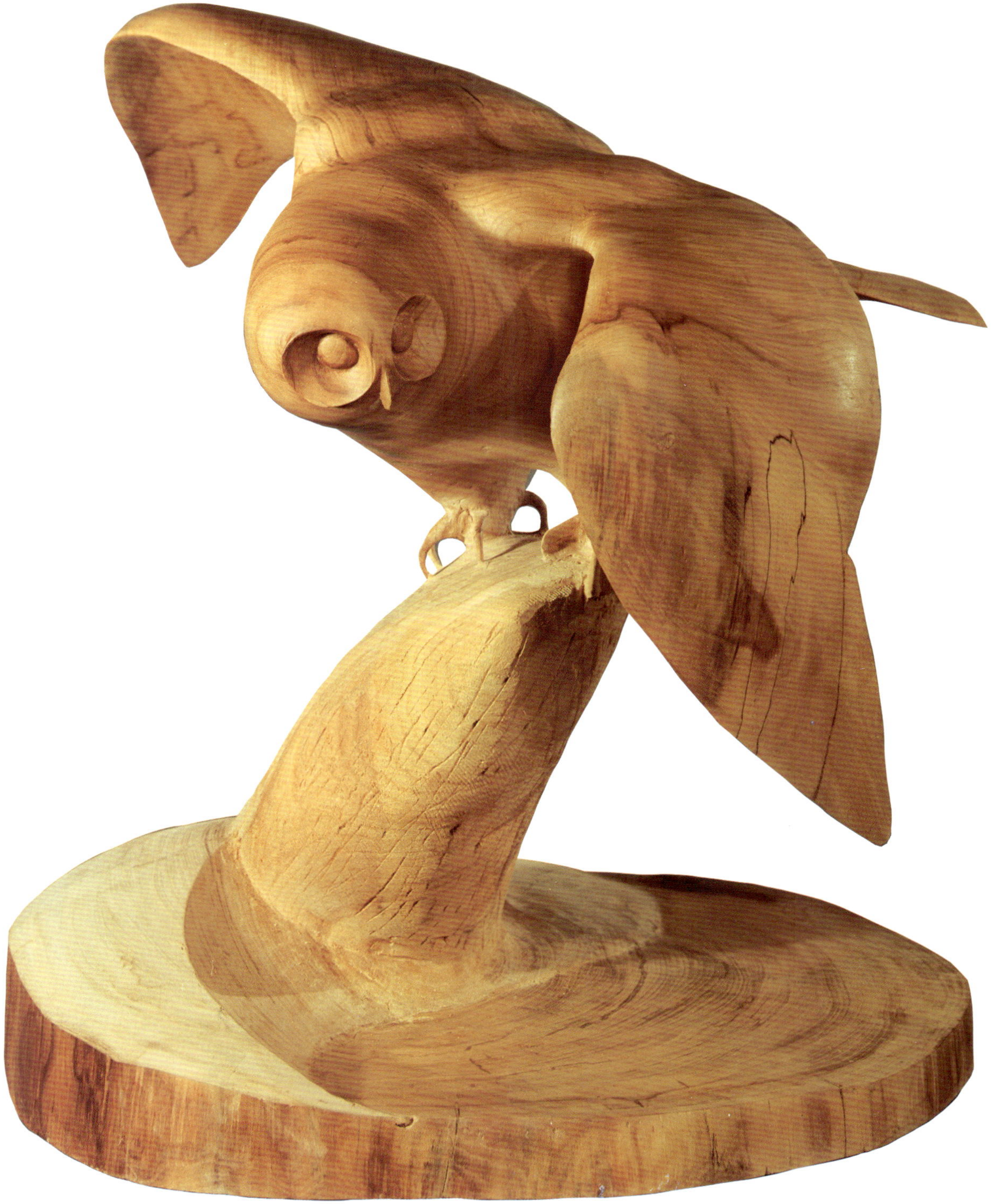

I like the wood to show just as it is. I like to see the great surface of polished wood. It's almost like a stone sculpture, and you wouldn't paint a stone sculpture.

Snowy Owl 1972, elm, 22 x 20 x 20 inches, private collection. *Birds in Art* 1984.

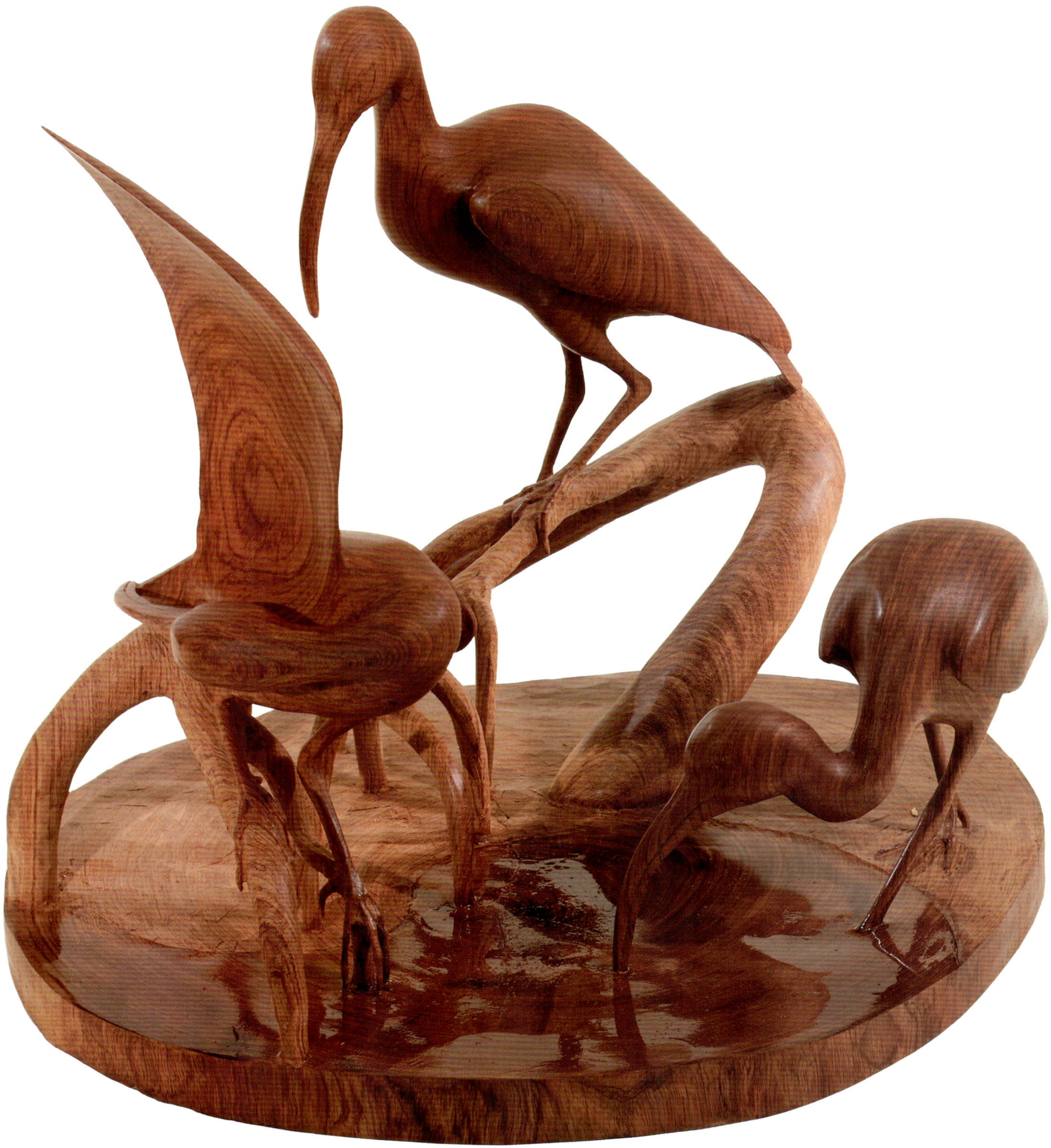

Scarlet Ibises *was quite a challenge. It involved three birds and a mammoth piece of bubinga wood. . . . In subtractive sculpture everything has to be planned ahead of time because you are cutting away, and once you cut away, it's gone.*

Scarlet Ibises 1979, bubinga, 21 x 19 x 19 inches, collection of Herbert Pratt. *Birds in Art* 1979.

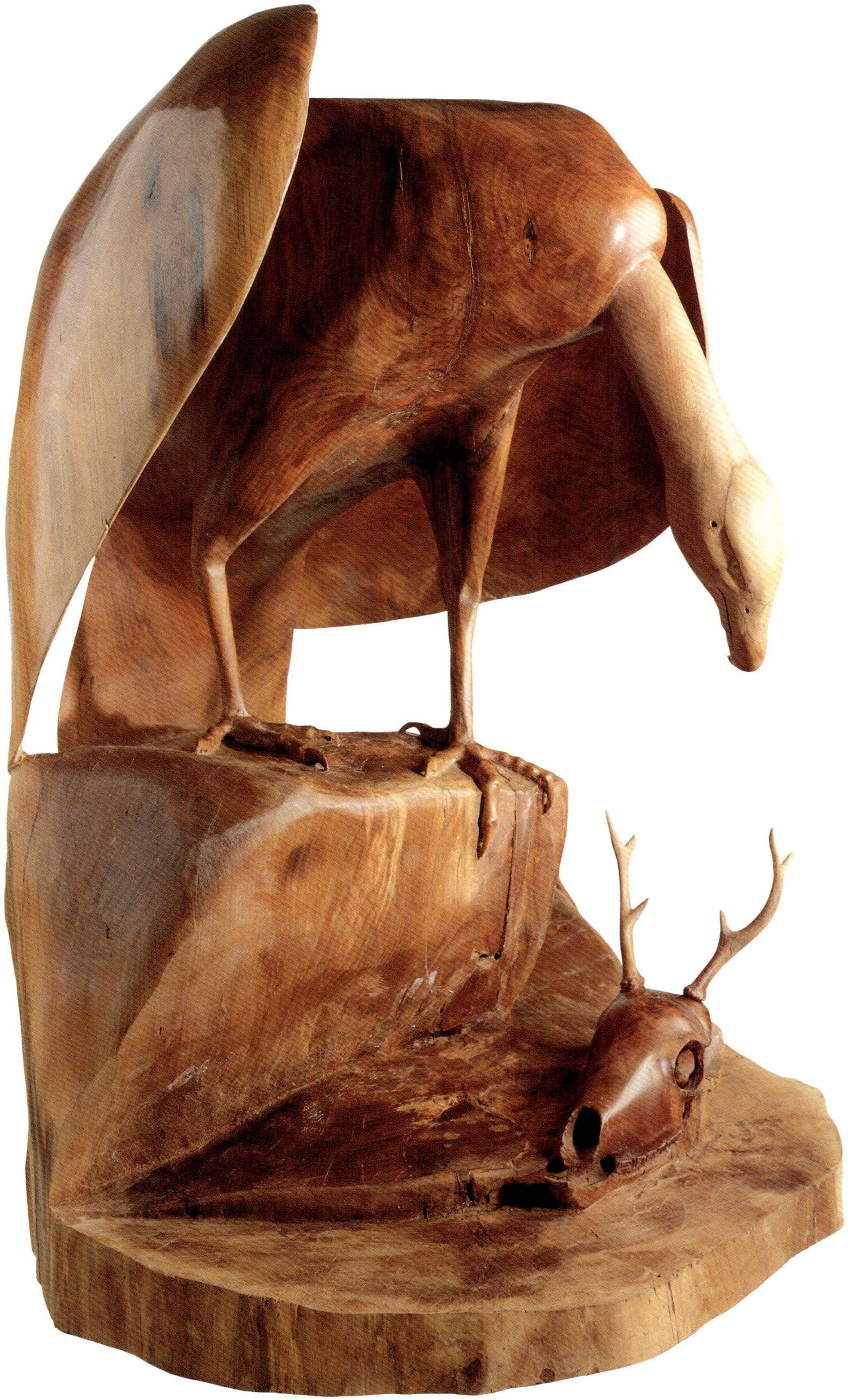

California Condor *was one of the most difficult sculptures I have ever done – he's so huge. The log was lying down, and I had to work on it a long time before I could even move it to an upright position.*

California Condor 1982, black walnut, 43½ x 27 x 28 inches, collection of the Leigh Yawkey Woodson Art Museum. *Birds in Art* 1983.

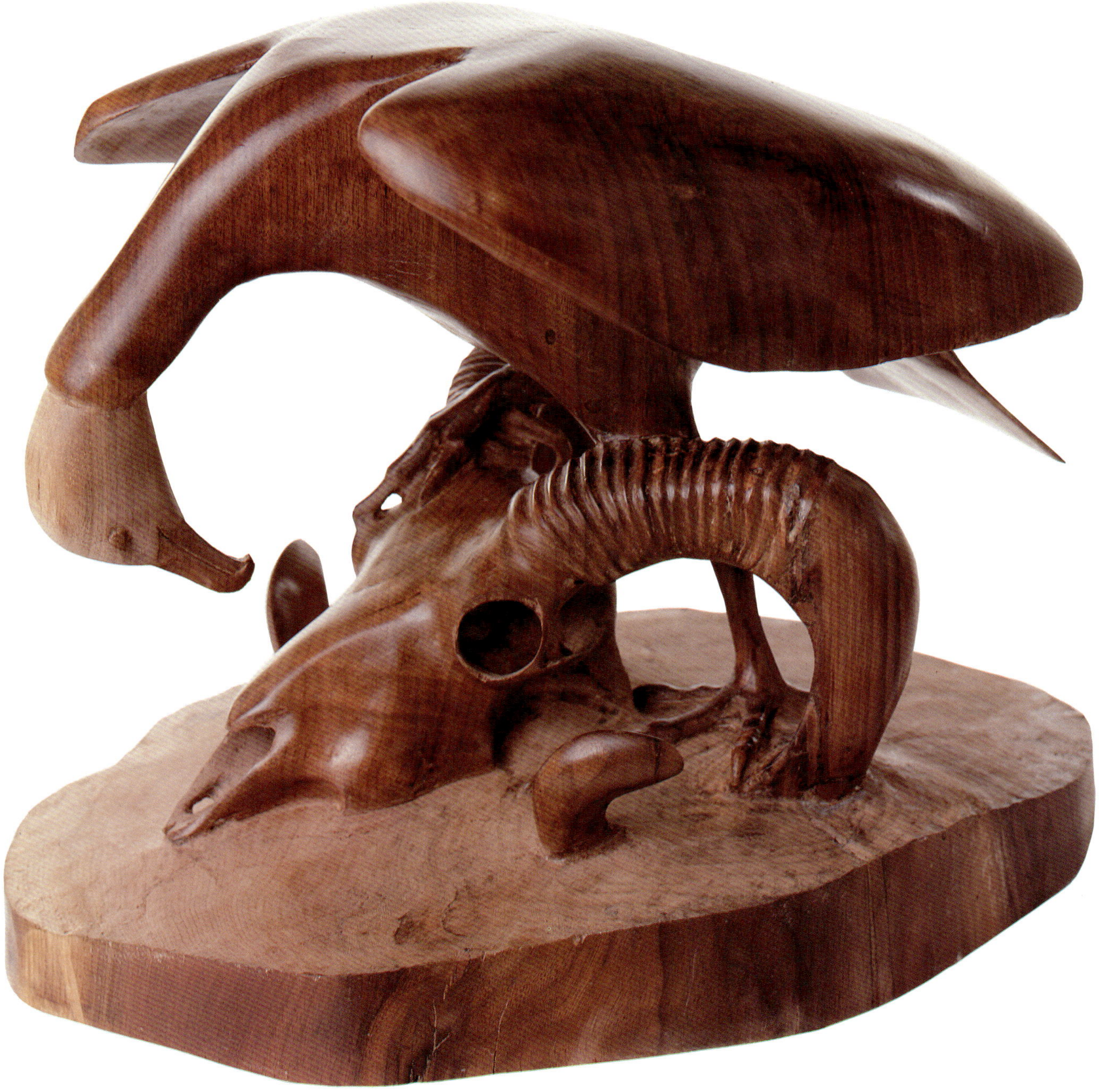

I love doing vultures on skulls. They are not only sculpturesque, but dramatic.

Black Vulture 1984, black walnut, 16 x 20 x 18 inches, collection of the artist. *Birds in Art* 1984.

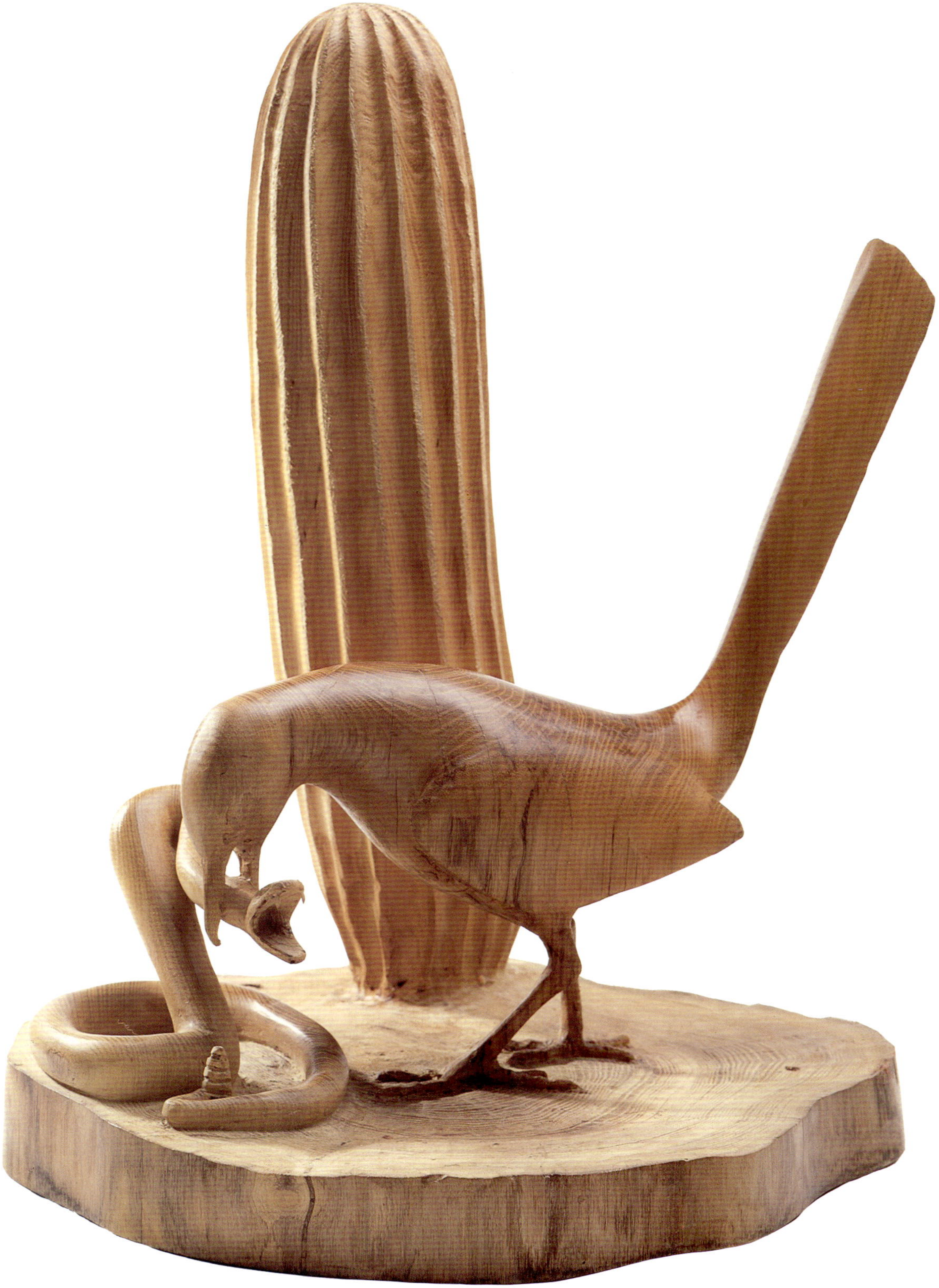

Bird sculpture should represent the artist's enthusiasm for birds by showing a typical pose of the bird in action with a suggestion of its environment.

Roadrunner 1988, locust, 19 x 15 x 14 inches, private collection. *Birds in Art* 1988.

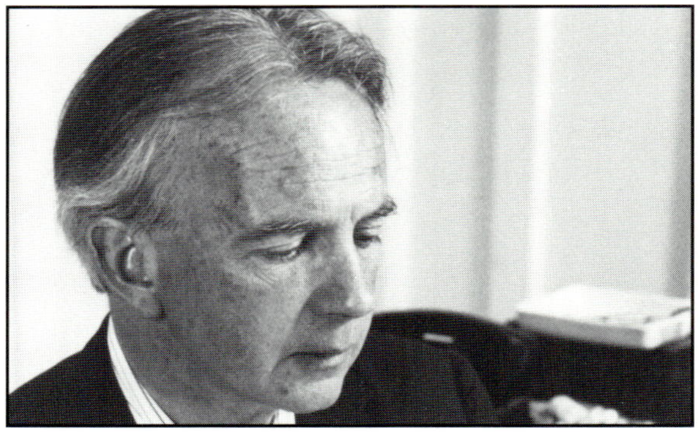

J. FENWICK LANSDOWNE

Master Wildlife Artist 1985
Born: 1937, Hong Kong
Resides: Victoria, British Columbia, Canada

The highest compliment anyone could give me is to say, "You're a good painter," not, "You're a good bird painter." I am a painter in the Audubon style. I am a delineator of birds. I don't do big canvases, big scenes. I do bird portraits.

I do fairly tightly controlled pictures with a lot of detail, a lot of exactitude. That may come from the fact that I do not have formal training and I was not taught to paint in broad brush strokes in a large expansive way. Also, the confines of the kind of painting I do tend to promote exactitude rather than interpretive expression. So it's a combination of the traditions of a tranquil art form and my nature which is fairly precise. I've had nearly thirty-five years experience now, and my painting is a lot freer and bolder than it was thirty years ago.

Each painter develops his own style and approach to his subject, though at first he may emulate the techniques of other artists. The heroes of my early painting days were Brooks, Fuertes, and Thorburn; much later came my admiration for John James Audubon. I took something from each of them and developed or adapted it in my own way, to fit my own needs. Others do this too, of course, and I find that some now base their styles on mine. It is easy to recognize one's own painting disguised thinly or not at all and passed off as an original work. At a certain level of competency, overt copying should be abandoned and a painter who publishes his work should be able to create his own pictures.

I'm quite old-fashioned now, because I don't paint in the currently popular style of full and detailed backgrounds and landscapes with the birds and animals less prominent.

If there is any abstract design in my painting, it comes quite unconsciously. I think painting usually does come unconsciously – especially the best kind. I am not conscious of Oriental influence either. I think the spareness of my paintings perhaps gives that impression. It's not a deliberate attempt to emulate Oriental artists. These things come in spite of myself.

When I see something in the field that gives me an idea for a painting, I may not go right back to the studio and put it down. I often carry it in my head for a long time, and when the opportunity arises, I try to translate it into a painting. I start with small sketches, doodles, rough drawings to fix the general composition in my mind. I use bird skins for the coloring, feather details, and measurements. Once I am certain of the measurements and feather patterns, I do a full-scale drawing of the bird, exactly as I wish it to be. Then I trace that onto the final sheet of paper. If I have more than one subject, I can move each tracing around until I get them exactly as I wish before I commit myself.

Most of my early sketches are in ball-point pen on a pad or on the back of an envelope. To me, they represent the idea manifest. Sometimes you're so hot, you can just bang that right onto the paper and do the painting. Mostly it goes from the rough sketch to a more formal sketch to putting in another bird and fitting them all together. Then I let it be for a couple of days – or certainly overnight. The next day I come in and it's fresh, or it's flat and I throw it away. But when it's working, I come in in the morning and I know I've got something really important. So that's transferred to a bigger drawing.

I paint mostly in gouache which is a species of watercolor with a slight opacity. I mix that with a bit of transparent watercolor, colored pencils, chalk, or whatever comes to hand. I paint on watercolor paper that has a fairly soft surface and a nice aesthetic. I prefer that to illustration board.

The bird is always completed first, and I drop the washing around it. The background is done much the same way, with multiple washes of one color or another built up and worked again and again. I do detail on top of washes, and washes on top of detail. I find this gives more richness of color and translucency.

Some people can paint for seventeen hours at a time. I find I burn out after five or six. If I'm doing something really complicated, a duck with fine venation, I'm exhausted after six hours. That night I go to sleep and the pattern comes again and again and again, and I keep repeating wigeon feathers, wigeon feathers, all night long, until the whole thing comes back again.

I think one should strive against too many fiddling brush strokes. If you paint with a bigger brush, instead of a little one, you often achieve a better effect and a more realistic effect. My paintings tend to tighten up against my unconscious, against my second nature.

F. LANSDOWNE

You can tell a good artist by the freedom of his brush strokes, the way he applies the paint, the color, and the obvious assurance of his work. Compare that with somebody who is not very good but is desperately earnest, whose brush strokes and texture and colors and drawing are not up to scratch. It's often a very fine line between a great painting and one that isn't.

Young artists should try to get some training in basic drawing and painting, which would serve them in very good stead, no matter what subject they chose to paint. You don't need special training to be a bird artist. There are simple things about birds you can learn very quickly yourself. But drawing and painting are so important that unless you are an absolute genius, if you don't have some training, you're really not going to be quite as good. And even if you are, it's going to take you a lot longer to learn the things that you could have learned at art school.

Art galleries don't usually think too much of bird painters, with some justification, I might add. There are many very good wildlife artists, but there are also many good wildlife painters who are not terrifically good artists. To draw fairly good birds does not make them great painters. In many cases, their work doesn't measure up to the standards used to judge other fine art. Good wildlife art should be judged not just by wildlife art standards but also by the finest art standards.

In 1956, when I was nineteen, the Royal Ontario Museum had an exhibition of my work. They were small paintings, little studies, and head studies I had done during the previous four or five years. It had quite an effect and received a lot of publicity in Toronto and throughout Canada. At the time, there wasn't a great deal of interest in wildlife painting and not many artists were doing it. Perhaps the exhibition encouraged other artists. Now there are hundreds and hundreds of people who do these things. Back then, you could have counted on two hands the number of people who were busy painting birds and animals.

Many factors may have contributed to the rising interest in wildlife art. People became concerned about the natural world and the environment, and they realized that many things were disappearing before their eyes. I think television brought these issues before the public. When I was a child, I remember seeing a nature film at a movie house. Nobody had ever seen that sort of film before and it was tremendously interesting. Now you can turn on the television almost every evening and see shows about nature, birds, and animals. People are better informed and take a greater interest in the natural world.

I can't remember when I wasn't interested in birds. I think my interest in birds was completely separate from the fact that as a child I was largely immobile and had a lot of time on my hands. There is something almost mystical about birds, perhaps because they can fly and we cannot. To me, the form of birds remains perennially seductive. The angularity of a heron and the sophisticated, subtle curves of waterfowl have always been both the material of my self-expression and my delight.

We lived near Cowichan and Mill Bay on Vancouver Island. It was there that birds began to attract my attention. I vividly recall the plummeting, erratic nighthawks of summer evenings, the flocks of plaintive waxwings, and the great, flame-crested pileated woodpeckers that hammered at the roadside stumps.

The winter of 1942 froze everything in our cottage, even a ruby-crowned kinglet seeking shelter in the woodshed. My mother found it as she went for fuel to feed the range in our orange-floored kitchen, and together we examined the tiny body and brilliant crown. That kinglet may have set the mold for my life's interest. Or perhaps it was already set.

I still remember it very clearly and it made a deep impression on me. I was very young, probably five. When she brought the bird in, I knew what it was and I was very interested in it. I must have already been keener than most five-year-olds in the subject.

I can't tell what starts these things. You are born with it, this tremendous interest – this obsession with birds. I used to draw when I was a child and I watched birds, and, at about fourteen years old, I inevitably started painting them. By the time the exhibition opened when I was nineteen, I had been painting birds for years and was well on my way.

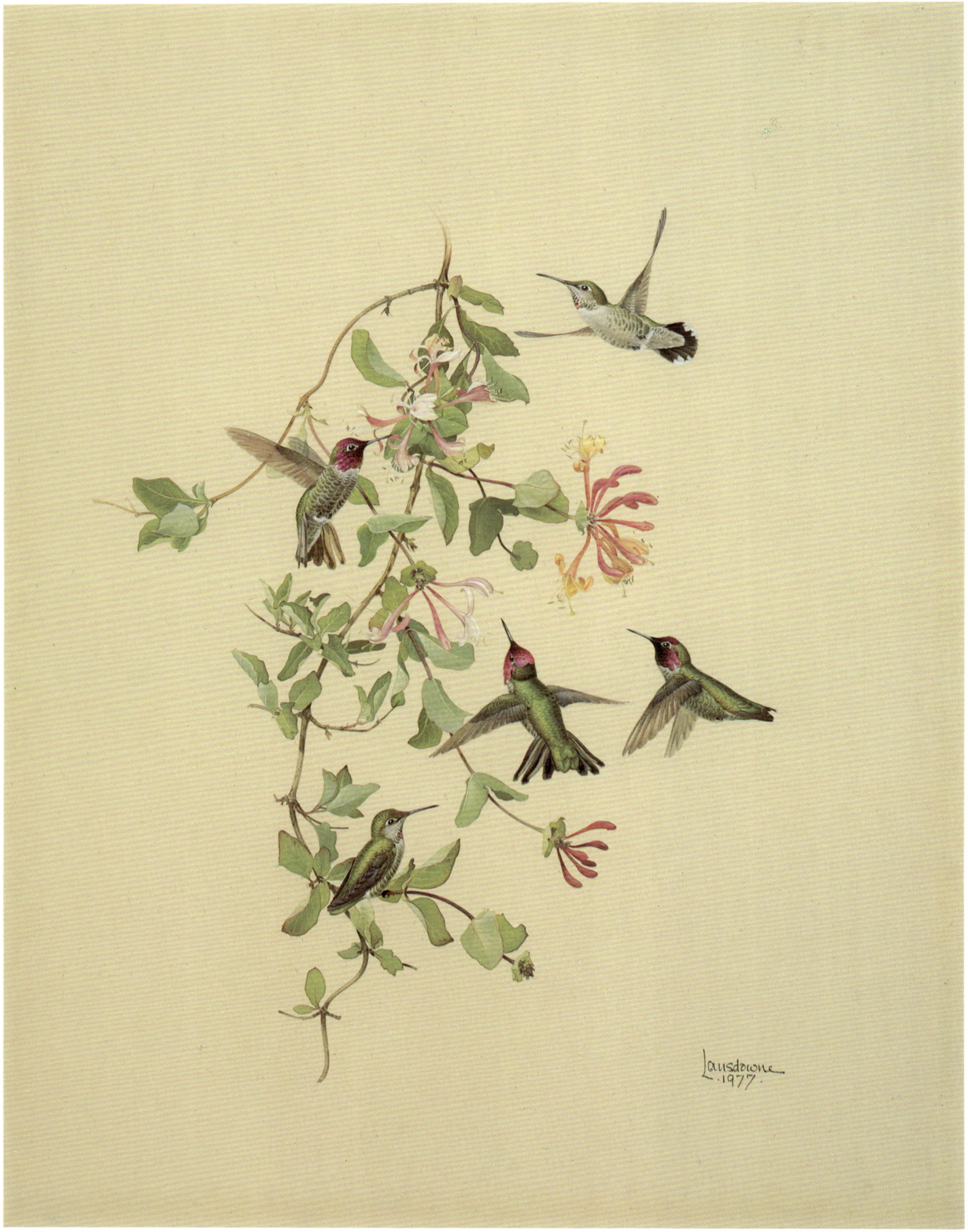

There is something almost mystical about birds, perhaps because they can fly and we cannot.

Anna's Hummingbird 1977, watercolor on paper, 30 x 21 inches, private collection. *Birds in Art* 1980.

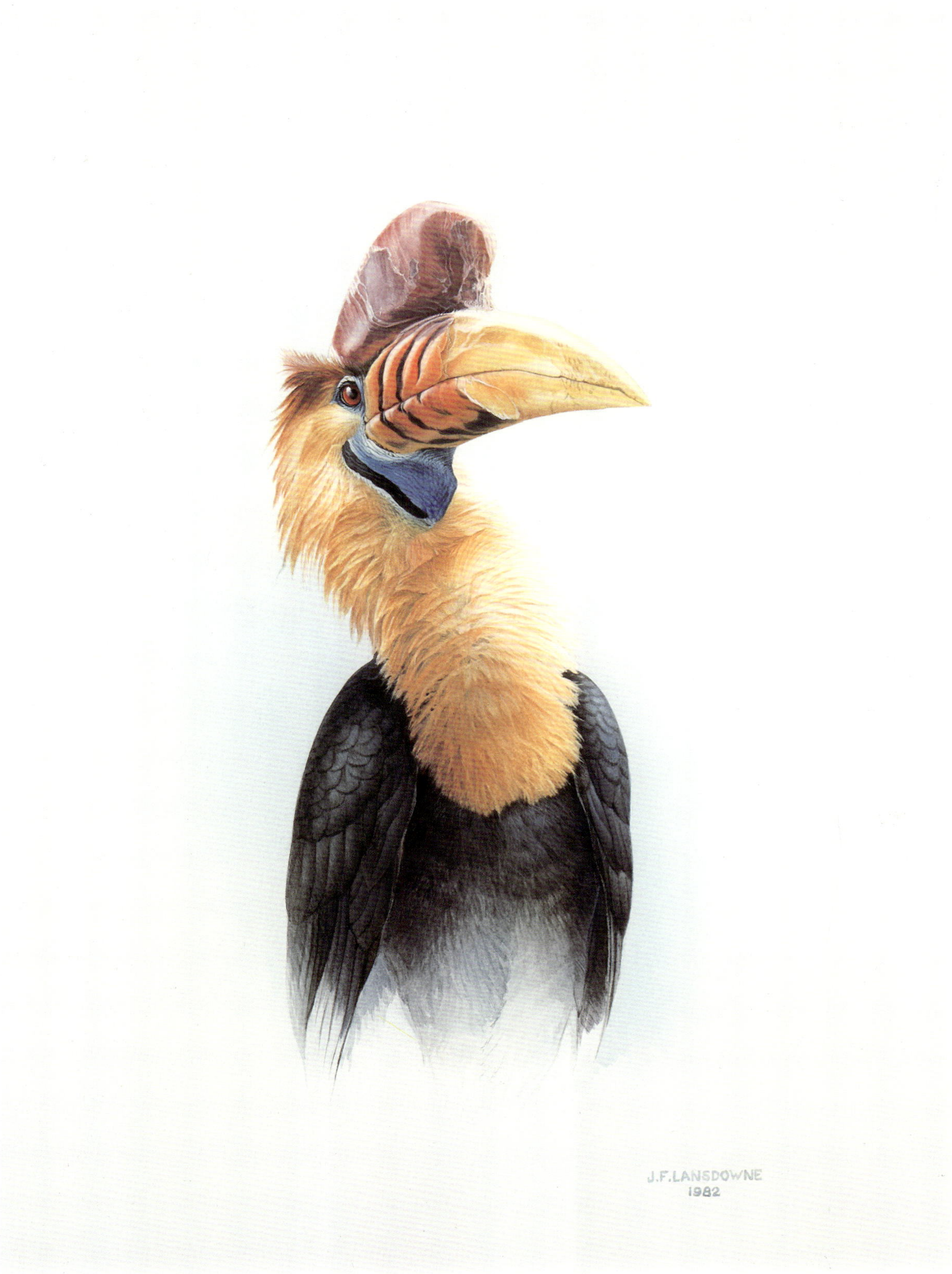

I can't tell what starts these things. You are born with it, this tremendous interest – this obsession with birds.

Celebes Hornbill 1982, gouache on paper, 25 x 20 inches, collection of M. F. Feheley. *Birds in Art* 1985.

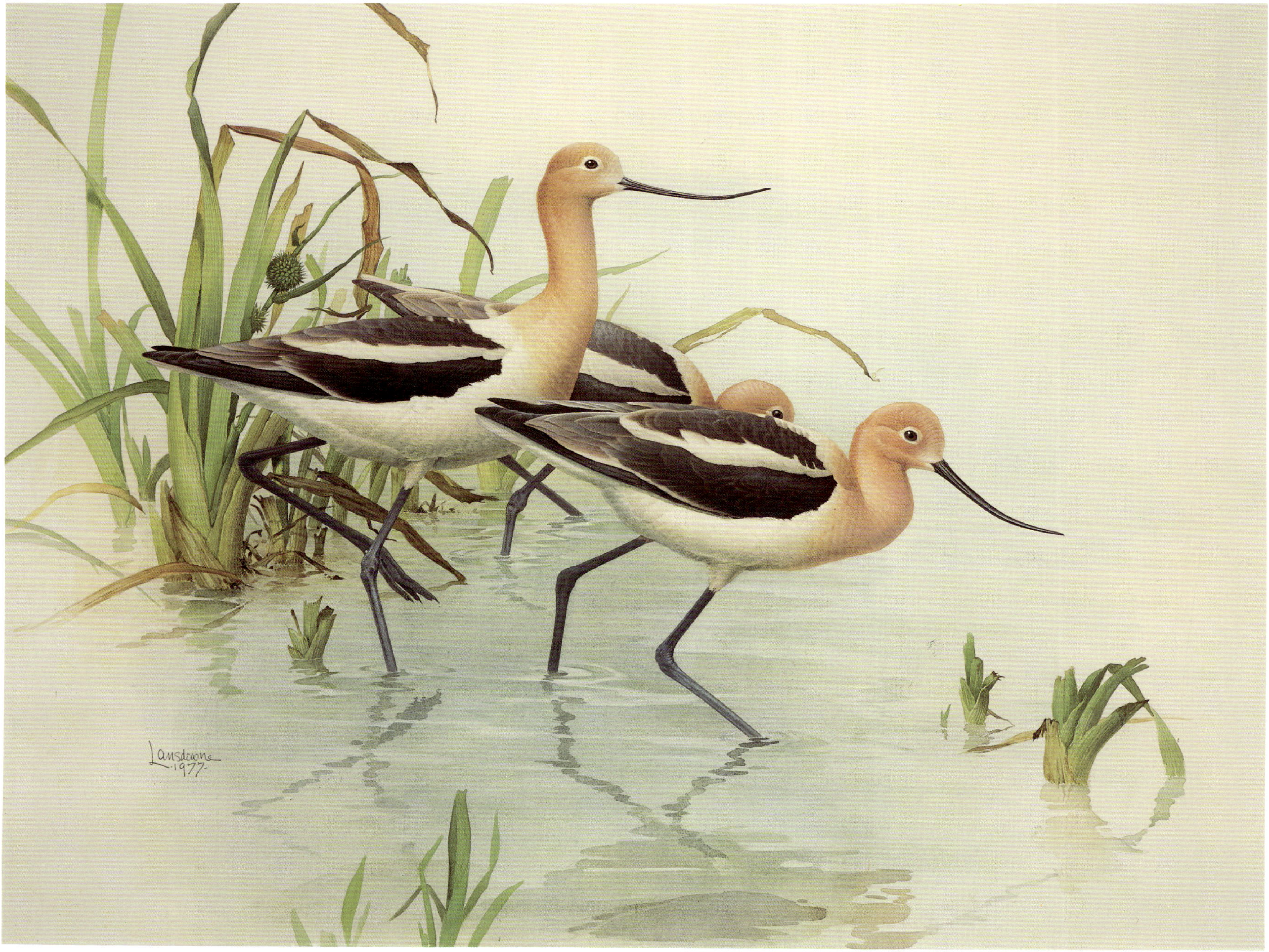

American Avocets 1977, gouache on paper, 24 x 31½ inches, private collection. *Birds in Art* 1979.

If there is any abstract design in my painting, it comes quite unconsciously. I think painting usually does come unconsciously – especially the best kind.

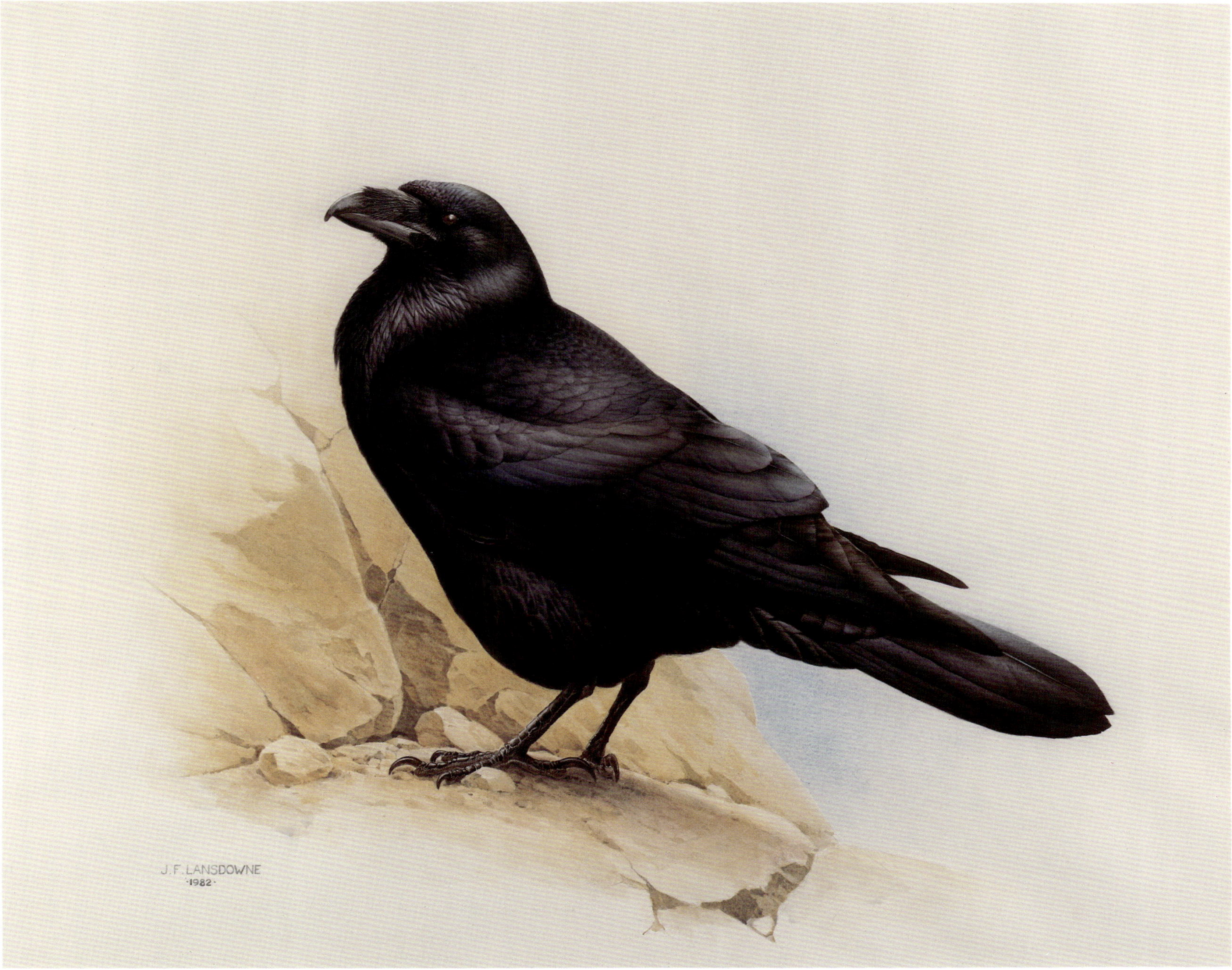

Raven (common raven) 1982, gouache on paper, 23¼ x 30¾ inches, collection of the artist. *Birds in Art* 1982.

My birds. . . tend to be fairly stationary. They tend to be birds more in repose than birds in action. . . . The looser, freer parts are often the backgrounds.

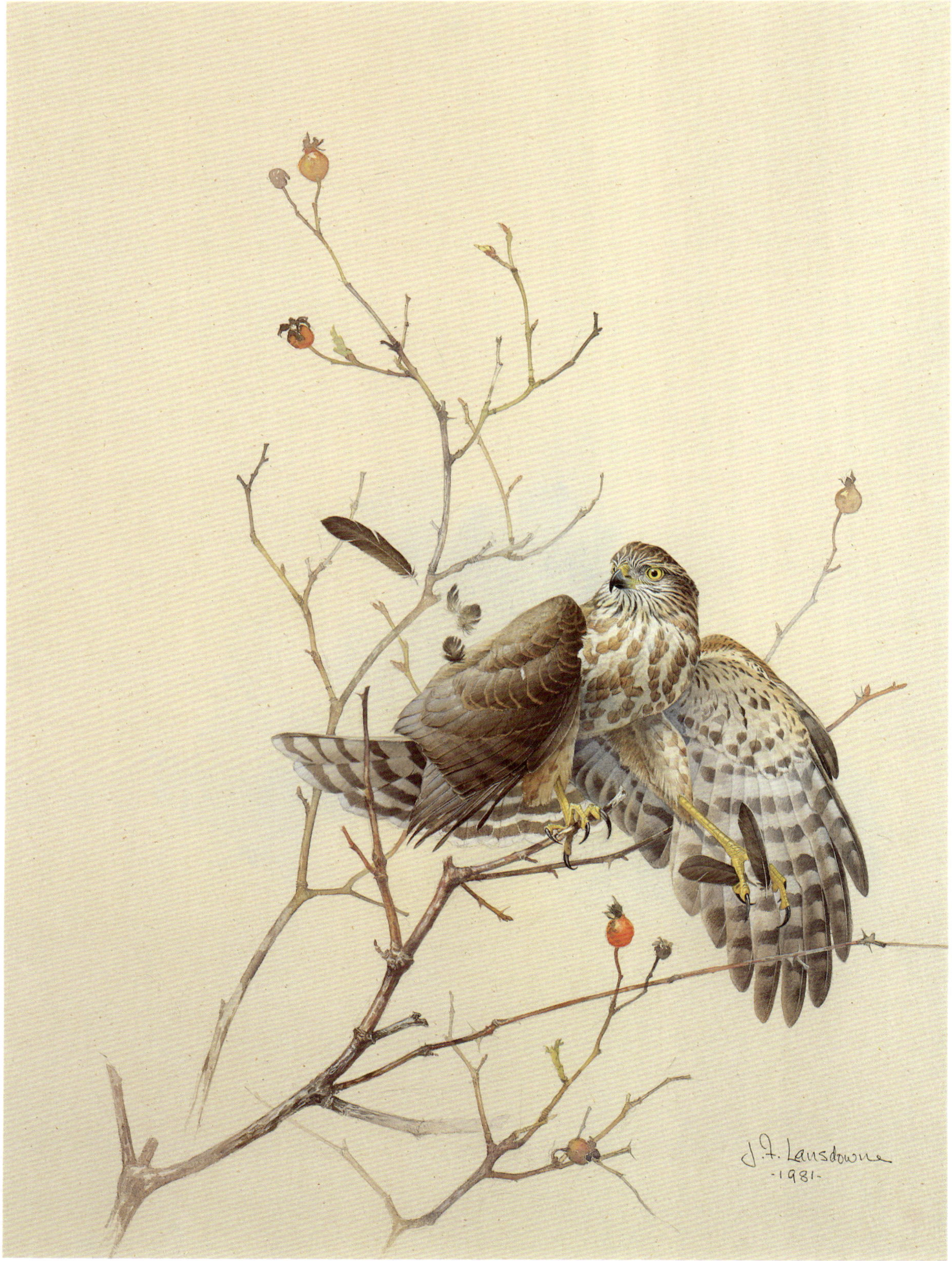

It is important to know the bird in life. The better you know it, the more certain you are of making it into something that is true to life.

Missed (sharp-shinned hawk) 1981, watercolor on paper, 27 x 20 inches, collection of The Greenwich Workshop, Inc., Trumbull, Connecticut. *Birds in Art* 1986.

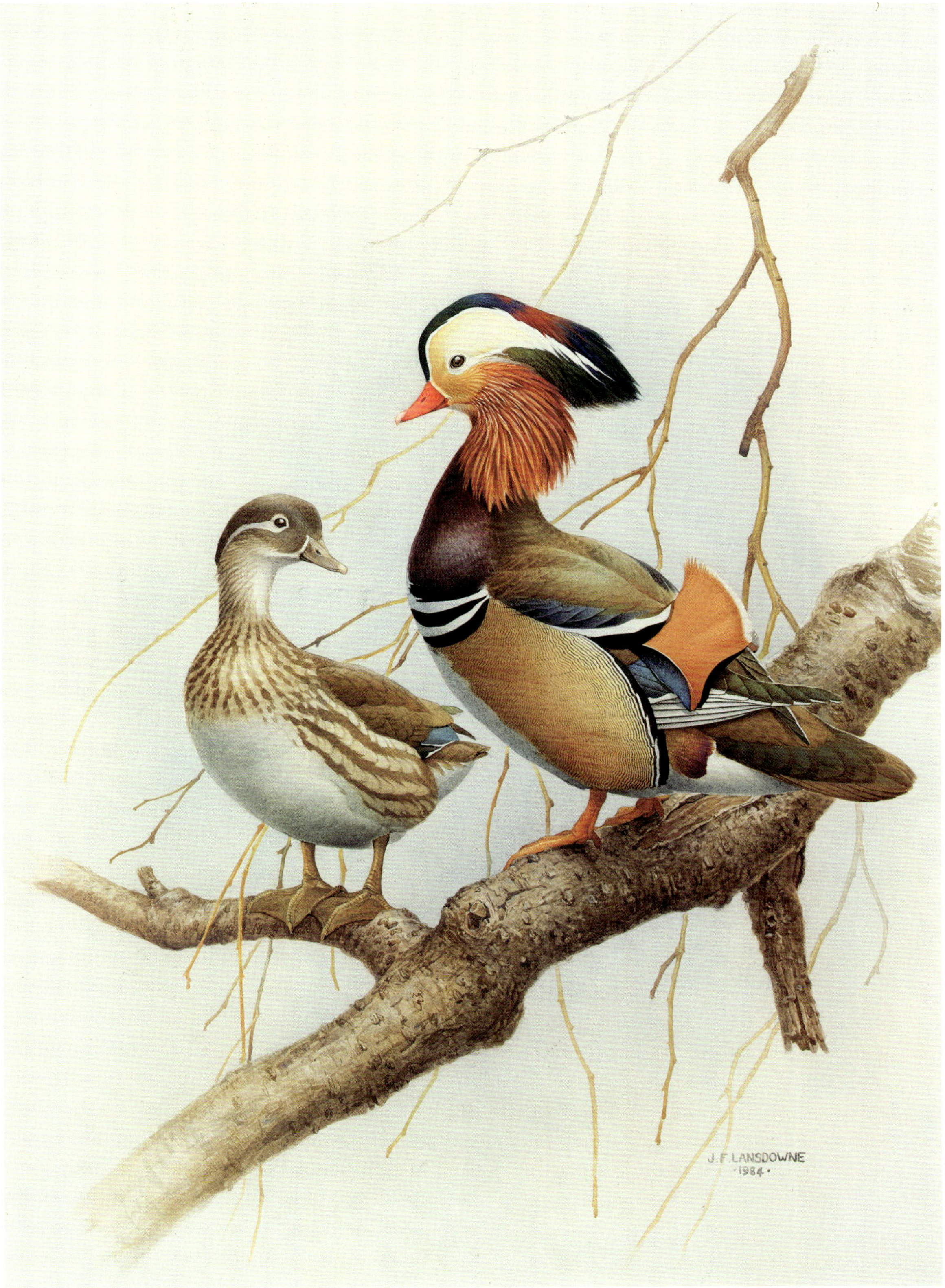

To me, the form of birds remains perennially seductive. The angularity of a heron and the sophisticated, subtle curves of waterfowl have always been both the material of my self-expression and my delight.

Mandarin Ducks 1984, gouache on paper, 25½ x 19¼ inches, collection of the artist. *Birds in Art* 1987.

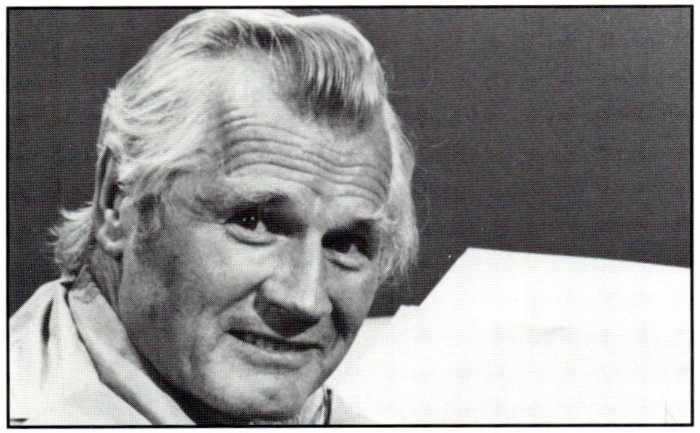

KEITH SHACKLETON

Master Wildlife Artist 1986
Born: 1923, Weybridge, England
Resides: Devon, England

We find beauty, quite simply, in what we love. Some of us love what others find ugly and forbidding. Perhaps it is ugly because they just cannot see – or perhaps it is beautiful because it has been treated with a very personal form of alchemy. But I can only speak for myself. . . . I just believe that landscape like this, savage, hostile, and unremitting though it may be by aesthetic standards, is still the most intrinsically beautiful landscape of all.

[Antarctica is] the only place I know that is absolutely, totally as it happened naturally. It's an intrinsic natural beauty. Everything you look at has been molded by time and wind and weather. It's just sort of part of the planet, inviolate. Elsewhere, there's always a feeling of human intrusion. Very often it's apparent in even the most beautiful rural landscapes: there's some sort of geometric shape that's been put there by people, be it a barn or a hedge or a bridge. Antarctica's like one great big abstract landscape, because it's all a natural happening.

A typical [painting for me] would be an extremely turbulent, wild ocean with just one albatross in it. This little albatross takes on an extraordinary importance, far outweighing its size, because it's the one living thing in this ferment, and it therefore is something that you reach out for, a little piece of living inspiration.

One of the joys of painting a sea is that you can design your own sea. There's such a wonderful freedom about it. I suppose seas appeal to me so much because they satisfy the frustrated abstract painter that lurks within most realistic painters: the longing to be able to create your own shapes. . . . Imagination can run riot, provided you remember what elemental forces make a sea. There is only one, and that's wind, supplemented by movements of currents or the depths. . . . You put waves in where you want them to be, with the shape you want and the emphasis you want. It's all very appealing.

Water is the most visually versatile stuff on this planet . . . . From ice with the consistency of rock to the buoyant clouds above, it will adopt any form, and it would be hard to decide whether solid, liquid or vapor commanded the widest repertoire of possibilities for a painter.

I don't remember a time in my life when I did not draw or paint, nor a time when I was not very fond of animals as a subject. The two went together, and I would not be able to say if I am an artist or a zoologist first. I just don't know where the priorities lie. I think I am such a lousy zoologist that probably the art side is stronger. I am prepared to manipulate the subject a little bit, to caricature it to make it look a bit more like itself, which pulls the rug out from under the idea of my being an accurate, scientific painter.

I never went to art school. The war started and that was that. This brings up the idea of who influences you; who makes you paint in the style you do? Obviously, it's the people you admire most, the people whose work you like. You may not know you are being influenced – that's the clever thing – but in the back of your mind something is saying, "That is lovely." I suppose in my formative mind it would have been Peter Scott who first gave me the idea that animal and environment are inseparable and equally important. It just rubbed into my subconscious and has been very much my attitude toward drawing.

Quite frequently, I find myself setting out to paint something with. . . an animal content, and finish up by finding that the scene itself will stand on its own, [so] the animal never materializes.

I paint in oils, entirely. I can't paint in watercolors because they're too difficult, but I do take watercolors along when I'm out in the wild, because they're the only thing you can carry. . . . My sort of painting activity is divided cleanly in half between the little rough sketches that I do in the field and the finished pictures, all of which are done in the comfort of the studio. I think this applies to a great many people. I think the only difference between me and most wildlife artists is that the field sketches of most wildlife artists I find really exciting and really lovely, and my own are absolutely ghastly. They're only of value to me to jog the memory. They're not, of themselves, of any merit whatever; at least, that's my view.

Oil suits me because you can just dash away. I like to feel my way with a picture and am very bad at visualizing things. . . I like oil painting because there are no rules. If I do not like something, I can wipe it out and start again.

If you paint on hardboard and you make a mess of a picture, just trundle it up to the workshop, run it over with a power sander, put it back on the easel, and you've got a surface that the power sander imparts on top of the lousy painting that is the most beautifully sympathetic surface to paint on that you can possibly imagine. Nearly every reasonably effective picture I've painted has got the mortal remains of several travesties underneath it. If you think the composition is wrong, you simply put it on the trestle and saw a piece off the bottom. I tend to see each one thereafter as endowed with the triumphant qualities of the phoenix.

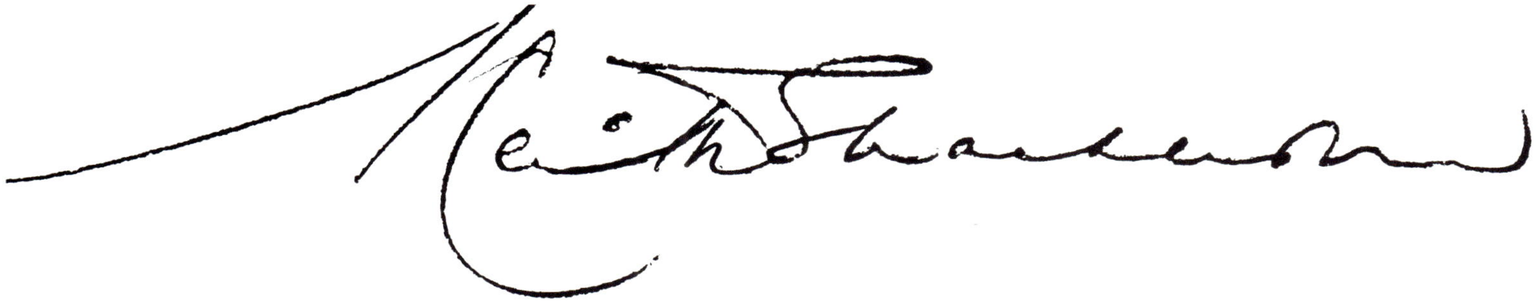

I am enslaved by a passion for painting big pictures. . . . Often I find myself painting. . . grotesquely large, as if dimensions for their own sake would add an element of artistic import. Alas, this is not the way it works, rather the reverse. If a picture is destined to be really bad, the smaller it is, the better for all concerned.

I have been telling myself for years that I must learn to paint little pictures, that there is no intrinsic merit in size. But. . . the habit is hard to break. Moreover, it is commercial folly. They call for wall space that is in ever shortening supply – and probably accounts for my owning the largest collection of original Keith Shackletons in Europe.

My father was an airplane designer, so as a child I drew airplanes a bit, and I drew birds, too. An airplane has an interesting lesson to offer about drawing birds. Airplanes are completely symmetrical, so you are tied to a rigid perspective. This helps you to understand what the living version of a flying machine is all about.

I noticed that in very early bird paintings, pre-Wilbur Wright paintings, the wings look like they could be used more effectively for hailing a cab than for actually lifting the bird's body through the air. It's only since Wilbur Wright that the concept of aerodynamics has influenced how artists portray birds flying.

Years ago, I toured the Piper Aircraft Company. They had a lot of wonderful slogans hanging up in the office. One said, "What don't go into an airplane don't cause no trouble." If you substitute picture for airplane – "What don't go into a picture don't cause no trouble" – you begin to build a good case for not bothering with much detail.

In England I get drawn in every now and again to serve on selection committees for art societies. One is the Guild of Aviation Artists. When you have a subject allegiance, you get people who feel very strongly about airplanes or ships or birds or what have you. They care so much about the subject that detail becomes the most important consideration to the art, not whether it's a lovely, powerful painting. For example, in a marine art show you may have a beautiful picture of a square-rigger rounding the Horn. Everything is working – the sea is going in the right direction, the wind is going in the right direction – it makes you want to reach for the Dramamine. All the exhibition jurors may have their hands up, "Yes. Yes. Yes." Then some guy says, "Ridiculous. Can't accept it. Everyone knows the *Cutty Sark* has seven futtock shrouds, not six." The same thing happens with wildlife art. It convinces me that if you can avoid detail, you've made a pretty shrewd move.

I am just not all that interested in the fiddle-de-dee on the surface. The underlying dynamism of living things and what can only be described as their character is much more intriguing. Detail is something that in practice you seldom see. If you feel obliged to put it in because you know it is there, the true conviction of reality is generally the first casualty.

I am not denigrating people who paint detail – actually I envy them, not only their patience but their ability. I have nothing against detail; it's just that it quietly scares the living wits out of me. The reason is, as soon as the painting is detailed, you're inviting criticism.

Of all the ingredients that go into making painters, good or bad, acclaimed or otherwise, the only one that matters is sincerity with oneself, and this simply means painting, or trying to paint, from the heart, and doing one's own thing. Influences are bound to raise their heads because this is the way life works.

As soon as we start trying to imitate something or, even worse, trying to avoid something because it is unfashionable, we get ourselves into double trouble. I think the only way you can measure sincerity is to carry on resolutely, painting what you want to paint, and it doesn't matter whether it's off the rails or not – the integrity will be there.

This, I find, is something worth clinging to. Art has a refreshing shortage of parameters for judgment. It cannot be accepted or rejected on any usual standards of weights and measures. It is a thing of personal preference and personal taste and thereby offers inexhaustible possibilities for painting, sculpting, writing, and talking the unintelligible. Against such a background, a simple ungarnished truth stands out like a jewel.

How a painting pleases the artist is the most important thing of all. I have never in my life painted a picture that I have been completely satisfied with, and I don't think that I ever will. Not just because I am self-critical, but because every time one looks at a scene, how ever many times it has been painted before, how ever many times one has tried to paint it oneself, there is always something new. It's like seeing it for the first time. I always feel I will have another go at it and maybe that next painting is going to be a little bit better. I would say to any young painter, if you have the philosophy that every unsullied rectangle that goes up on your easel is going to be your masterpiece, when it is finished, allow yourself to be pleased with it. Because that's what encouragement is made of.

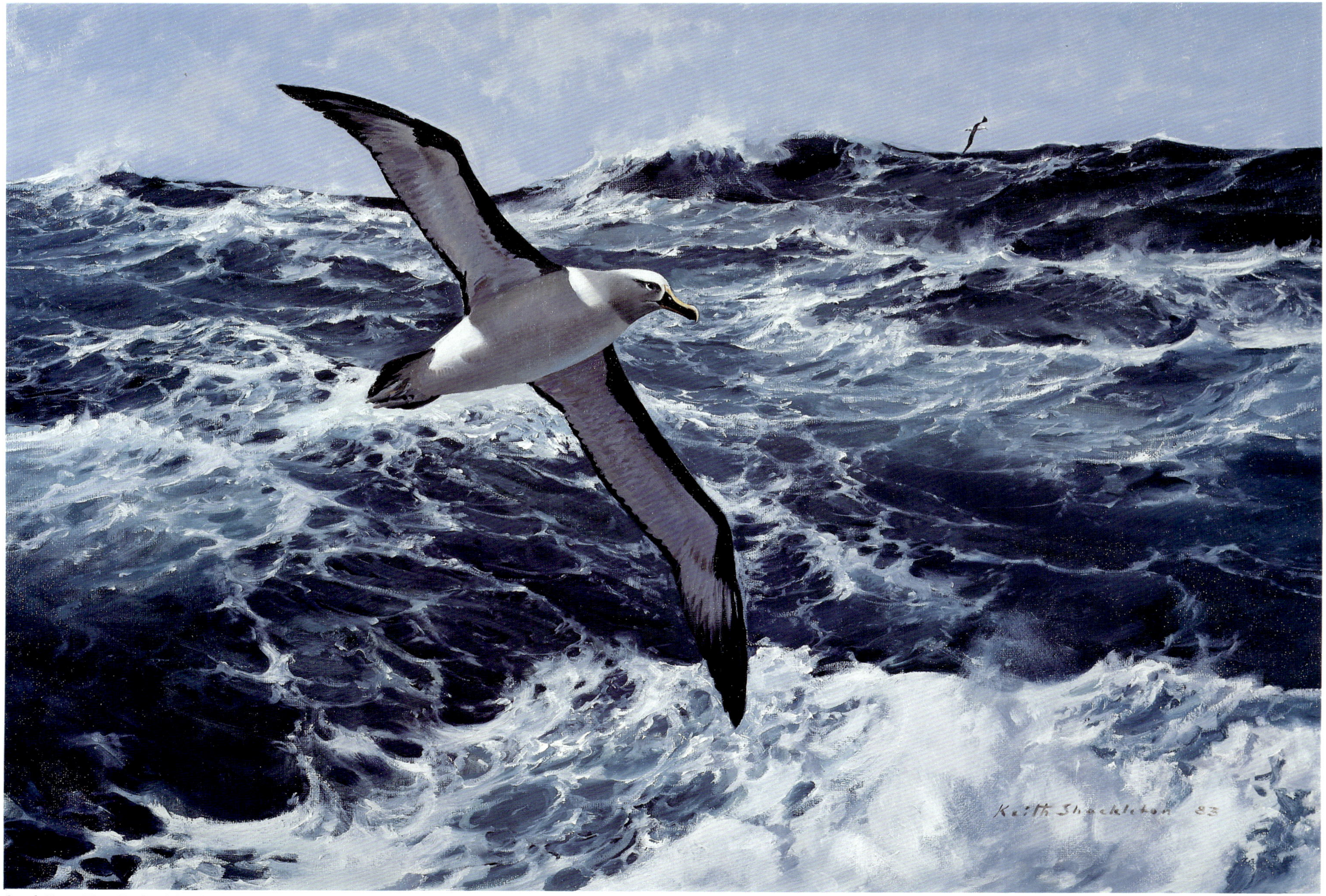

South From New Zealand (Buller's albatross) 1983, oil on board, 24 x 36 inches, collection of the Leigh Yawkey Woodson Art Museum. *Birds in Art* 1984.

Nothing can hold the eye and the attention longer and more restfully than the ocean. It is not unlike gazing at a fire with free-range thoughts.

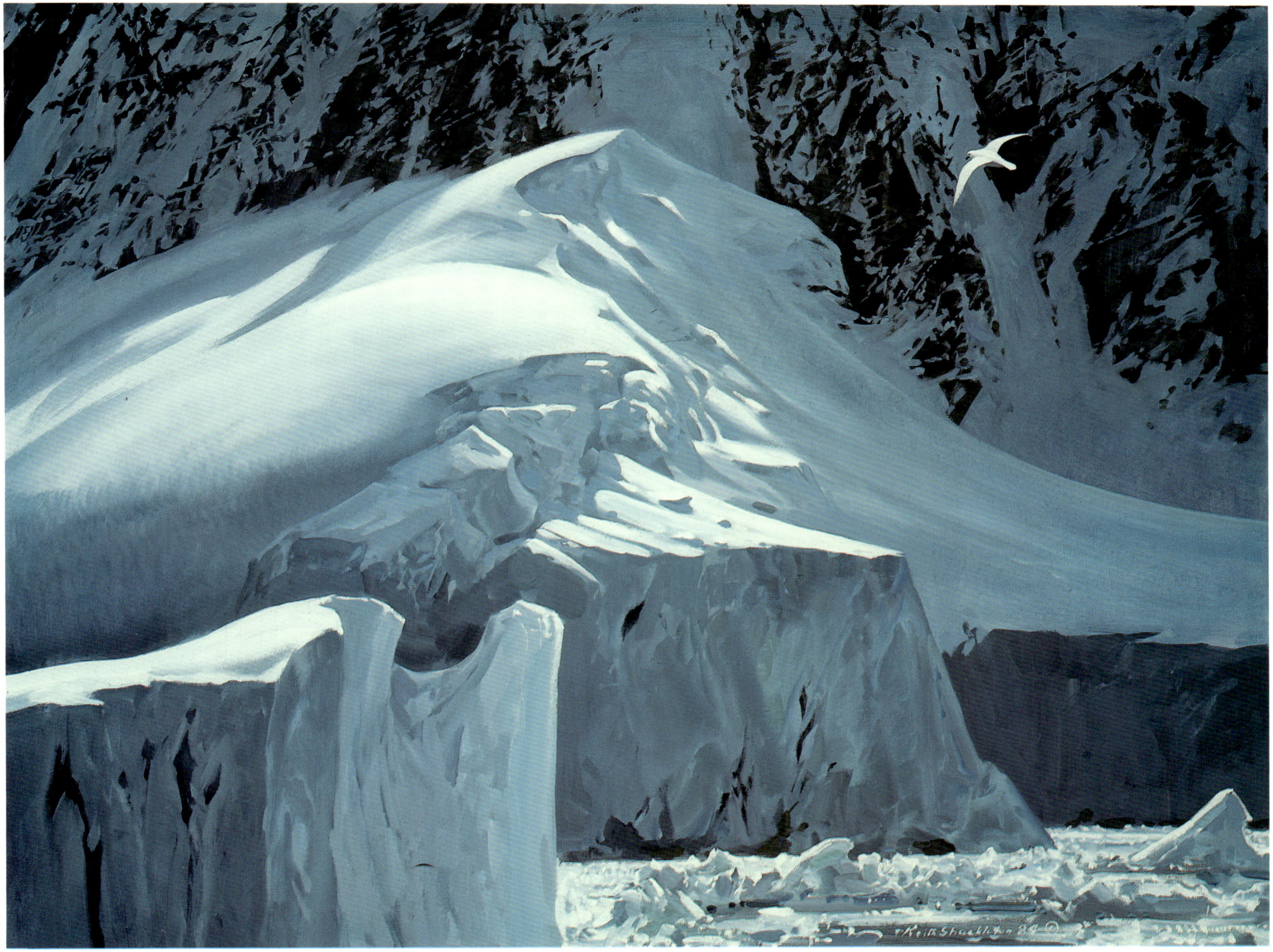

Along the Graham Coast (snow petrel) 1984, oil on board, 24 x 48 inches, private collection. *Birds in Art* 1985.

There are no sweeter curves in nature than those produced by wind. Sometimes the agency of water is involved, as with ripples on sandflats after the ebbing tide.

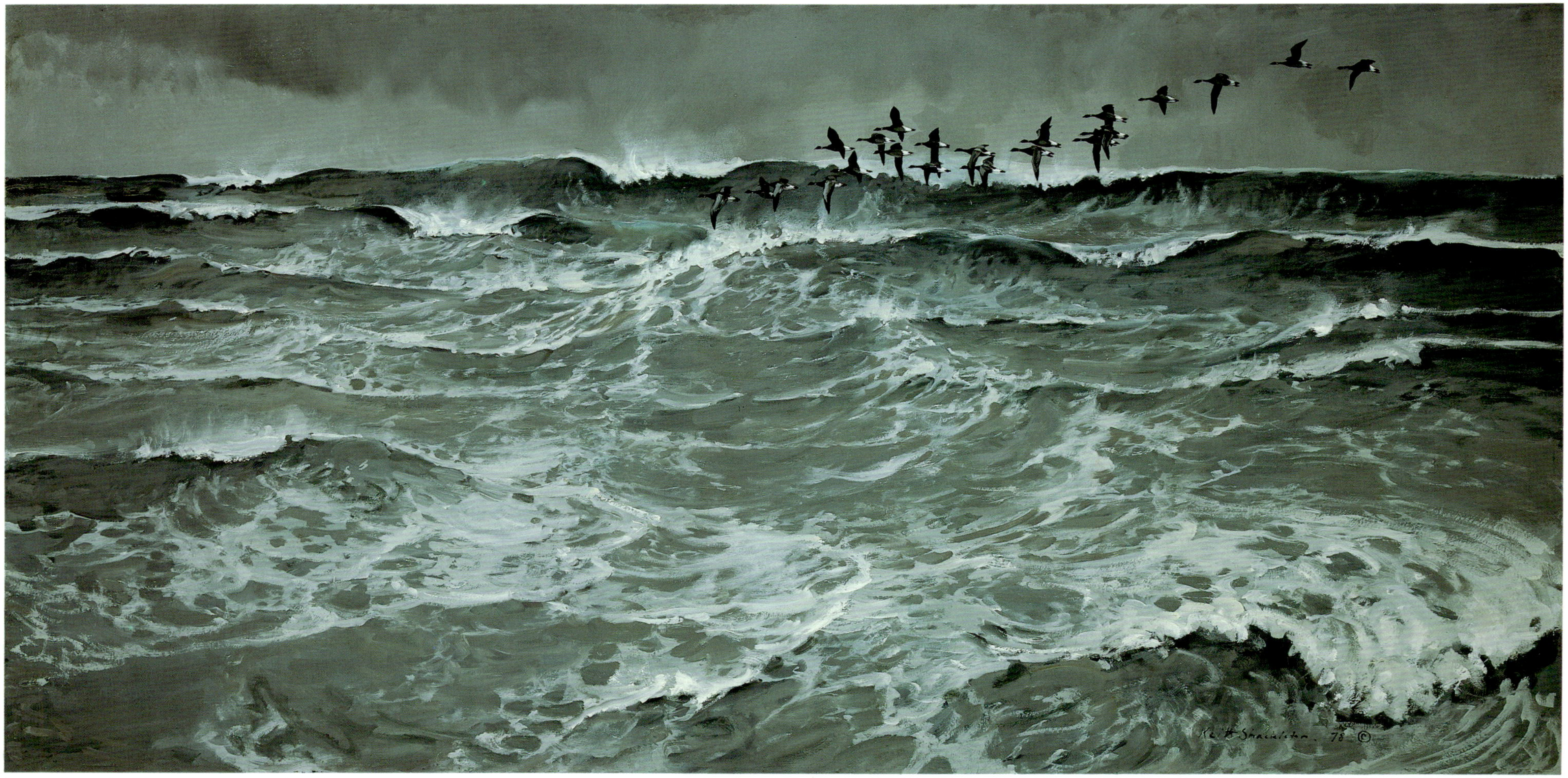

Brants Over the Harbor Bar 1978, oil on board, 30 x 40 inches, private collection. *Birds in Art* 1985.

You can paint nothing on a picture lighter than white, so it follows that there is no way of painting an actual source of illumination, only the effect of it when it falls on objects.

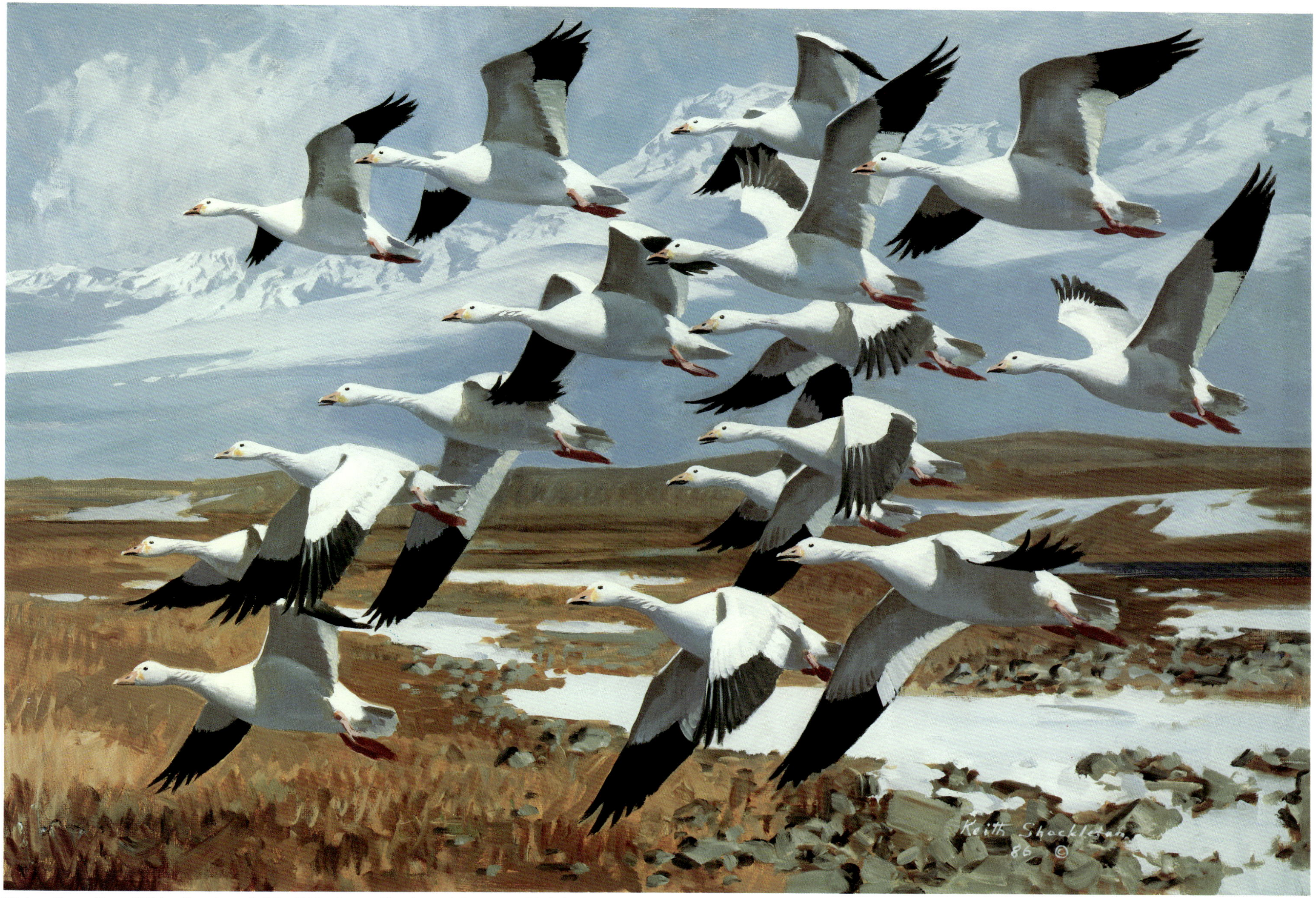

Sixteen Snow Geese 1986, oil on board, 24 x 36 inches, collection of the artist. *Birds in Art* 1988.

If you're painting something you see with your own eyes, it doesn't matter if it's been painted before; it hasn't been painted through your eyes.

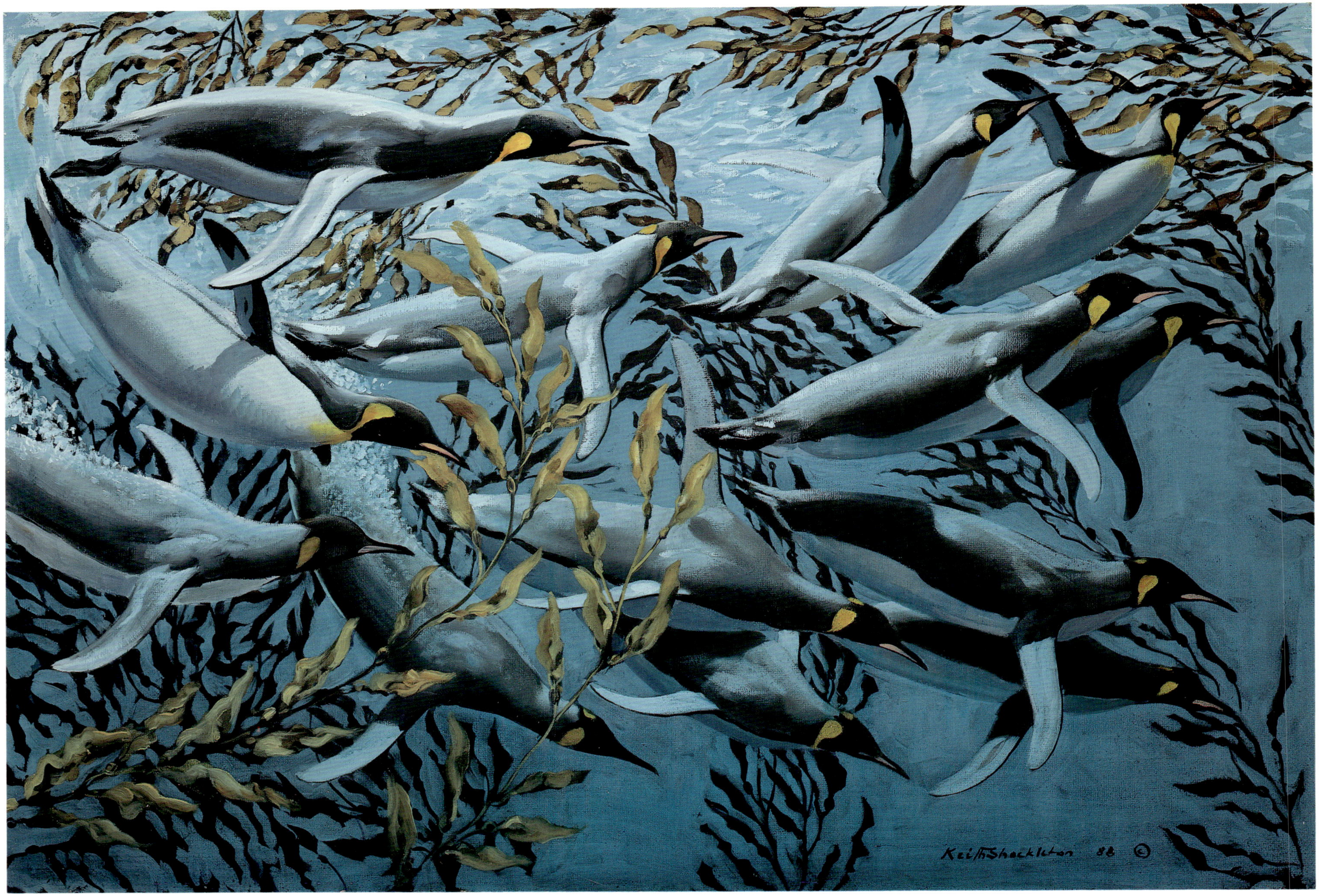

Flying Through Kelp (king penguin) 1988, oil on board, 24 x 36 inches, private collection. *Birds in Art* 1989.

We find beauty, quite simply, in what we love. . . . Art has a refreshing shortage of parameters for judgment. . . . a simple ungarnished truth stands out like a jewel.

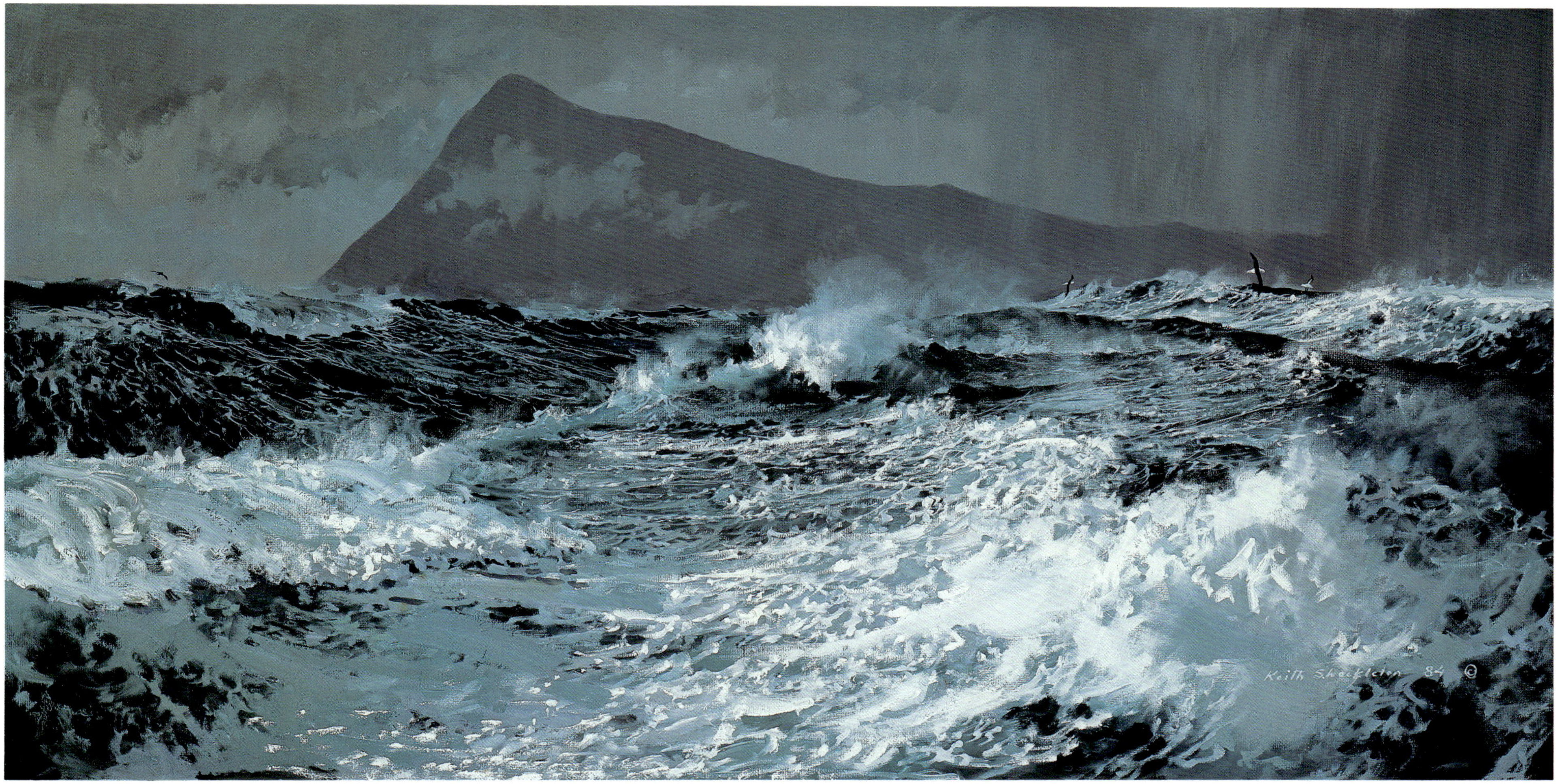

Cape Horn (black-browed albatross) 1984, oil on board, 24 x 48 inches, private collection. *Birds in Art* 1986.

I think a man would need to be a little short on imagination to feel no trace of awe and unease in such places, and a monumental conceit not to feel humbled by it.

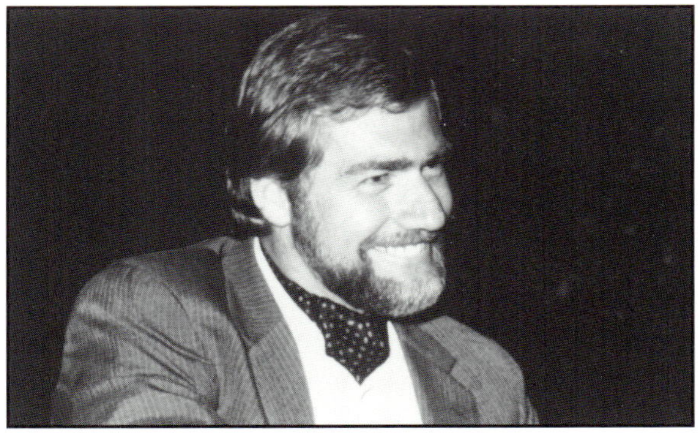

Kent Ullberg

Master Wildlife Artist 1987
Born: 1945, Gothenburg, Sweden
Resides: Corpus Christi, Texas

Underlying each of my sculptures is an abstract form. Sometimes I could make the same sculptural statements with purely abstract shapes without having to make them look like birds. But, by using nature as a vehicle, my art communicates on more levels. More important, it communicates about my aesthetics, about my sense of beauty and design. It also communicates about my love for nature and about the preciousness of nature. On the most fundamental level, my sculptures are recognizable objects. Some viewers never go beyond that. They say, "Hey, how cute. What a pretty heron." But that is only one level.

On the other hand, if I am sculpting a pelican, I could quit with an abstraction. I could title it *Pelican* and, whether you would see a pelican or not, I would have communicated my aesthetics and the shape I fell in love with. But I may not have shown you how beautiful pelicans are in themselves nor how important it is to take care of them. Realism adds this message. It is a conscious decision to take the statement far enough to add this other level of communication. Invariably, I think I go too far. I always wish I had quit earlier, but I want to communicate about the special quality of each species. And this seems to be the only way I know how.

There is a vast difference between noodling – putting in detail for detail's sake – and the degree of realism I am talking about. Sometimes in my early work, you could barely recognize the subject matter. I work closer to nature now. But to put in every feather does not add to my art. It is really a decision more of what to leave out than what to put in. That is probably the most difficult decision an artist faces, and it comes down to individual aesthetics. You could noodle until you are blue in the face, and you still cannot put in as much detail as nature has.

Art is personal communication about what you see and feel. With a beautiful work of abstraction, you can communicate your aesthetics, and that is most important, regardless of what we paint or sculpt. Wildlife art must not lose touch with that. Making a great rendering of nature is not art. The Creator already did that, you know! The artist translates nature and makes the viewer see it in a new way – through the artist's soul.

When I was in art school in the sixties, pop art was big. My teachers said to me, "This stuff you are doing has been done. It's old art; it was done a long time ago and it's not relevant." But this is where my heart is. I am a romantic person. For a while I felt I had been born a hundred years too late. I felt very displaced. I had a contemporary art education, and I had to embrace modern idioms and speak that language. I studied it and I worked in it, but I always wished naturalistic language was acceptable to the art establishment. I despaired for many years, but, by living and working long enough and being damned lucky, it looks like history is turning around. Today, for the first time, I do not feel I was born a hundred years too late. I have come to realize that representational and nonrepresentational art are just different artistic languages. To argue one is better than the other is to say English is better than French, and Swedish is better than German. They are different ways of expressing yourself. That is why I think it is absurd when promodernists refuse to look at realistic art as art.

Realism is again becoming acceptable. Modernism has run out of steam because modernism's big thing is newness, new expression, and it has run out of newness. There is retrospection in postmodernism. To a great extent, it is classical art, but not all the way back to Greek and Roman heroes. It is representational – realism with a strong modern consciousness for having experienced pure abstraction. It is art that could not have been done in the 1800s. One of the reasons I have been commissioned to do many large public sculptures is that they work well with post-modernist architecture.

Historically, animals were seldom subjects for public art. If they were used, it was only as allegories or as adjuncts to man. Nobody stuck a monumental fish in the middle of a city before. You may have seen an eagle as an allegory representing the armed forces, but you have seldom seen an animal used for its own sake as an element for architectural sculpture. So, here I am, putting my cranes, my fish, and my eagles all over the country in front of post-modern buildings. Twenty years ago I would not have received commissions for large public monuments. It is a sign of changing aesthetics. Monumental sculpture gives me a bigger voice to speak passionately about nature and conservation.

I am drawn to monumental expression because composition, if properly conceived, tends to gain strength when translated from a model. I have to be honest – when it is unveiled, it's certainly an ego trip, but I also feel very humble. I feel an acute responsibility to give people something that speaks to them. I find it difficult to defend the arrogance of an artist who uses public space and money to put up something that has no meaning to anybody but himself.

The public pieces require many considerations other than my personal sentiments. I never design a piece without first viewing the space. Sometimes I have only flat ground and blueprints to work from,

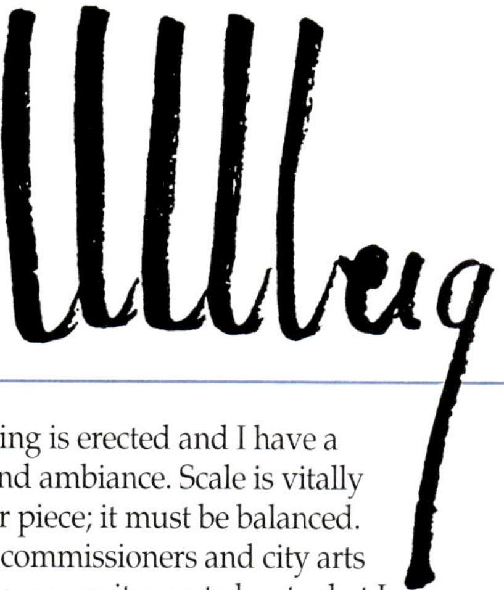

but more often the building is erected and I have a good feel for the space and ambiance. Scale is vitally important for an outdoor piece; it must be balanced. I have to work with arts commissioners and city arts boards and communicate my excitement about what I want to do. And, I have to work within their budgets. The entire process is sometimes very difficult and worrisome.

The foundry work is mostly drudgery. There's a certain satisfaction in seeing the finished piece, but it is hard work. I have a work ethic that if you have not worked hard, you do not deserve success. So, after a day of hauling water and clay up and down ladders, when I am dead tired and dirty and worn out, I kind of think that I have earned my success.

When Roger Tory Peterson's field guide to the birds of Europe came out in Sweden in 1955, I was ten years old and had just started birding. For me, more than anything as a kid, that book brought the world to my fishing village – mystical, beautiful birds with exotic names from Southern Europe and the Mediterranean, the hint of the beyond and the longing to travel. Of course, I thought he was just a chap up the road who had written the book because "Roger Petersson" is my cousin, so he couldn't be a really big deal. As I grew up, I realized who Roger Tory Peterson is, and his influence has been with me through Europe and in my travels through Africa, and it is still with me today. So you can imagine the incredible feeling for me to receive the Master Wildlife Artist Award from his hand. Just to be able to show my work with artists I have admired all of my life is enough. That is a tremendous thing. I think that is where the Leigh Yawkey Woodson Art Museum makes a fantastic contribution to younger artists.

My Dad really wanted to make a landscape painter of me. He took me on all his field trips. While he painted, I watched birds and that is the foundation for my interest in nature. When I went to art school, I enrolled in painting, sculpture, and drawing. When I got my hands in clay, I fell in love instantly – really never looked back. I put myself through art school working as a taxidermist for the Swedish Museum of Natural History. It was a perfect combination of my emerging skills as a sculptor with my interest in nature.

After art school I bought an old VW bus because I wanted to see the art in Europe. In Paris I discovered Rodin. Nobody ever treated bronze as a medium of modeling like Rodin. I will never forget the impact his sculptures had on me when I viewed them for the first time. I think that is the most deeply moved I have ever been. The most important part of art education is seeing art.

Every wildlife artist dreams of going to Africa, and it's not easy when you don't have any money. I wrote letters extolling my virtues to any address I could lay my hands on. I was offered a taxidermy job in Botswana. It was 1967, Botswana had just gained independence from Britain. Here I came, a romantic kid, always dreamed about Africa, over-read on Hemingway, to a country that was basically pristine. My last four years there, I was curator at the National Museum and Art Gallery. It was my job to collect ethnographic material from the tribes, to put together a scientific collection of birds and mammals, and to arrange exhibitions of local and historical art.

I first came to this country on the invitation of an American museum director I had met on safari. America is the freest country I had ever been to. I decided I had to live here permanently.

When I lived in Africa, Scandinavian animals faded from my work because the African imagery just grabbed me. When I lived in Colorado, I almost had a heart attack the first time I saw a bison. I mean, there's a walking sculpture. It is said an artist reflects his environment, but it is always understood to mean the curious cultural currents in large cities. For me, with seven years in the bush and growing up close to nature, to do anything else than what I am doing would be insincere. Contemporary art reflects the concerns of its culture, and one of mankind's biggest concerns today is the natural environment, so what could be more logical for a contemporary artist than nature's images?

All artists are mystics in a way. You deal with symbols and language and you try to communicate through your work. When you create, sometimes it feels as if you are not doing it, that it is coming through you. You look at something you have done, and there is almost a strangeness, an alienation. You wonder, "Did I do that?" When I first started out, I sometimes found it very frightening – now I find it exhilarating. I feel an intense joy. When a sculpture really works, it is like you are communicating with nature, and you become a translator somehow. When I do good things, I never for one moment think it is just me sitting there slapping that stuff together. I always know that it comes through me, that I am a vehicle. I think as one matures as an artist, one learns more and more to get out of the way, to get your ego out of the way, to let it happen.

I believe life is eternal, so I do not worry about fame. But I hope others see in my work the beauty I have seen in nature. I want them to feel how incredibly beautiful creation is, how there was one man who walked this path and loved it.

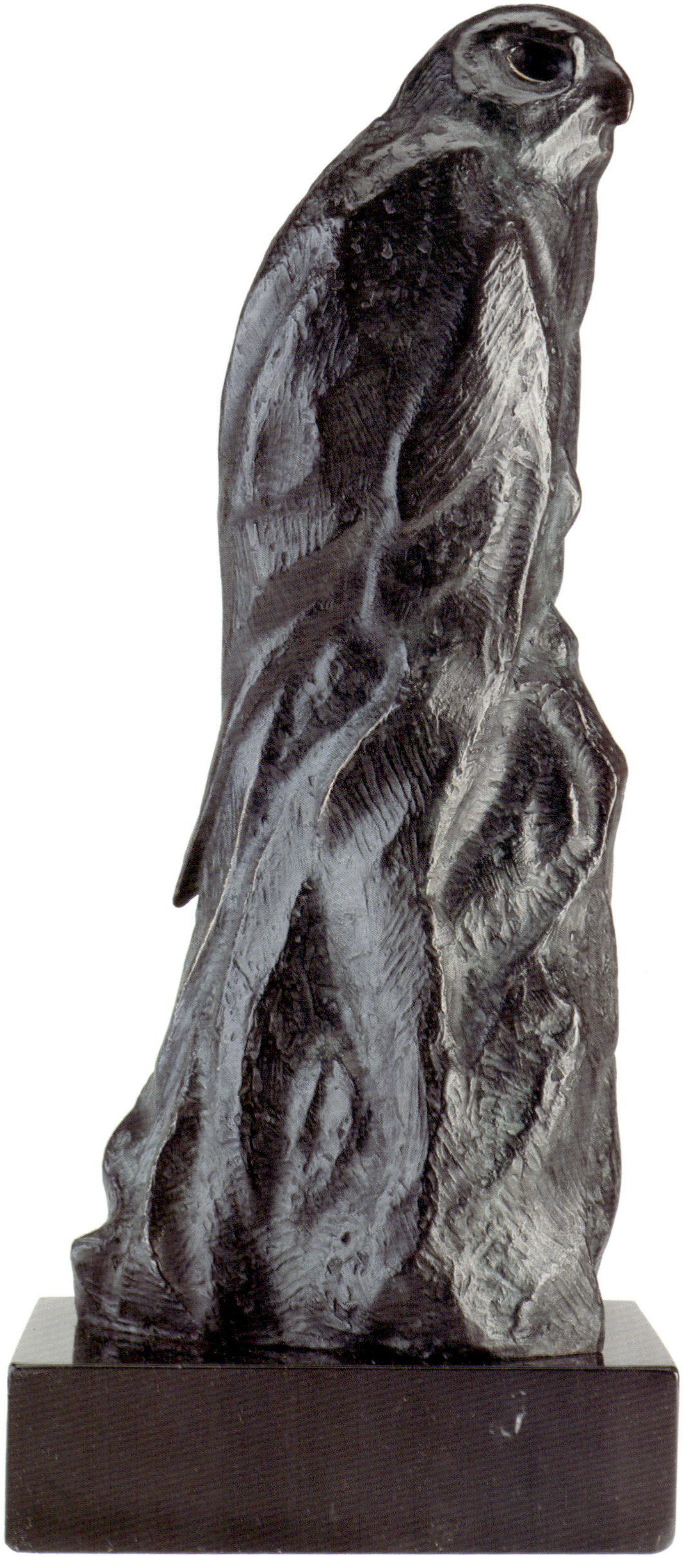

A painter works with color while a sculptor works in the gray scale. On the sculpture surface, the raised points capture light and the recesses capture shadow. The deeper the hollows, the darker the grays. In between these levels of highlight and deep shadow is where a sculptor works.

Falcon (gyrfalcon) 1972, bronze, 17½ x 8 x 8 inches, collection of the artist. *Birds in Art* 1987.

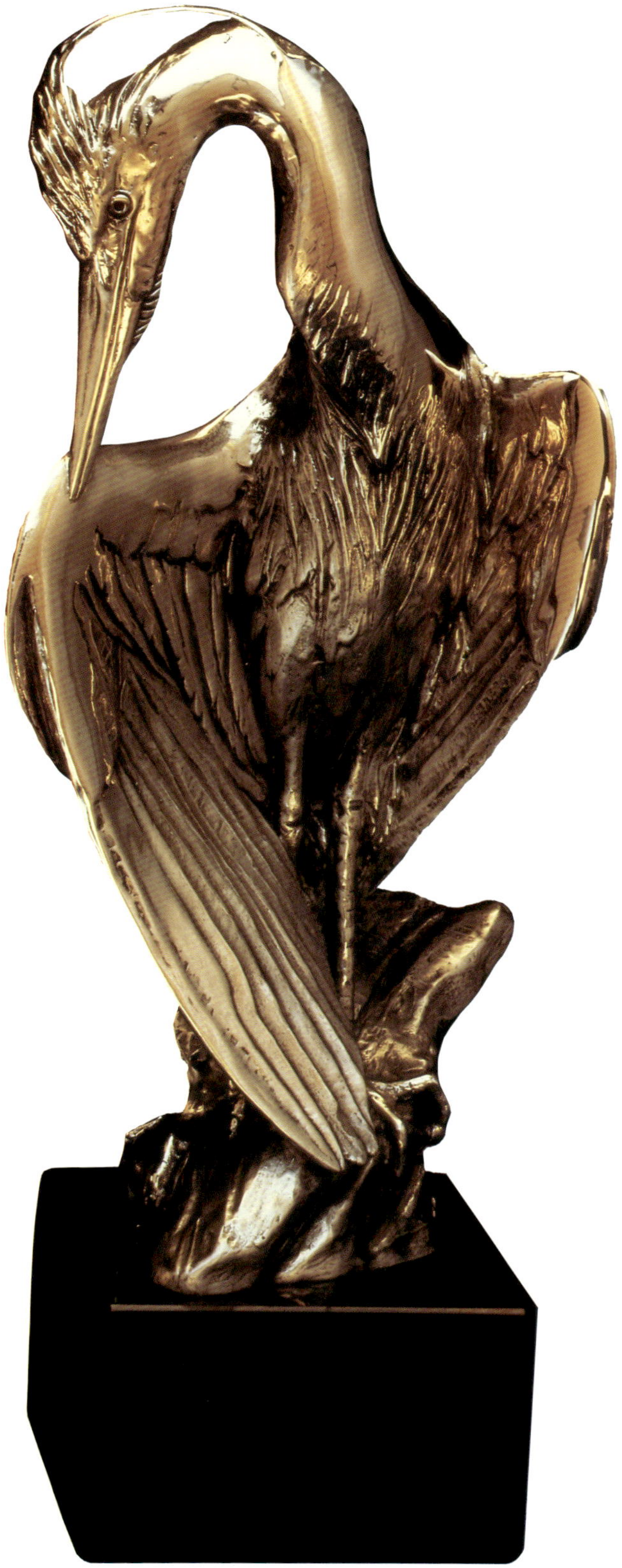

A painter has a symphony of color at his command while the sculptor has a more limited range. But, to me, sculpture is sometimes a purer, deeper emotion. I can think of nothing more beautiful than the unaccompanied cello.

Spring Plumage (great blue heron) 1985, stainless steel, 14½ x 8 x 6¾ inches, collection of the artist.
Birds in Art 1986.

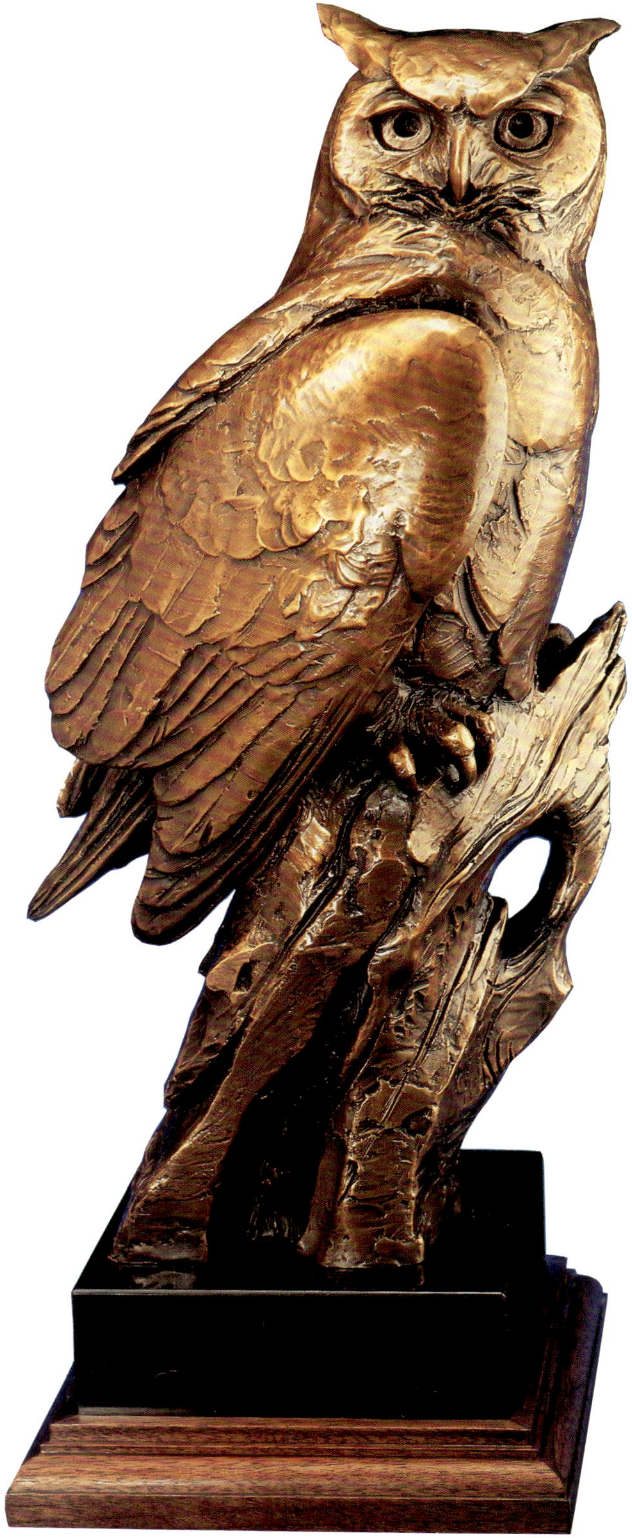

For me, nature is a vehicle to communicate my aesthetics, the shapes and abstract forms I love.

Nightwatch (great horned owl) 1988, bronze, 19½ x 9 x 8 inches, private collection. *Birds in Art* 1988.

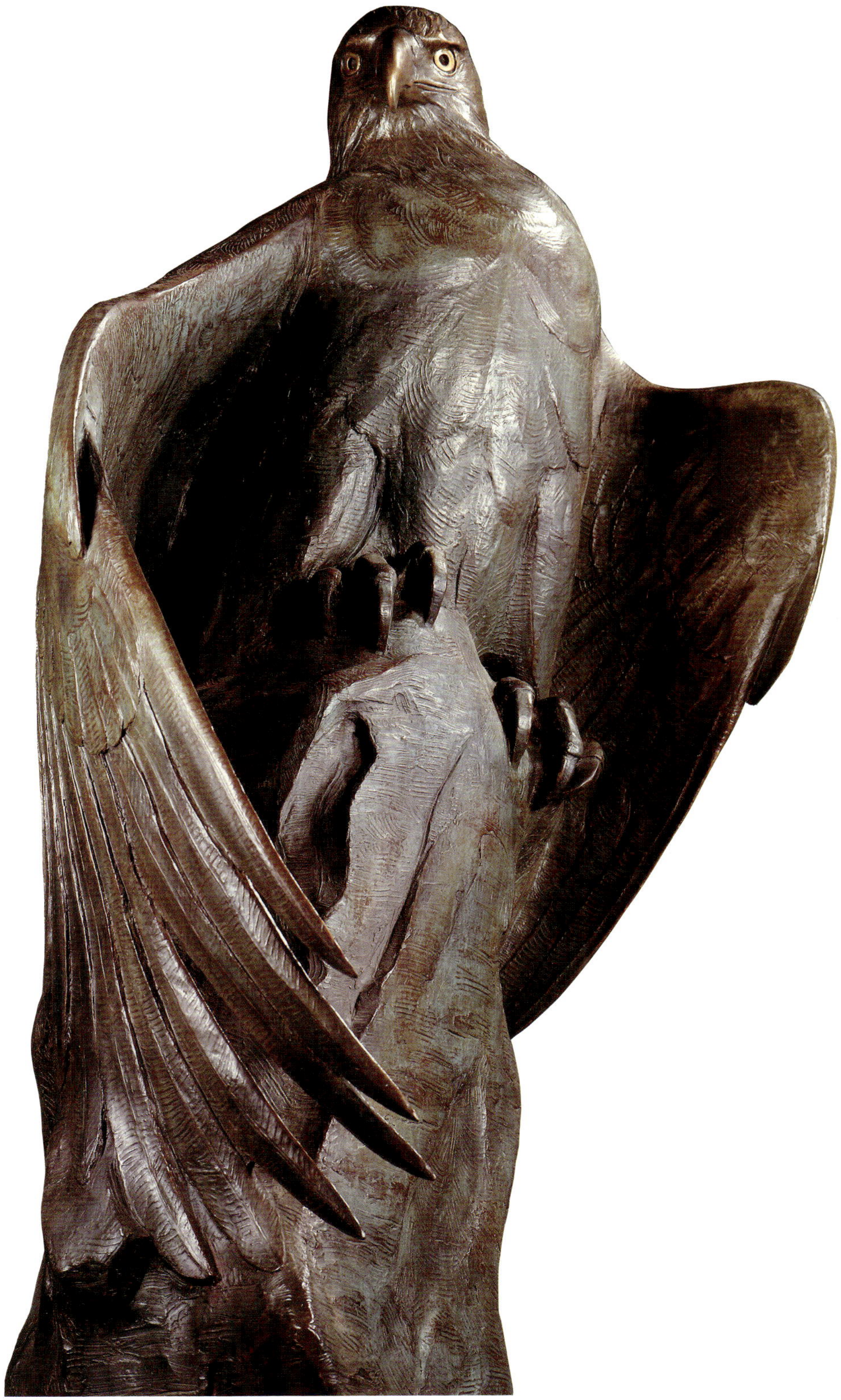

Monumental sculpture gives me a bigger voice to speak passionately about nature and conservation.

Eagle Rock Monument (bald eagle) 1983, bronze, 74 x 45 x 45 inches, collection of the Leigh Yawkey Woodson Art Museum. *Birds in Art* 1983.

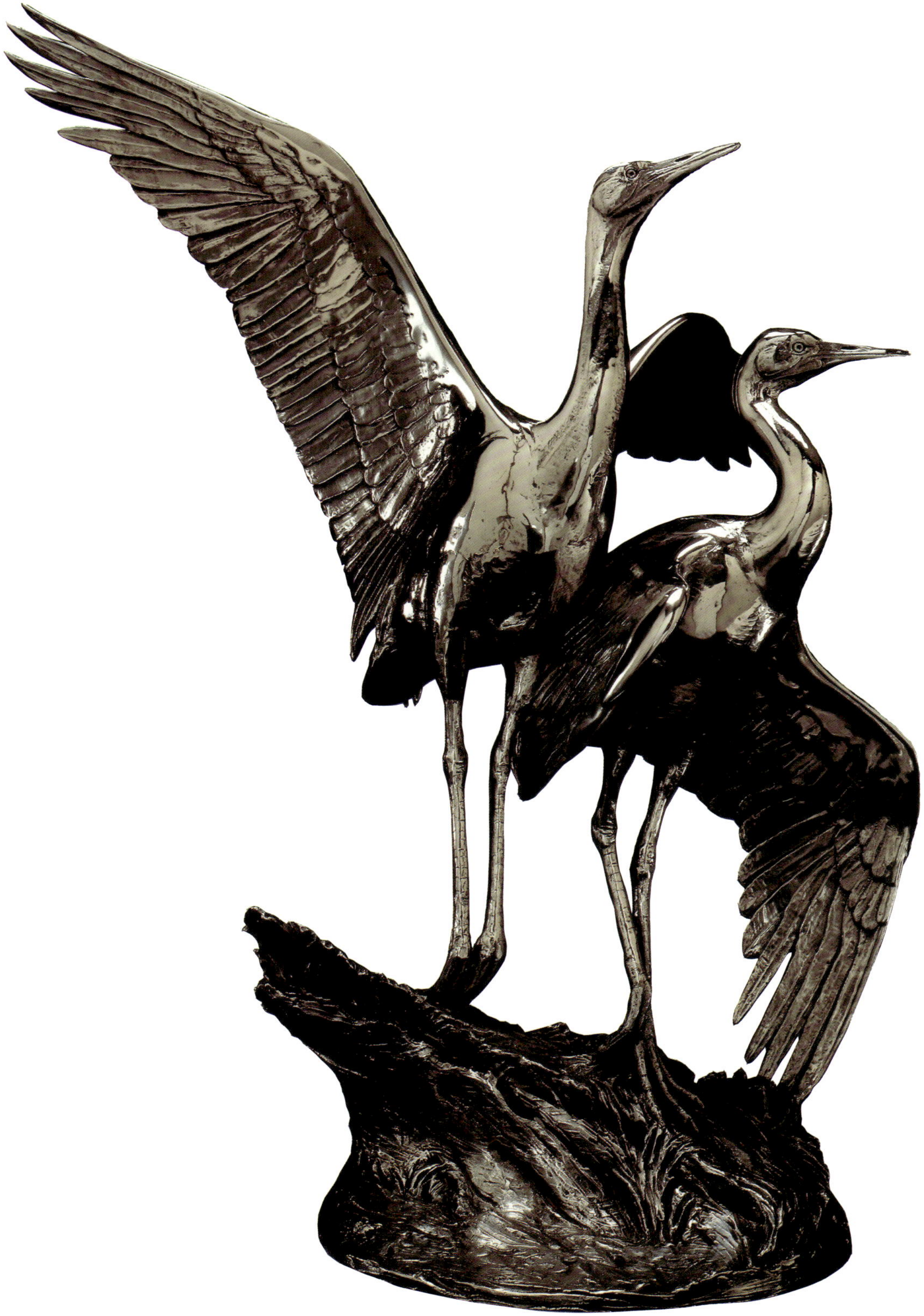

In this day of tremendous concern for the environment, natural images are completely logical for a contemporary artist.

Whooping Cranes 1987, stainless steel, 27 x 21 x 18 inches, collection of H.R.H. Prince Bernhard, The Netherlands. *Birds in Art* 1987.

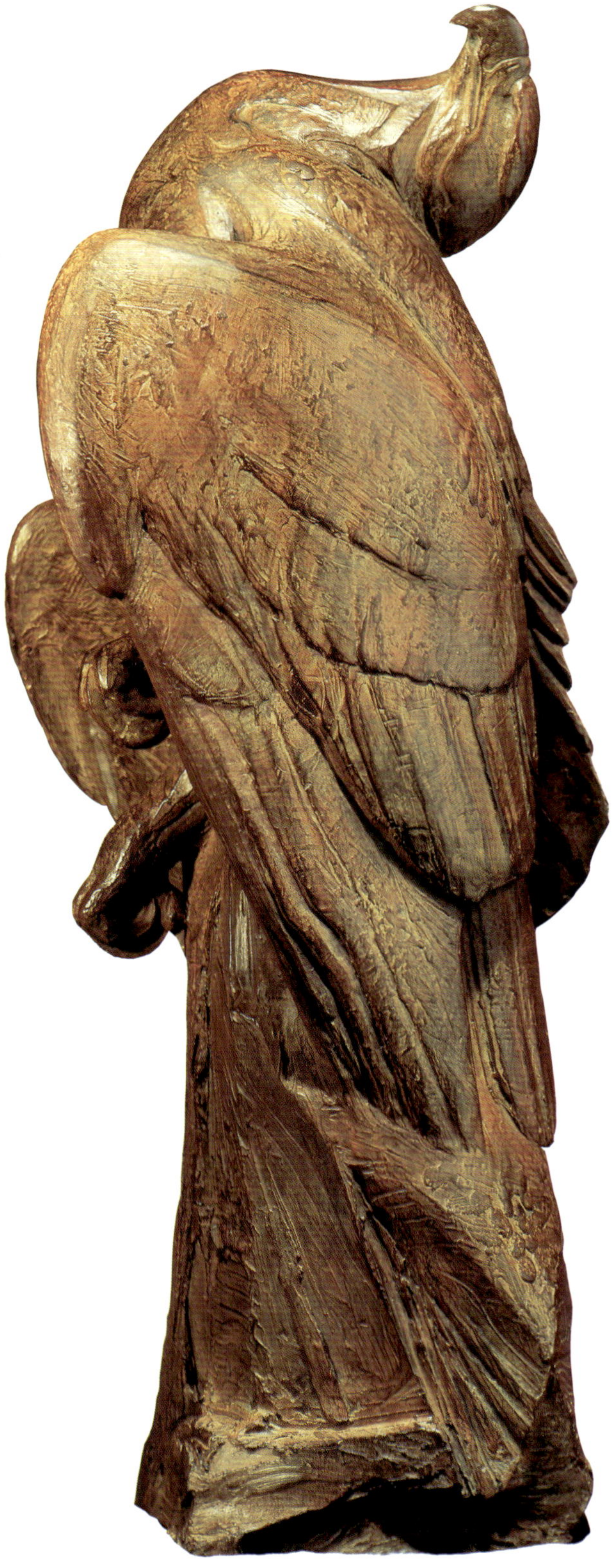

I am a conservationist and I want my work to speak about nature. I was so angered by the spill in Prince William Sound that I grasped for expressionist language. It would have been more logical to depict a sea bird soiled with oil, but that would limit the expression to pity. I wanted to make a much wider statement, so I picked the bald eagle – because it is the symbol of America, and I felt we were soiling our nation with our disregard of nature.

Requiem for Prince William Sound (bald eagle) 1989, bronze, 26½ x 8 x 8 inches, private collection. *Birds in Art* 1989.

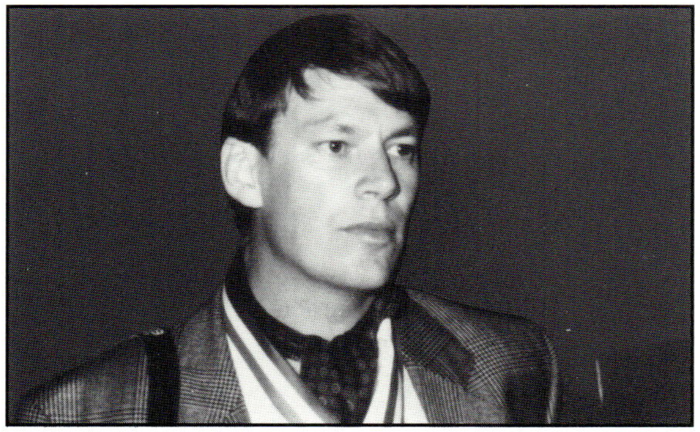

LARS JONSSON

Master Wildlife Artist 1988
Born: 1952, Stockholm, Sweden
Resides: Hamra on Gotland, Sweden

There are so many good things about birds. They have their own spirituality – the way they lift from the earth and seem to fly weightlessly – something humans always dream of doing. They migrate and mix with different winds. Then one day suddenly they all disappear and go down to Africa. It intrigues the imagination, the strength they carry in such small bodies and how they find their way back. They're so beautiful, so aesthetic, the way they move, the way their wings move, all the colors, all the variations, all the species. Birds are very approachable; they're rather easy to get in contact with. All these things add together. For me, it is a special love.

Bruno Liljefors, the Swedish painter, was among the first to paint the animal as a part of nature, to put the animal and its habitat into a unit, as one whole thing. Traditionally, the animal was painted and a background added later, more like a theater backdrop. Liljefors was one of the first ecologists in painting. He depicted nature and animals as being dependent on one another. More important, there is a lot of spirit, a lot of emotion in his paintings which springs from the impressionists and the awakening of the modern era in art. The wild wood is so vital to our emotional life in Sweden.

Swedes and Scandinavians are more dependent on wild nature than is continental Europe, where the land has been cultivated hundreds of years longer and where nature has been forced to adapt to humans. Into modern times, Swedes relied on picking berries and mushrooms, hunting wild animals and birds, and cutting timber. If you are dependent on wild nature for your living, you learn to treasure it and, to tell you my view, you also put spirit into it.

No specific event turned me into a painter. I was interested in birds and wildlife and was already painting before my earliest memories. I do remember several occasions that put me on the right trail. When I was five years old, we first went to Gotland where we lived very close to the coast. There were lots of birds so I spent much time walking along the shore. When I was six years old, I learned I could paint a white spot in the eye of a bird to give it life. And when I was seven years old, my parents sent several small paintings of mine to a children's art competition. I must have been pretty good at drawing birds, because the paintings were returned as fakes. The judges didn't think a child could have done them.

Painting is a way to express my emotions. Sometimes it is more intentional, when I have several thoughts I want to express. Other times I do it unconsciously. But, without emotions, painting gets uninteresting and is seldom very good. I spend a lot of time outdoors, and, when I see something that pulls strings in my life, my emotions are awakened. It could be very simple, like two shades of color or a bird that walks into a certain type of mud where the lines and the colors come together. And this *means* something to me; this *is* me. And I get very inspired to paint. This is very much how I work.

One summer I spent a great amount of time just looking at a pair of common gulls. They did not succeed in raising young, but I just watched them walking around. I painted them in the field. I got acquainted with these beautiful animals, how their heads turned different angles. It became an obsession to get so close to them that I could foretell what they were going to do.

What could be better for painting wildlife than painting out-of-doors? But to me, sketching in the field is not primarily a way to produce nice sketches to use in a show; it is a way to experience wildlife. Often when artists field sketch, they do not look at the subject; they paint an image they have in their heads. For every osprey you see in the field, you probably have seen many photographs of ospreys in books. So you already have an image in your head and you do not trust your eyes. You will not improve or develop. You will repeat that image all the time. A hundred years ago, they sketched to learn how a bird looked. Today, people know how a bird looks because they have seen the bird in photographs, but they don't know their own impression of it.

The impressionists trusted their eyes and really looked at the subject they were painting. I think it is very important to trust your eyes and to improve your sight power – that is the importance of field sketching and painting outdoors.

I often look though a telescope while I paint. You simply cannot paint a goose from ten yards away, but if you view it through a telescope, you can construct it as if it were near you. The telescope also simplifies the background; objects and colors are blurred and a lot of detail is lost, which is good for a background. It is almost like having a frame around the subject.

Watercolors and oils are different mediums and they express different things. Watercolor is fast. I actually painted the sparrow hawk while viewing it from my window through a telescope. I do some of my best work this way, being spontaneous when I don't have a lot of time to think. Before I paint in oil, I often make several sketches and then try to rediscover a fresh emotional spirit. I might work the surface too much

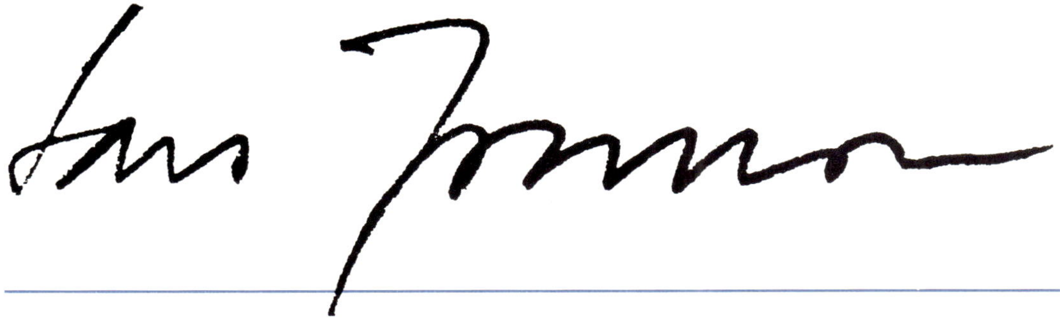

emotional spirit. I might work the surface too much and end up with details. This is very common, especially among wildlife artists. Often my oil paintings are not better than my watercolor sketches. It is harder for me to part with a very good field painting or field sketch than with a finished oil. I treasure the field sketch sometimes more than the finished painting.

I have not had any formal training so, for me, art is instinctive. With training, some artists may come to a certain stage earlier than they would without training. There is a point in one's development when you start to paint because you love it – you think it is just such a nice thing to do. Then you see a master, someone whose work you like, and you try to achieve his skill. I think that is actually a very lucky period of your life because you have a goal. But one day you realize you have reached a certain amount of skill, and it is no longer interesting to try to paint a bird or a wood in the way Liljefors did. You cannot get any further on that line. You have to get the power from inside; you have to open your mind and follow your own eyes and imagination. You have to find your own way. That is where the hard part comes, when you have to express *yourself*. Then your art will grow in a slightly different way, if you open up your heart.

The market – trends, critics, and what the public wants – obviously pushes artists in different directions. I would say I am not influenced by the market, but every artist would like to think that. It is not always easy to be aware of outside influences. You can paint just to sell your work, or you can be true to yourself and paint what you like the most. The problem with wildlife art might be that it is so commercially successful, we never take the time to question what we are doing. I am trying to be as honest to my own feelings and emotions as I can.

In Sweden, Liljefors is very highly treasured. We have a tradition of wildlife art, and I feel accepted by most artists and galleries. I know there are many wildlife artists who are frustrated by not being taken seriously by the art community, but I would say many wildlife artists do not take art seriously. There are so many artists in the general field of art who are not accepted, that for every frustrated wildlife artist, there are probably a thousand frustrated artists painting landscapes, abstracts, or any other art form.

A lot of artists tell me they would like to get away from detail and paint more impressionistically. But when I look through galleries and exhibitions of wildlife art, I see mostly detail work. I guess that's because of the market; but if you see too much that looks the same, it gets boring in the long run. I do not dislike detail; detail can be good. A really good painting, which is honestly made and has a lot of emotion and power in its design, can almost never be destroyed by too much detail. It might not gain from detail, but it won't be destroyed. In most cases, however, bad designs and bad themes and bad constructions of the animals are masked with details.

I think there is so much more we can do as artists, instead of blaming the art establishment. It is part of our work as artists to question what we are doing, to criticize ourselves to see what more we can do. Wildlife art that does not reveal something about the artist is very seldom significant. I don't think we have ever touched the limitations of what painting wildlife might be about.

When I paint, I am searching for an expression and something about the birds which appears evident, as though I have not influenced them; they must have their own life, their own soul. Only then do they become of interest to me and are able to tell me something that I cannot formulate myself. In many cases, I need to search deeply for this aspect; other times, it falls into place by itself, almost without my involvement. On those occasions when "the evident" occurs, it strikes me afterwards that I have been working unconsciously, almost instinctively, on a subject that has fascinated me. I gain most satisfaction when I experience myself as a medium, when the physical friction in my body and in the material, from the impression of the eye to the emergence on the paper, is almost nonexistent.

I have done paintings in one day that I like very much; and I have done paintings that took weeks, where I struggled and I struggled. Some very quick paintings and sketches can be good, sometimes the very best. Sometimes everything comes together in a painting; all your emotions and everything fit perfectly; it just works and you cannot answer why. That is what's so beautiful about art. When you succeed, you cannot really say why. If you could extract the ingredients of what is good in a painting and distill some formula for success, then you could endlessly produce good paintings, but your art would die, because art is the life you give to each painting. That is why it is so terribly exciting to paint; it is always unpredictable. You always think maybe *this* will be the ultimate painting.

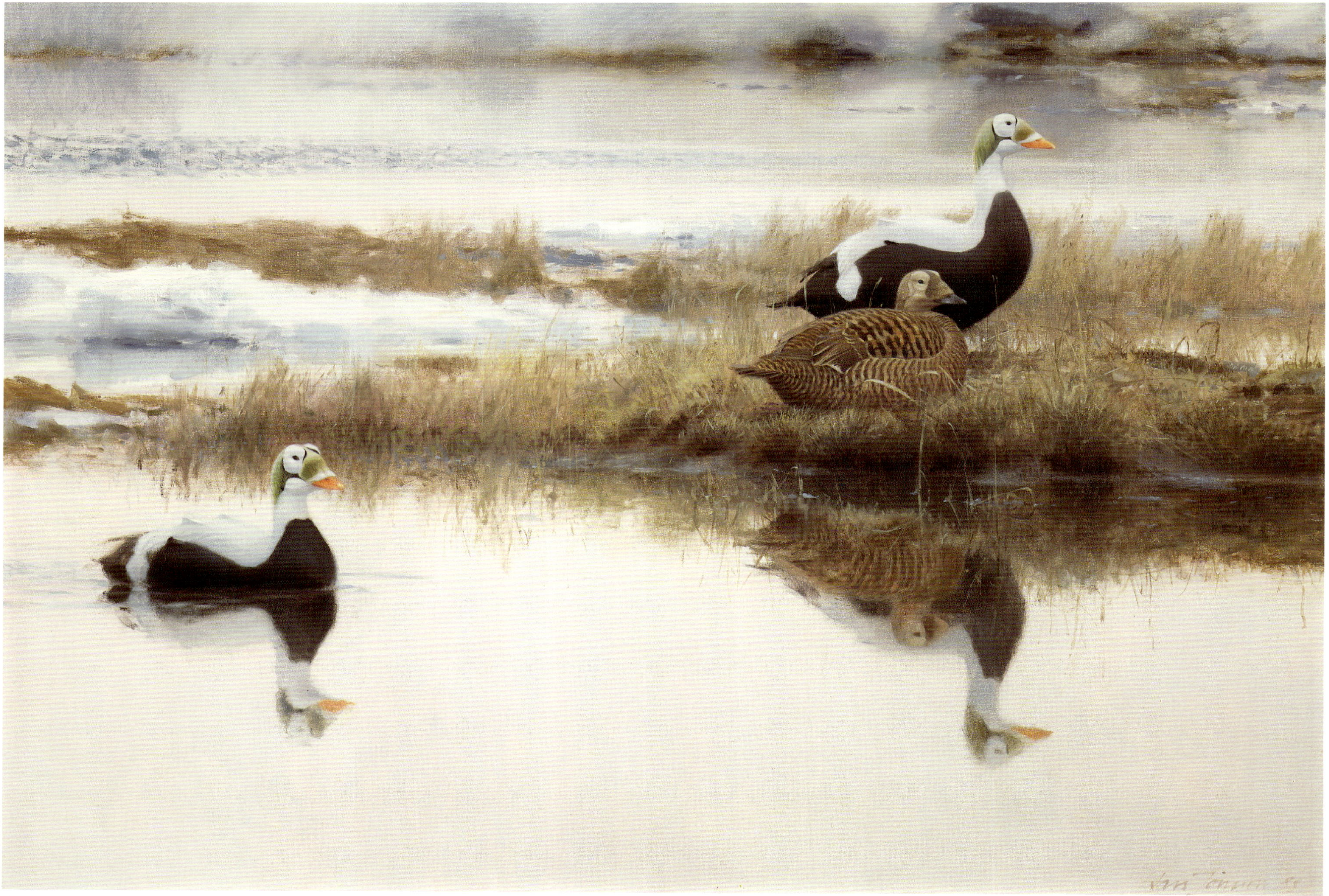

Arctic Spring (spectacled eider) 1988, oil on canvas, 33 x 49 inches, private collection. *Birds in Art* 1988.

Birds are the bearers of my message. They are the mirror which gives perspective to my inner being.

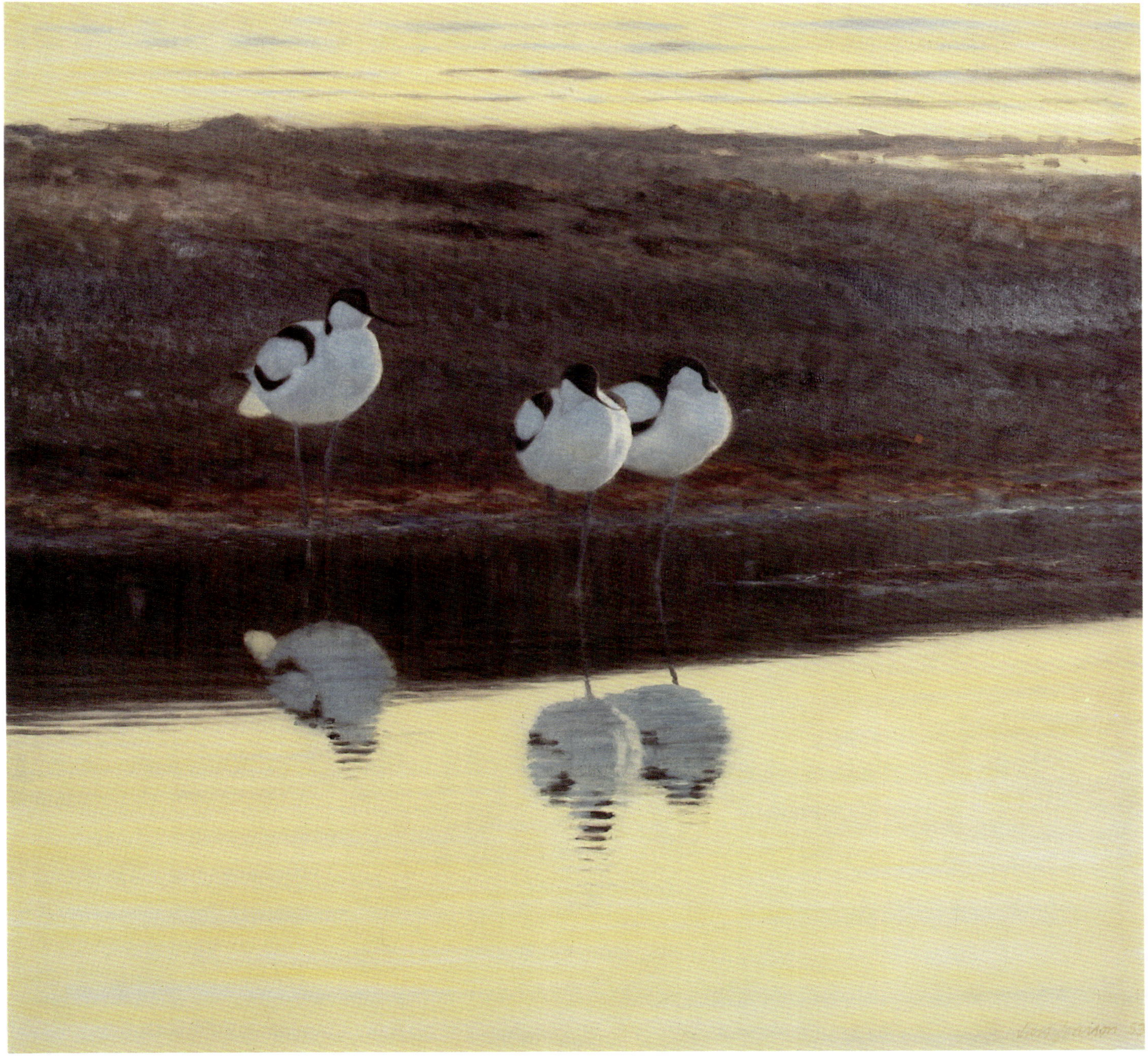

At the Dawn (European avocet) 1983, oil on canvas, 43¼ x 47¼ inches, collection of the artist. *Birds in Art* 1984.

The twilight or the early morning light often inspires me, maybe because in Sweden we simply have so much of it. There is a mystery and a spell while everything is not truly visible, when colors are still to be born out of a shivering darkness. The intense and yet subtle colors of dawn and dusk are a rich mold for my art.

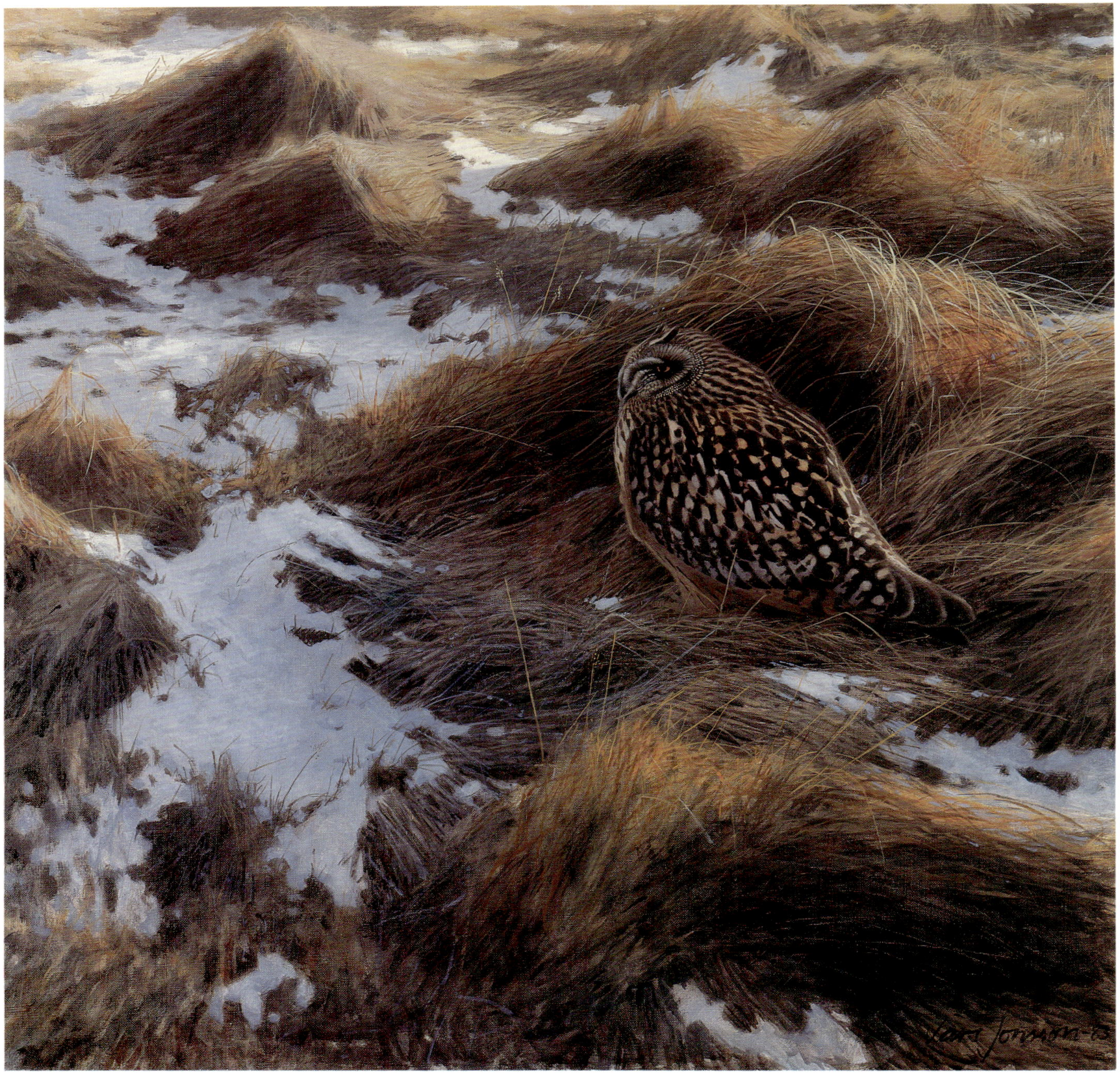

Early Spring Morning (short-eared owl) 1983, oil on canvas, 37½ x 39½ inches, collection of the Leigh Yawkey Woodson Art Museum. *Birds in Art* 1984.

Spring is in such a hurry; the land is impatient for summer so that although spring's vitality and beauty intoxicate me, I seldom manage to do much painting. . . . My sketchpad is filled with half-finished drawings that partake of the restless, unfinished spirit of the season.

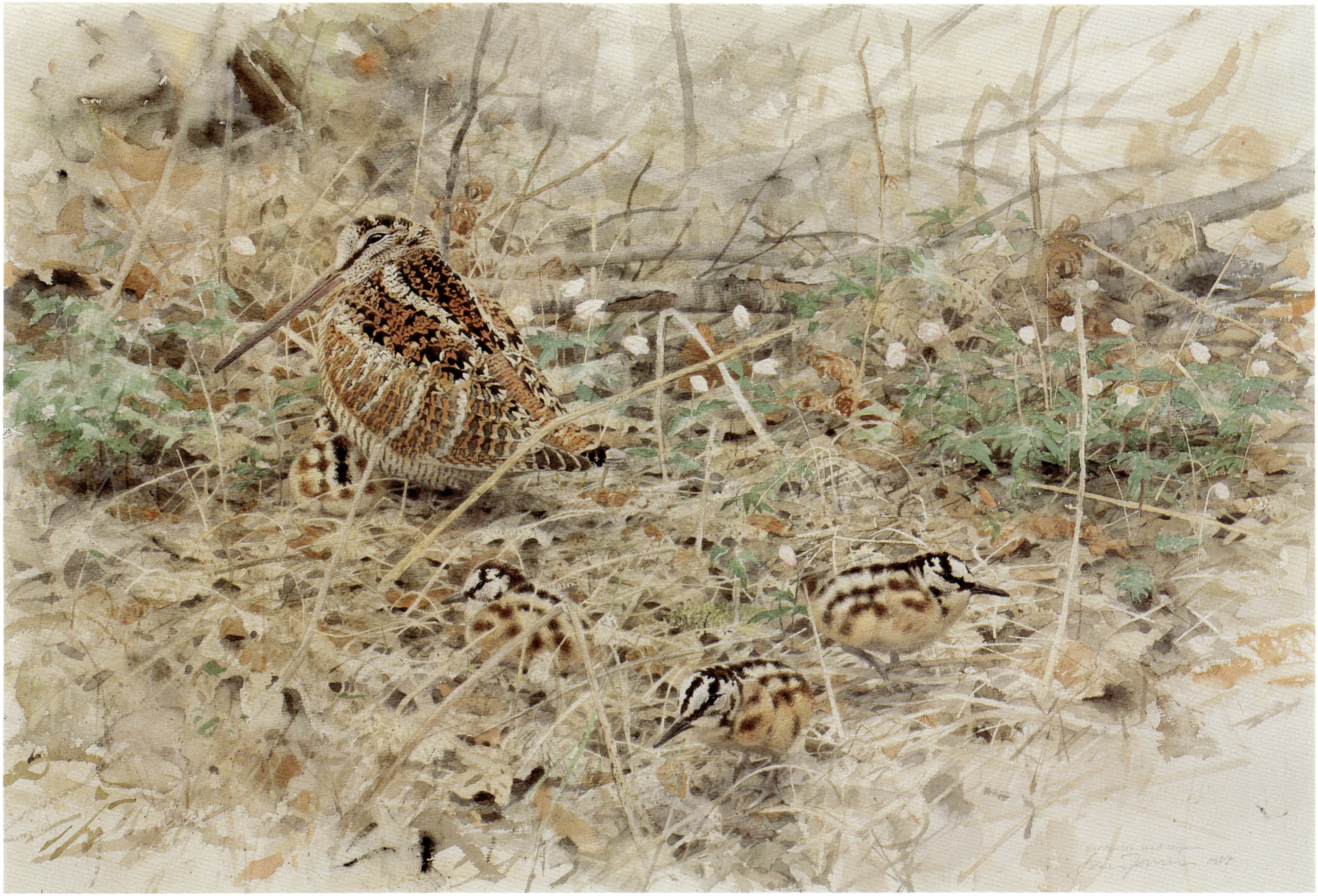

Woodcock With Young (European woodcock) 1987, watercolor on paper, 18 x 27 inches, collection of Mr. and Mrs. Göran Lundström. *Birds in Art* 1988.

After midsummer, I achieve a calmer tempo; I accept the passage of time; I pause to rest on my oars, to look around, to reflect – and to paint.

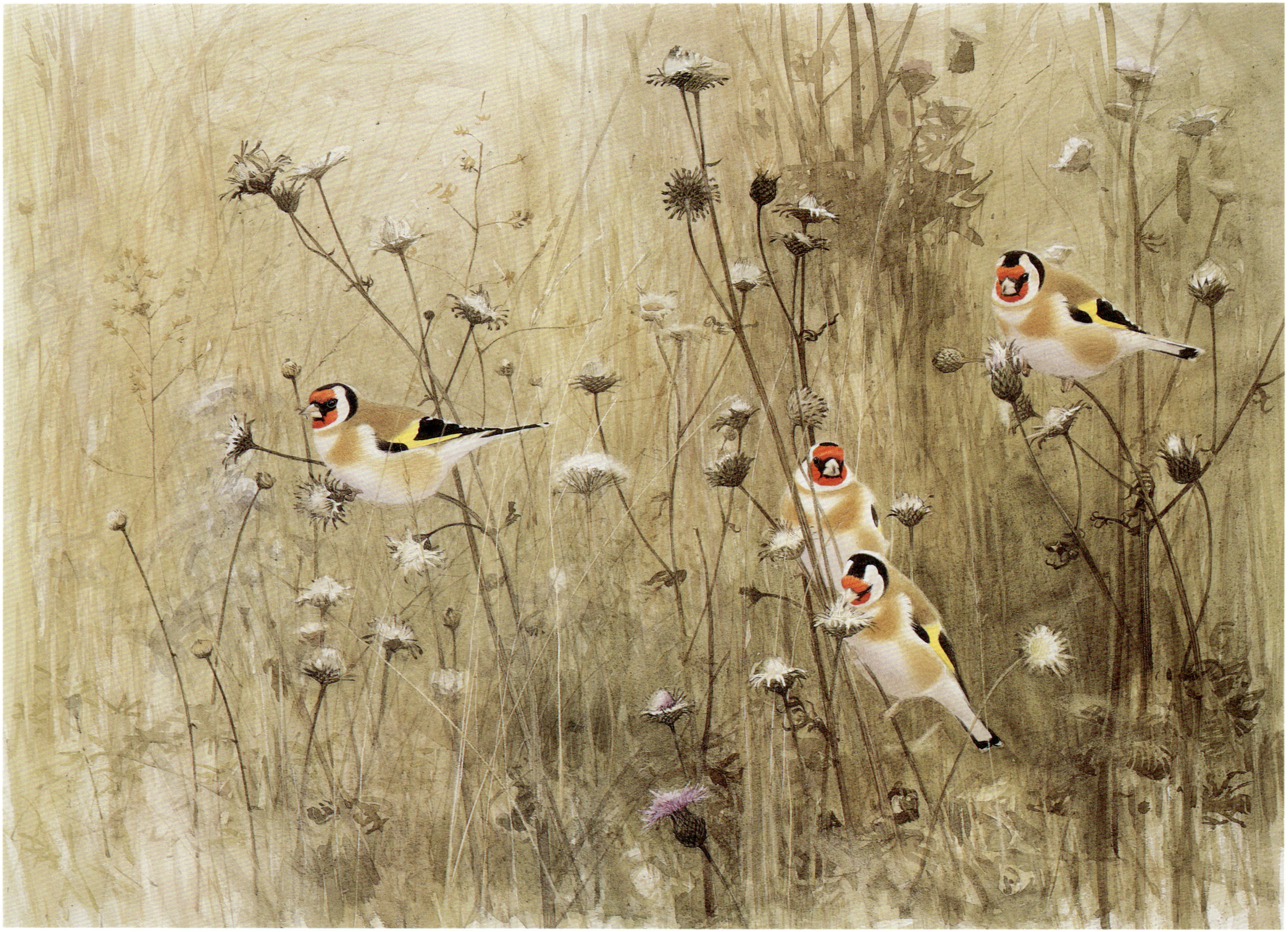

The Golden Season (European goldfinch) 1985, watercolor on paper, 22 x 30 inches, collection of the artist. *Birds in Art* 1986.

The relentless circle of nature is like a human life: We are born with the first spring thaw when the migrant birds return, and we die in the late autumn darkness.

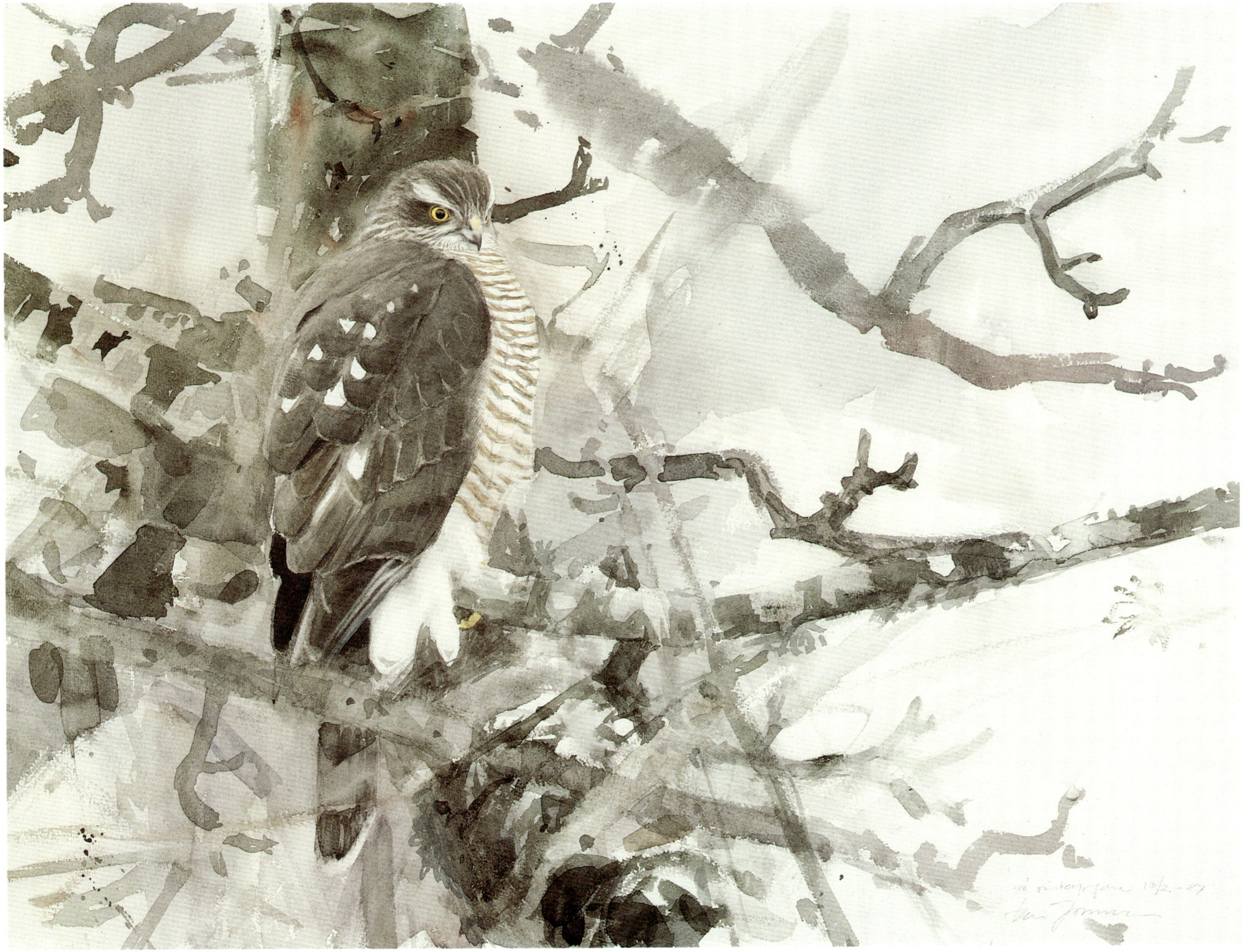

Sparrow Hawk (Eurasian kestrel) 1987, watercolor on paper, 16½ x 22 inches, collection of the artist. *Birds in Art* 1987.

As far as I am concerned, the time spent on a painting bears no relation to its spiritual content, in the same way that the number of words does not determine the intensity of a poem.

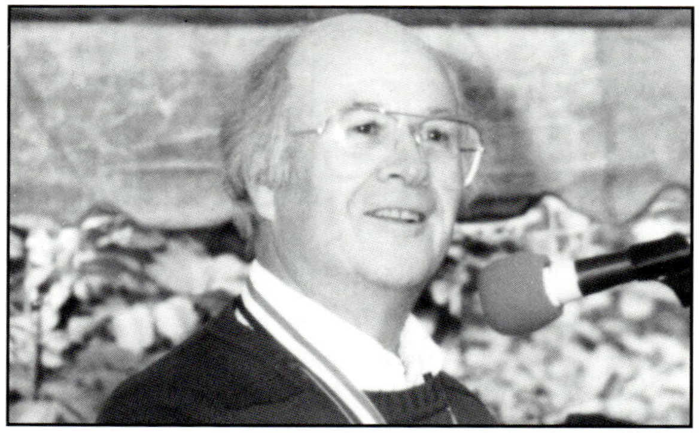

MAYNARD REECE

Master Wildlife Artist 1989
Born: 1920, Arnolds Park, Iowa
Resides: Des Moines, Iowa

I have had an interest in natural history as far back as I can remember. My father was a fisherman so I was fishing by age three. We lived in the lake region of Iowa, and I've had a lifelong interest in water and water birds. When I first began painting, I drew pictures of water and sand beaches.

When I was in the seventh grade, my teacher saw my interest in art and sent away for instructions on how to paint. We didn't have art classes in school so she taught me as much as she could about watercolors. She encouraged me to enter a pencil drawing of mallards in the state fair. I received first prize of $1.50. I just couldn't imagine that much money, and I spent it all on art supplies. Until then, the only oils I had were house paints. My sister saved the ribbon and gave it to me years later. I still have it.

At one time I wanted to be a museum background painter so I visited museums of natural history. That led to visiting art museums where I started to see the masters. I was intrigued by Winslow Homer's seascapes and powerful use of light and shadow. While stationed in France during World War II, I studied the paintings at the Louvre. You would think they'd have taken them down because of bomb scares, but they didn't. They even had the *Venus De Milo* out. I learned a lot from studying the masters' techniques and ways of handling paint.

I was a very compulsive sketcher and wherever I was, in every spare moment, I sketched everything I saw – trees, rocks, troop ships. I still use some of those sketches forty-five years later. A lot of my art supplies and sketches were sunk in the English Channel. I felt rather bad about that, but if I had to decide between staying alive or losing my sketches, I'd stay alive any day.

After the war, I went back to Des Moines to work at the Museum of Natural History. I continued to illustrate books and I did a lot of study skin collections. This allowed me to hunt birds both spring and fall for museum specimens. By preparing hundreds of bird skins, you learn every muscle and bone. It's very valuable when you paint.

When I first started out, I could not make a living doing artwork in my community so I worked in commercial art. I did natural history assignments for magazines and conservation organizations, and I did some of my best work, although it might be classified in the gray area between illustration and art. About the same time magazines switched to photography instead of art, people became more interested in original art and limited edition prints. So then I could earn a living painting what I wanted because there was a market for it.

I object to being called "self-taught" because it sounds like I became an artist without any help, and this is not accurate. I read books, visited museums, and observed nature. I picked up information and design ideas from every place I could. I learned the commercial aspects of painting from magazine art directors. I received assistance from many artists, especially Francis Lee Jaques and Jay "Ding" Darling.

I met Francis Lee Jaques and was invited to his apartment on many occasions where I watched him paint. He had a vast knowledge of waterfowl and helped me a lot. Jaques taught me to rough in the birds first. After laying out a painting and getting the flow of the birds in flight, it is important not to lose the design by covering it up. So it's just a matter of roughing in the birds to establish position, then painting the background and coming back to complete the birds. I still use this technique.

Ding Darling was a friend of mine for twenty-five years. I made a painting of a pronghorn antelope running and took it to Ding one morning. He said, "Maynard, pronghorn antelope run flatout like a racehorse. They run smooth. They don't jump up and down." He said I'd better do more research and more watching. He was correct, and I learned the value of thorough research.

Artists in the East may have an advantage in marketing, but I feel the Midwesterner has the advantage of being right on the scene of the natural world. I do a lot of pencil sketches in the field and a lot of observation, just absorbing what I see. It may be something I've seen a thousand times, but by looking at it again, I see new ways of handling things I've painted many times before. I can't get that new twist or fresh approach at the drawing board in my studio. My best paintings are based on fieldwork.

I also field sketch in oil paint. These sketches are mostly landscapes to show the colorations of atmospheric conditions and how the light works on the

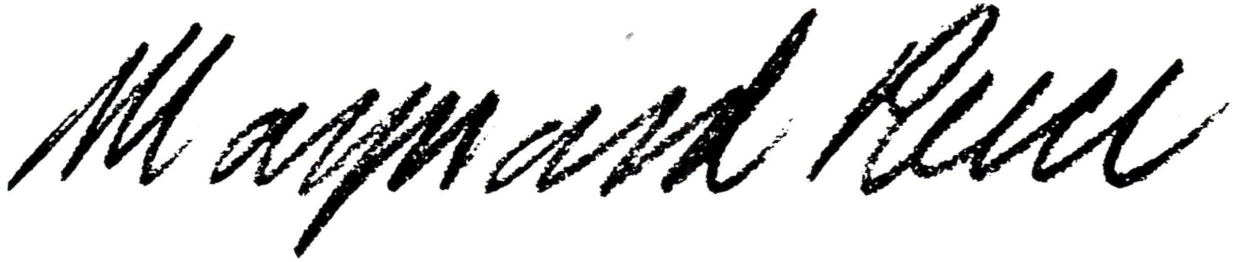

trees and plants. The birds or mammals are introduced later. I have always been fascinated with lighting over open landscape – where shadows of clouds hit one area and sunshine hits another and how objects in the foreground are silhouetted against the brilliant color behind. I am most interested in painting nature as it appears in natural light, subdued shadow, fog, and with long shafts of sunlight hitting the landscape. I use oil paints because I can control the mood and color value more closely than with other mediums.

Most people who relate to my work like the habitats as much as the birds. To me, the bird is part of the whole scene; the clouds, the trees, and the water are equally important. People like to reminisce. My paintings may remind them of some favorite place and transport them from mundane activity to a place they like to be.

I always try to tell a story in my paintings. I try to paint more than just a portrait of a bird. I try to tell something about the bird, the way the bird lives, and what it does. A good painting goes beyond just photographically recording a bird. An artist interprets what he sees, and his thoughts and feelings are revealed in his paintings. It is very subtle and difficult to explain, but it gives meaning to a painting.

Any time you have vast knowledge of your subject, you are more comfortable painting it, and the painting comes out a lot fresher and with more feeling. You are able to show the essence of the bird. If you are not intimately acquainted with a bird, you more or less just record the various shapes and colors. That's the difference between doing a portrait and doing something that is alive.

Accuracy is most important. You don't paint seven fingers on a human hand. It's just as important to know the individual shapes, proportions, and colors of each species of waterfowl.

Years ago, I did a grouse painting for my hunting partner. He liked the sketch but pointed out that my trees were wrong. Grouse in the north country are never far from aspen, which is a major source of winter food. His criticism made me aware that the bird and habitat must be compatible or your work will lack credibility. We paint for critical eyes these days, but I enjoy the challenge of doing it right.

We don't want to be known as "wildlife artists"; we want to be known as "artists." Whether we paint people or deer shouldn't make any difference, but some people try to make one art and the other illustration. Wildlife art is art. It's frustrating, but I don't think being militant about it is productive so I just paint and let other people worry about it.

I think the distinction between illustration and art has been overemphasized. Good illustration should be good art. Just because an artist is limited by art directors in the way he handles a certain subject doesn't necessarily mean his painting is any less art than if he had full freedom. Under those rules, Michelangelo would be known as a commercial artist because the Pope told him exactly what he had to paint and when he had to get it done.

Ding Darling taught me about conservation. He was doing cartoons about what was happening to our planet long before people were even interested in it. He made a believer out of me, and I've been trying to find some way to save our planet ever since.

I think all nature artists try to interest people in the outdoors to get them concerned about saving our planet. Not every painting has a direct message, but by painting the beauty we see in the world around us, we hope to interest others in helping to save wildlife habitat from utter destruction.

In the early days, northwest Iowa, where I grew up, was one of the big migration routes of waterfowl through the central United States. The birds were so plentiful that market hunters used to ship waterfowl by the barrel to New York restaurants. Today, only a small percentage of the birds still come through. It's just devastating to think of the millions that once migrated through that area. It's not due to hunting as much as agriculture destroying the marshlands. What was once a big marsh is now all corn fields.

I won the Federal Duck Stamp competition five times. A lot of attention is focused on the money the artist makes, but the real purpose of the competition is to raise money for waterfowl and habitat restoration. I have a love for waterfowl, and I am always honored to help the conservation effort.

The best part of art is the challenge. You are always striving to do better paintings and to try new things. You just never arrive; there is always a new plateau. I look forward every day to painting, and, as long as I have health and my eyesight, I will continue to paint. I find the challenge both invigorating and fun.

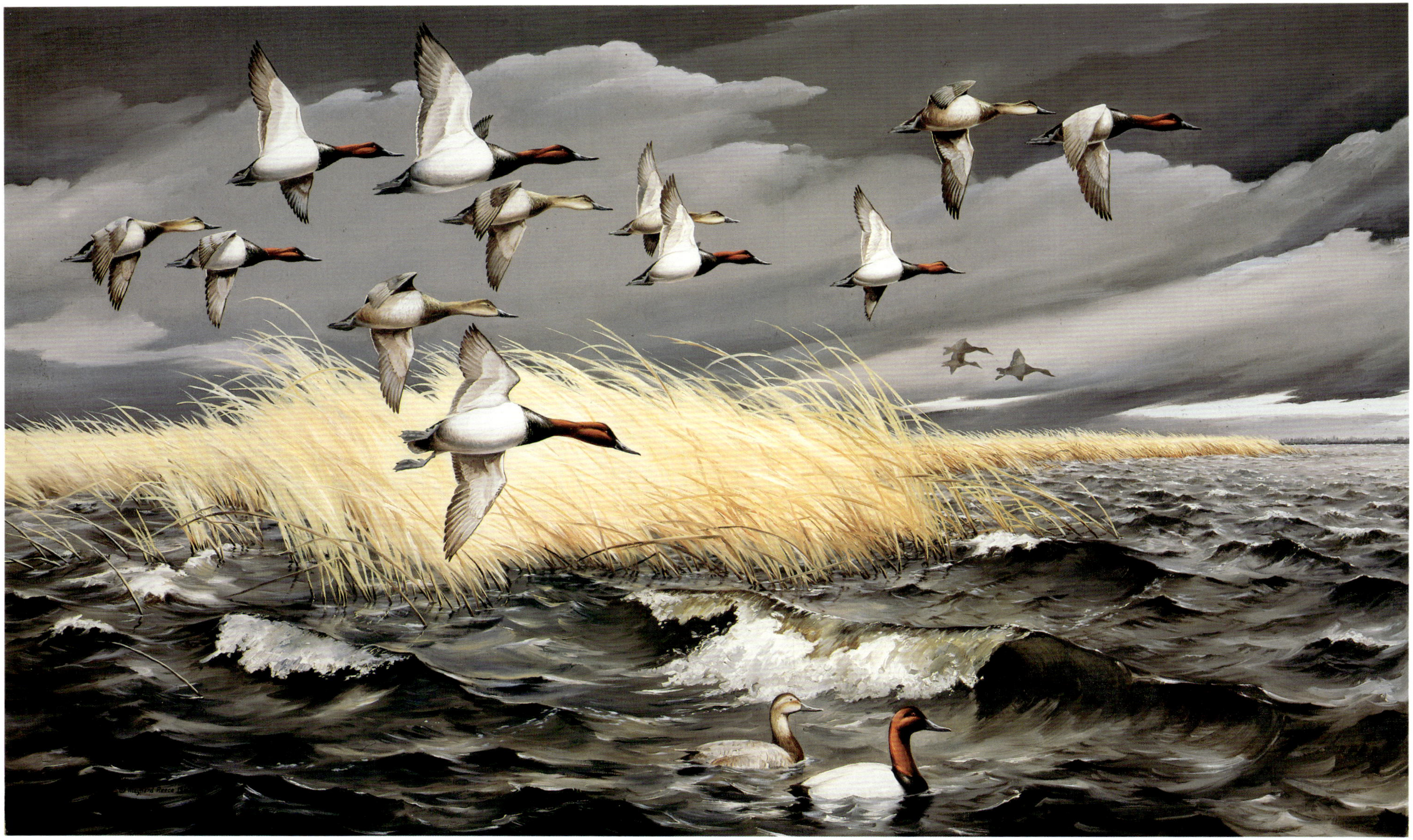

Dark Sky (canvasback) 1980, oil on canvas, 36 x 60 inches, private collection. *Birds in Art* 1982.

I have a love for waterfowl, and I am always honored to help the conservation effort.

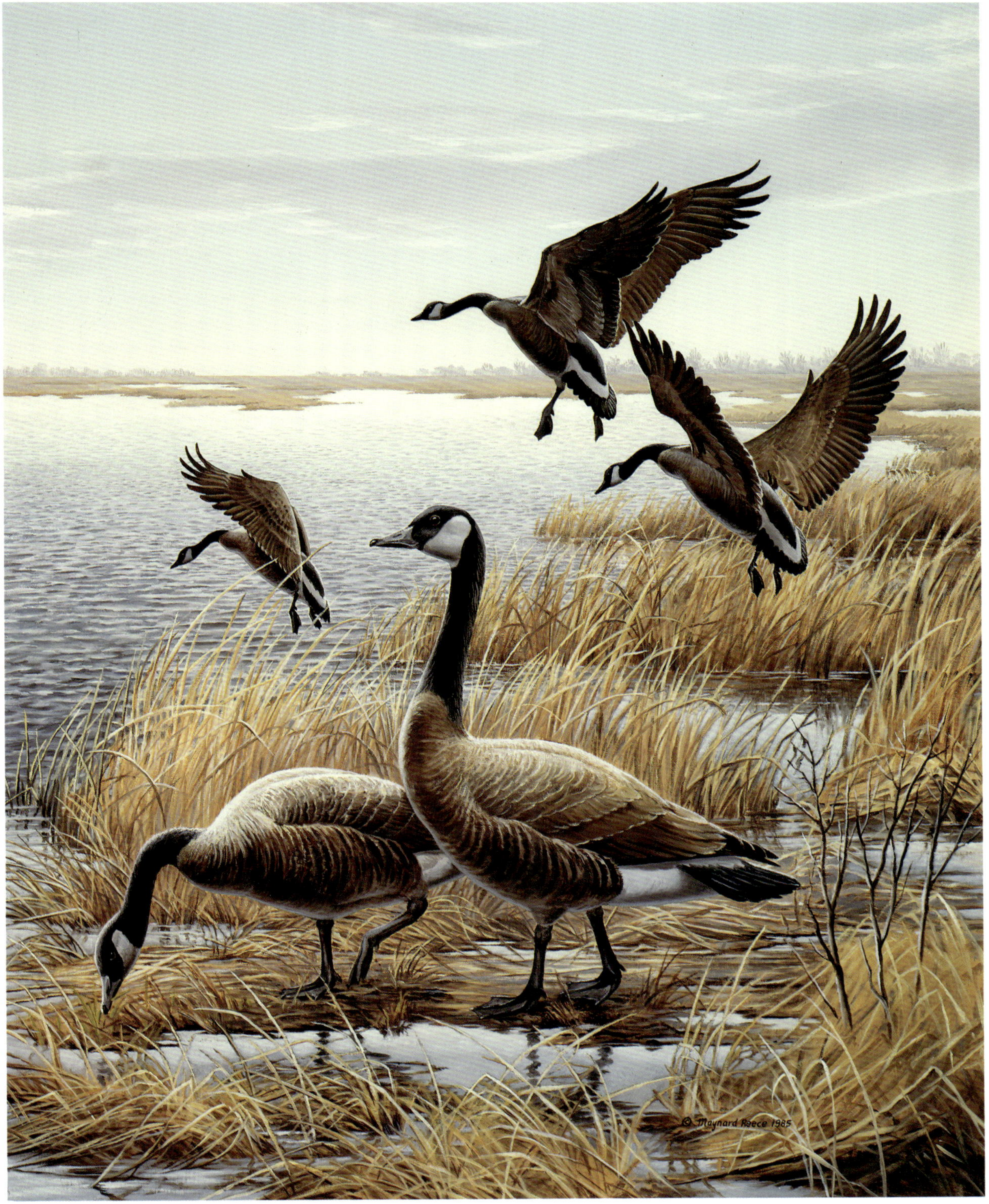

Art is my living and my love. I hope to leave something behind that is worthy of our heritage.

Water's Edge (Canada goose) 1985, oil on canvas, 34 x 28 inches, private collection. *Birds in Art* 1986.

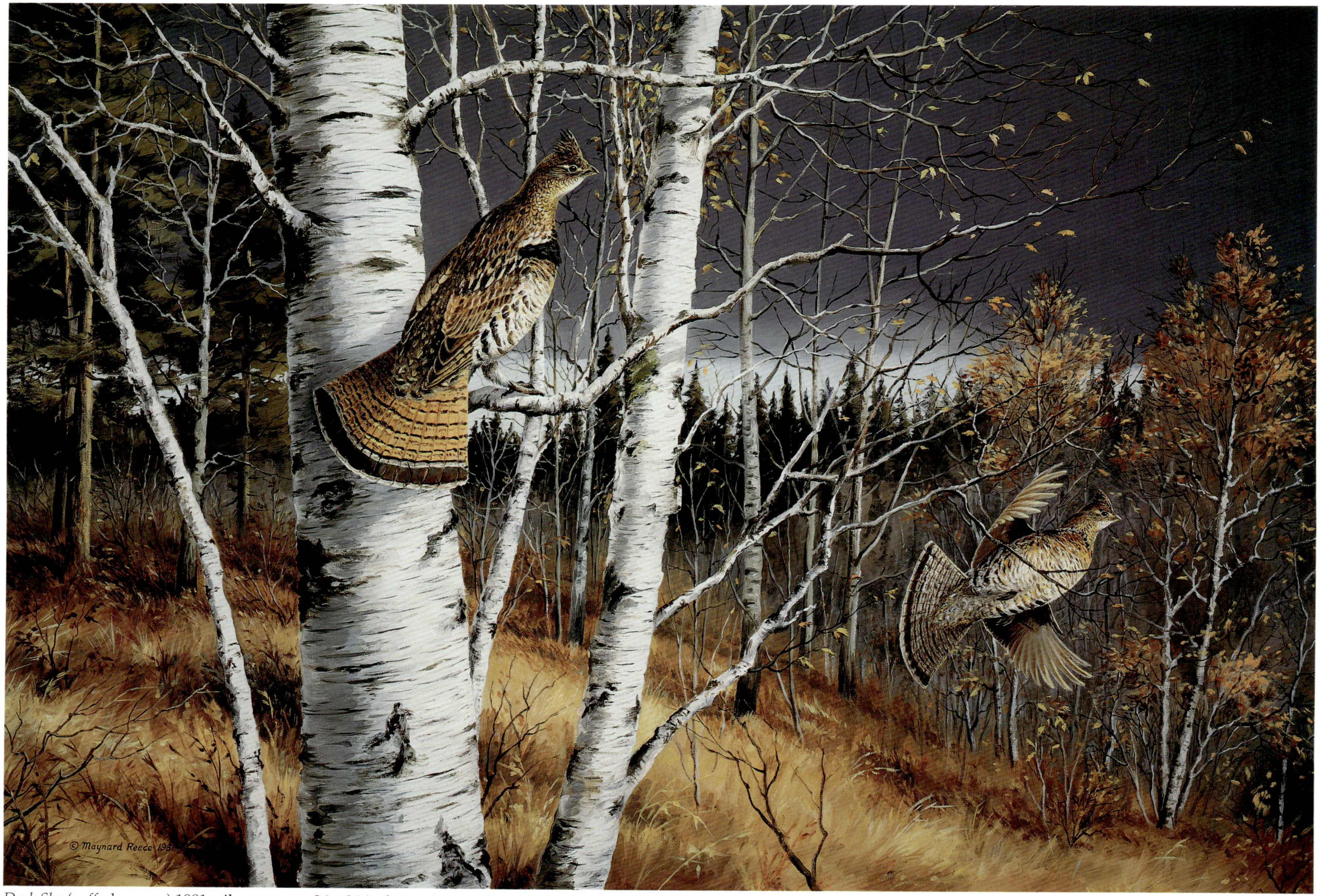

Dark Sky (ruffed grouse) 1981, oil on canvas, 24 x 36 inches, private collection. *Birds in Art* 1981.

An artist interprets what he sees, and his thoughts and feelings are revealed in his paintings. It is subtle and difficult to explain, but it gives meaning to a painting.

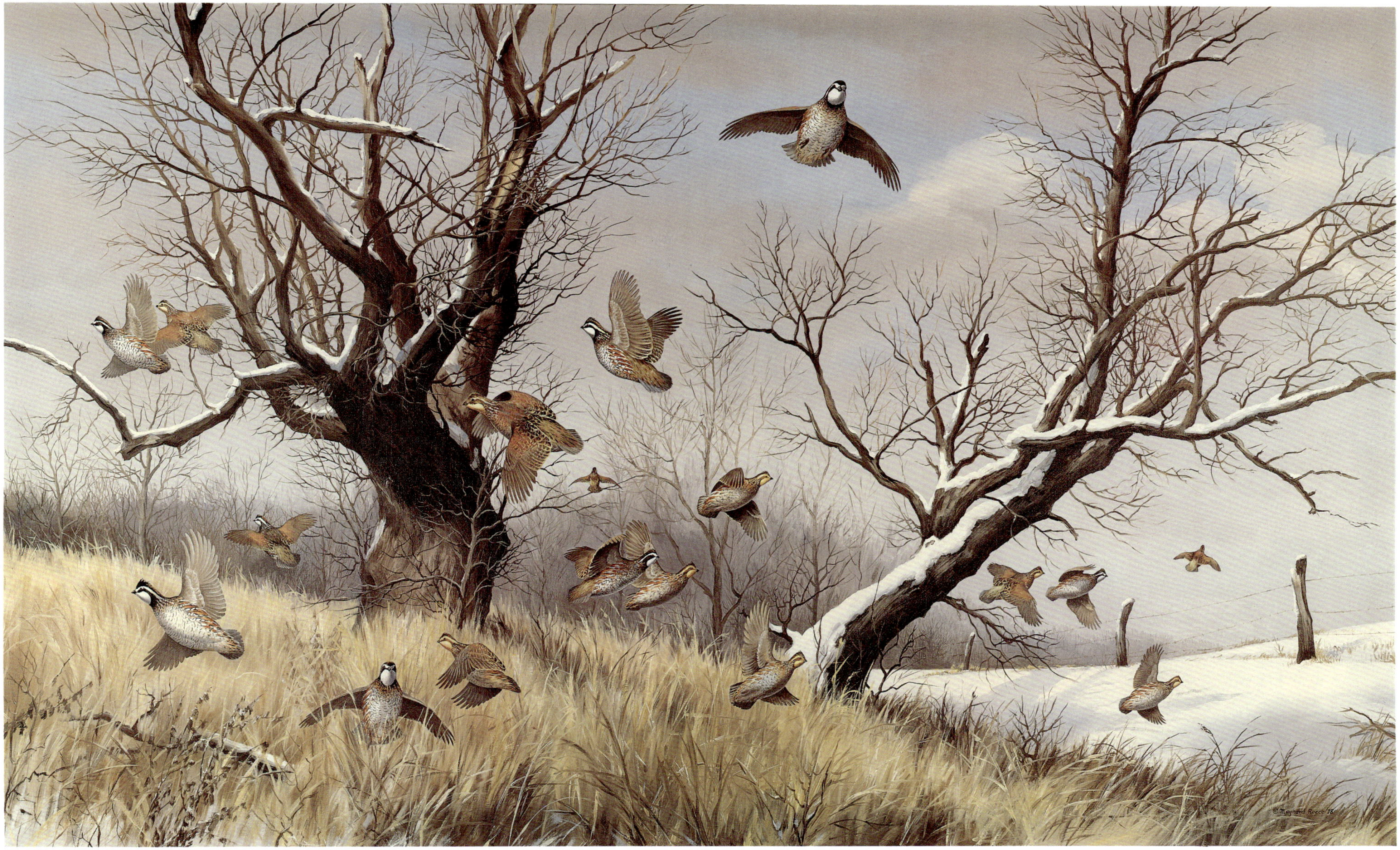

Winter Covey (northern bobwhite) 1978, oil on canvas, 36 x 60 inches, collection of Dr. and Mrs. Joel D. Teigland. *Birds in Art* 1978.

The bird is part of the whole scene – the clouds, the trees, and the water are equally important.

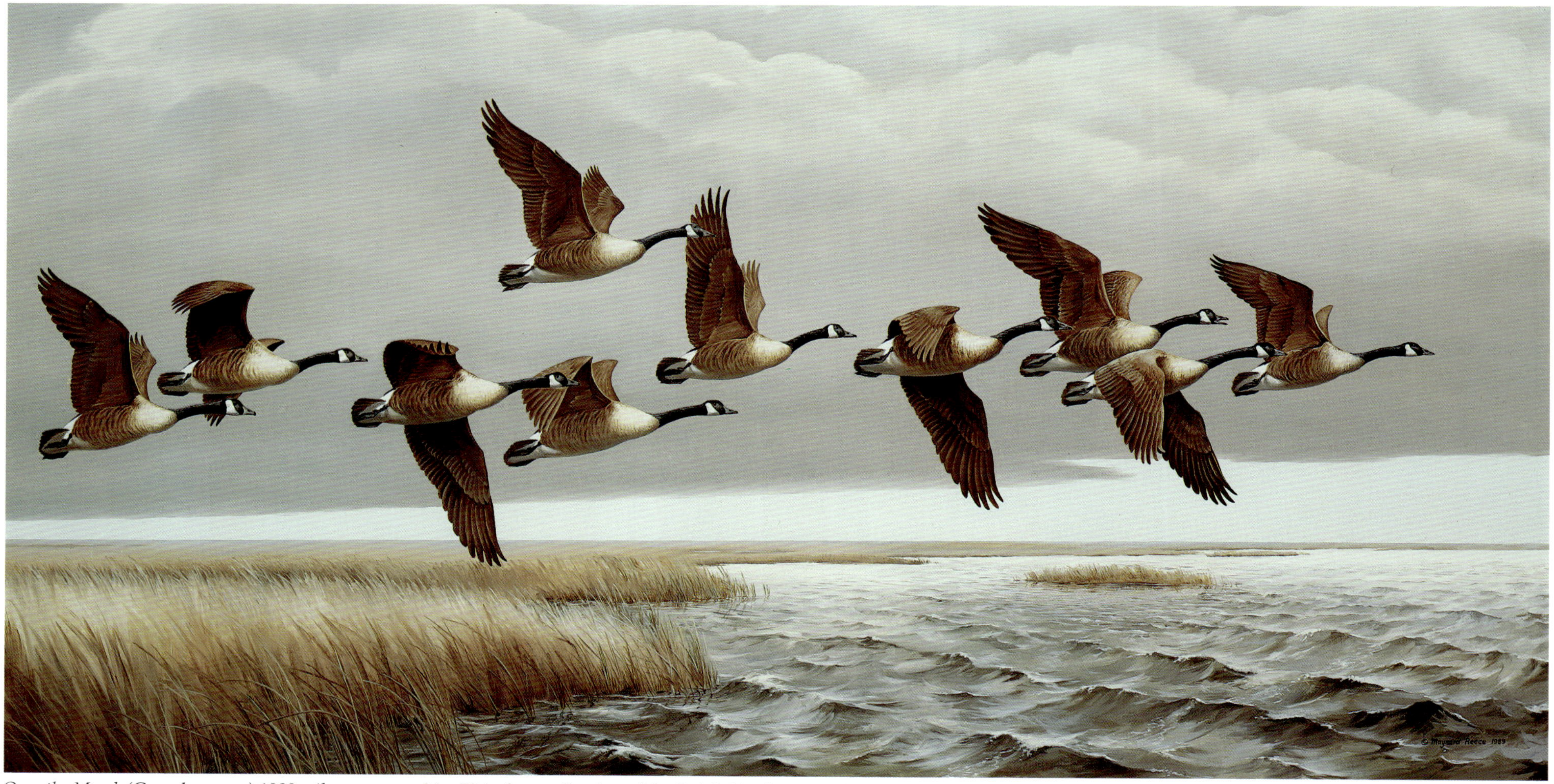

Over the Marsh (Canada goose) 1989, oil on canvas, 36 x 72 inches, collection of the Leigh Yawkey Woodson Art Museum. *Birds in Art* 1989.

Canada geese are most beautiful when they are flying over a wide, open marsh. Geese hold power and freedom in their wings.

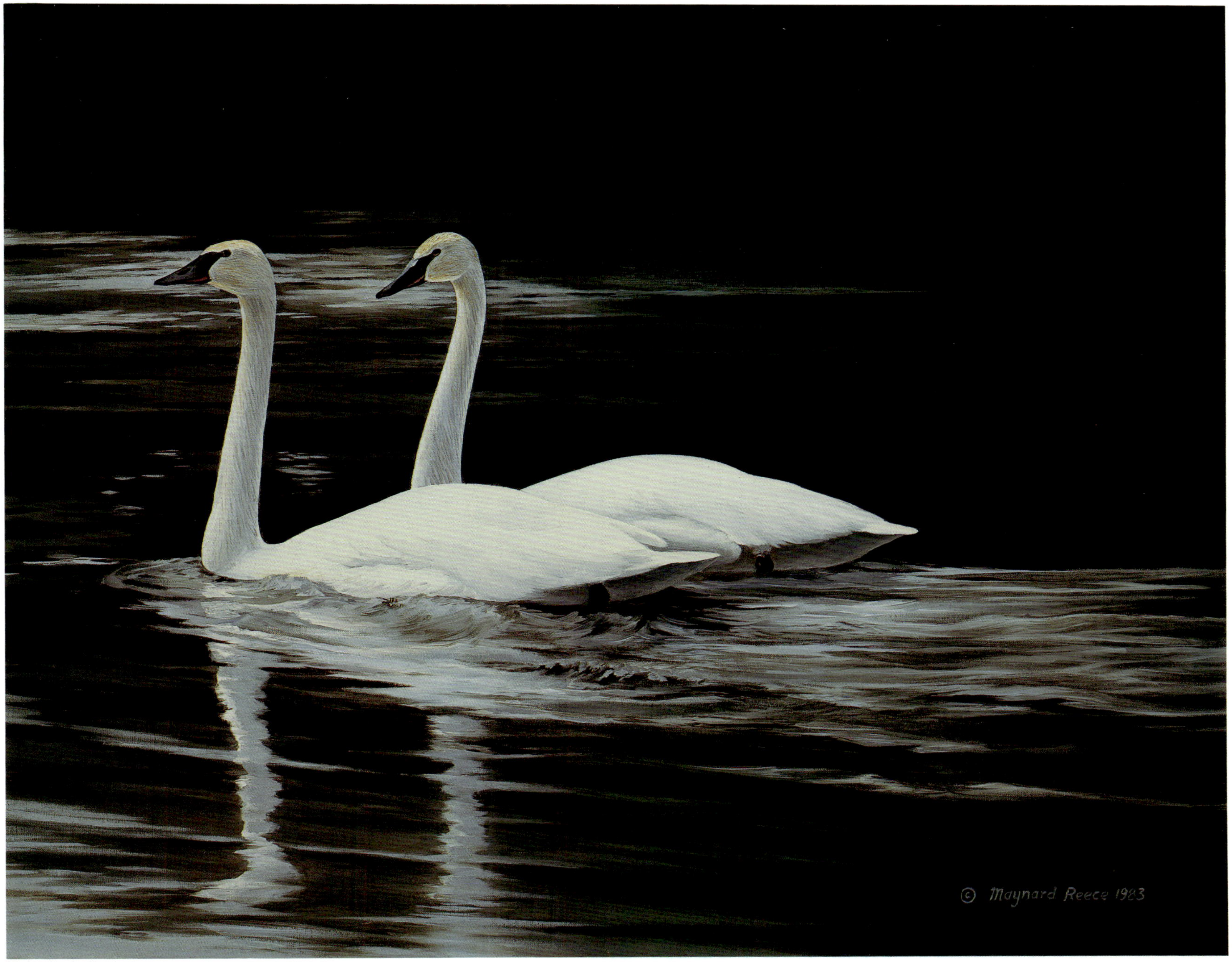

The Pair (trumpeter swan) 1983, oil on canvas, 20 x 24 inches, private collection. *Birds in Art* 1989.

Waterfowl. . . do not exist for us, but with us. At least we can make sure that suitable habitat is saved for them and for ourselves so that our children can enjoy the wonderful experience of watching the flight of waterfowl.

References

Preface

Fish and Wildlife Service, Department of the Interior. *1975 National Survey of Hunting, Fishing, and Wildlife Associated Recreation*. Washington, D.C., 1977.

Fish and Wildlife Service, Department of the Interior. *1985 National Survey of Fishing, Hunting, and Wildlife Associated Recreation*. Washington, D.C., 1988.

Hill, Martha. *Bruno Liljefors: The Peerless Eye*, Kingston upon Hull, England: The Allen Publishing Company Limited, 1987.

Nissen, C. *Die illustrierten Vogelbücher.* Stuttgart: Hiersemann Verlag, 1953. Quoted from Mengel, Robert M. "Beauty and the Beast: Natural History and Art." *The Living Bird*, 1980.

Turner, Frederick Jackson. "The Significance of the Frontier in American History" from *Frederick Jackson Turner: Wisconsin's Historian of the Frontier*, edited by Martin Ridge. Madison: The State Historical Society of Wisconsin, 1986.

Wexler, Mark. "Wildlife Art Comes of Age." *National Wildlife*, October/November 1980.

Birds in Art – Taking Flight

Forester, Alice Woodson, and John E. Forester. Personal correspondence and interviews with Inga Brynildson and Woody Hagge, March/April 1990.

Harrison, George H. Telephone conversation with Woody Hagge, February 1990.

Hughes, Judy A. "*Birds in Art:* With Flying Colors." *Wildlife Art News*, September/October 1988.

Leigh Yawkey Woodson Art Museum. *Birds in Art* exhibition catalogues, Wausau, Wis.: 1976 - 1989.

Leigh Yawkey Woodson Art Museum. Scrapbooks 1976 - 1989.

Savage, George, and Dorothy Doughty. *The American Birds of Dorothy Doughty*. Worcester, England: The Worcester Royal Porcelain Company Limited, 1962.

Wagner, David J. Telephone conversation with Inga Brynildson, June 1990.

Wexler, Mark. "Wildlife Art Comes of Age." *National Wildlife*, October/November 1980.

The Flight of the Painted Bird

Allen, Elsa Guerdrum. *The History of American Ornithology Before Audubon.* King of Prussia, Penn.: W. Graham Arader III, 1951.

Audubon, John James. *The Birds of America.* New York: American Heritage Publishing Co., Inc., 1966.

______. *My Style of Drawing Birds.* Ardsley, N.Y.: The Haydn Foundation, 1979.

Cantwell, Robert. *Alexander Wilson: Naturalist and Pioneer.* Philadelphia: J. B. Lippincott Company, 1961.

Danzker, Jo-Anne Birnie. "Avian Images in Western Culture" from *J. Fenwick Lansdowne.* Vancouver: The Vancouver Art Gallery, 1981.

Deuchar, Stephen. *Sporting Art in Eighteenth-Century England: A Social and Political History.* New Haven: Yale University Press, 1988.

Egerton, Judy, comp. *British Sporting and Animal Paintings: 1655-1867.* London: The Tate Gallery, 1978.

Gould, John. *John Gould's Birds.* New York: A & W Publishers, Inc., 1981.

Hammond, Nicholas. *Twentieth Century Wildlife Artists.* Woodstock, N.Y.: The Overlook Press, 1986.

Hyman, Susan. *Edward Lear's Birds.* New York: William Morrow and Company, Inc., 1980.

Lank, David M. Introduction to *From the Wild: Portfolios of North America's Finest Wildlife Artists*, edited by Christopher Hume. Richmond Hill, Ontario: GWA Group Publishing Company, 1987.

Lindsey, Alton A. *The Bicentennial of John James Audubon.* Bloomington: Indiana University Press, 1985.

Lysaght, A. M. *The Book of Birds: Five Centuries of Bird Illustration.* New York: Exeter Books, 1984.

Marcham, Frederick G. "The Hands of an Angel." *The Living Bird Quarterly*, Autumn 1989.

Mengel, Robert M. "Beauty and the Beast: Natural History and Art." *The Living Bird*, 1980.

McCabe, Robert A. *The Bird in Natural History: Before, During, & After Audubon.* Madison: University of Wisconsin, Elvehjem Museum of Art, 1983.

Norelli, Martina R. *American Wildlife Painting.* New York: Watson-Guptill Publications, 1975.

Peck, Robert McCracken. *A Celebration of Birds: The Life and Art of Louis Agassiz Fuertes.* New York: Walker Publishing Company, Inc., 1982.

Peterson, Roger Tory, and Virginia Marie Peterson. Introduction to *Audubon's Birds of America* by John James Audubon. New York: Abbeville Press, Inc., 1981.

Oster, Maggie, ed. *The Illustrated Bird.* Garden City, N.Y.: Dolphin Books, 1978.

Rawls, Walton. *The Great Book of Currier & Ives' America.* New York: Abbeville Press, Inc., 1979.

Schmitt, Victoria Sandwick. *Four Centuries of Sporting Art.* Mumford, N.Y.: Genesee Country Museum, 1984.

Simpson, Lisa A. *From Arcadia to Barbizon: A Journey in French Landscape Painting.* Memphis: The Dixon Gallery and Gardens, 1987.

Sullivan, Scott A. *The Dutch Gamepiece.* Totowa, N.J.: Rowman & Allanheld Publishers, 1984.

THE MASTERS

Interviews conducted by Inga Brynildson and Woody Hagge unless specified. Additional material from *Birds in Art* catalogues, 1976-1989, and correspondence in Leigh Yawkey Woodson Art Museum archives. Brackets [ ] indicate text paragraphs and pages of quoted material from sources listed below. For consistency, spelling and punctuation have been corrected to *The Chicago Manual of Style.*

Robert Bateman

Sources:

Interview, April 1990.

Birds in Art Master Wildlife Artist lecture, September 1982.

Davis, Tom. "Robert Bateman: The Good Thought and Other Abstractions." *Wildlife Art News*, November/December 1986. [Text ¶ 18; Page 65]

Derry, Ramsay. *The Art of Robert Bateman.* Markham, Ontario: Penguin Books Canada Limited, 1981. [Text ¶ 3]

______. *The World of Robert Bateman.* Markham, Ontario: Penguin Books Canada Limited, 1985. [Text ¶ 1, 6, 7, 20, 21]

Reproductions:

Ghost of the North, collection of the Leigh Yawkey Woodson Art Museum. All other photographs courtesy of the artist and Mill Pond Press, Venice, Florida.

Charles Greenough Chase

Sources:

Interview, April 1990.
Birds in Art Master Wildlife Artist lecture, September 1984.
Stegmaier, Mark E. "Naturalistic Carvers." *Wildlife Art News,* November/December 1985. [Text ¶ 5]

Reproductions:

California Condor and *American Oystercatcher,* collection of the Leigh Yawkey Woodson Art Museum. All other photographs courtesy of the artist.

Guy Coheleach

Sources:

Interview, April 1990.
Birds in Art Master Wildlife Artist lecture, September 1983.
Brakefield, Tom. "Guy Coheleach: The Reach of an Artist." *Southwest Art,* November 1981. [Page 75]
Coheleach, Guy. Foreword to *Masters of the Wild: Coheleach* by Terry Wieland. Camden, S.C.: Briar Patch Press, Inc., 1989. [Page 74]
Gelbach, Deborah. "The Fast and the Beautiful." *Midwest Art,* Fall 1983. [Page 73]
Hughes, Judy A. "Guy Coheleach: A Brush with Excitement." *Wildlife Art News,* September/October 1987. [Page 70]
Van Gelder, Patricia. *Wildlife Artists at Work.* New York: Watson-Guptill Publications, 1982. [Text ¶ 6]
Wechsler, Chuck. "Guy Coheleach: An Artist of Contrasts." *Wildlife Art News,* July/August 1984. [Text ¶ 9]

Artist's Photo:

Courtesy of M. J. Castle Studio.

Reproductions:

Brightwaters Creek, collection of the Leigh Yawkey Woodson Art Museum. All other photographs courtesy of the artist.

Don Richard Eckelberry

Sources:

Interview, April 1990.
Eckelberry, Don Richard. "Birds in Art and Illustration." *The Living Bird,* 1963. [Text ¶ 4, 5; Pages 38, 40, 43]
_____. "Of Animals and Art." *Audubon,* September 1978. [Page 39]

Reproductions:

Spruce Grouse, collection of the Leigh Yawkey Woodson Art Museum. *Pintail Drakes,* courtesy of the National Wildlife Federation, Washington, D.C. All other photographs courtesy of the artist.

Owen J. Gromme

Sources:

Davis, Tom. "Owen J. Gromme: A Lifetime of Preparation." *Wildlife Art News,* November/December 1985. [Text ¶ 7, 10, 13, 22, 23, 28; Pages 15, 16]
The Fond du Lac County Conservation Alliance. "A Portrait of Our 'Owen.'" Fond du Lac, Wis.: The Fond du Lac County Conservation Alliance. [Text ¶ 16]
Gromme, Owen J. "Songs of Spring." Old Frontenac, Minn.: The American Museum of Wildlife Art, 1988. [Text ¶ 11]
Hughes, Judy A. "*Birds in Art*: With Flying Colors." *Wildlife Art News,* September/October 1988. [Text ¶ 3]
Hume, Christopher, ed. *From the Wild: Portfolios of North America's Finest Wildlife Artists.* Richmond Hill, Ontario: GWA Group Publishing Company, 1987. [Text ¶ 4; Page 14]
Leroux, Charles. "Fight for nature is a work of art." *Chicago Tribune* (16 August 1984). [Text ¶ 6, 25, 26]
Mentzer, Michael. *The World of Owen Gromme.* Madison, Wis.: Stanton & Lee Publishers, Inc., 1983. [Text ¶ 5, 8, 9, 12, 17, 18, 19, 24, 27]
Milwaukee Public Museum. *A Retrospective Exhibition: The Wildlife Art of Owen J. Gromme.* Milwaukee: Milwaukee Public Museum, June 1980. [Text ¶ 2]
Sanders, Donna. "Owen Gromme: Wildlife Art's Grand Old Man." *Air Destinations,* May 1988. [Text ¶ 20]
_____. "Look Closely, It Is All on the Canvas." *The Living Bird Quarterly,* Winter 1989. [Page 18]
Seaborg, Walt. "*Birds of Wisconsin* author combines beauty and scientific accuracy in his wildlife paintings." *Wisconsin Rec News* (February 1967). [Text ¶ 14, 15, 21]

Artist's Photo:

Courtesy of Donna Sanders.

Reproductions:

Departure From Lake Katherine, collection of the Leigh Yawkey Woodson Art Museum. *Salute to the Dawn, Sharptails Dancing,* and *Distant Thunder,* courtesy of Stanton & Lee, Madison, Wisconsin. *Ruffed Grouse* and *Getting Even,* courtesy of Wild Wings, Inc., Lake City, Minnesota.

Lars Jonsson

Sources:

Interview, April 1990.
Birds in Art Master Wildlife Artist lecture, September 1988.
Jonsson, Lars. *Bird Island: Pictures From a Shoal of Sand.* Beckenham, Kent, England: Croom Helm Limited, 1983. [Pages 112, 113, 114]
_____. "Reflections." *Lars Jonsson: Bird Reflections.* London: The Tryon Gallery, 1987. [Text ¶ 16; Pages 110, 115]

Reproductions:

Early Spring Morning, collection of the Leigh Yawkey Woodson Art Museum. *Arctic Spring* photographed by A. Kilbertus, Montreal, Canada. All other photographs courtesy of the artist.

J. Fenwick Lansdowne

Sources:

Interview, April 1990.
Birds in Art Master Wildlife Artist lecture, September 1985.
Lansdowne, J. Fenwick. *Birds of the West Coast.* Vol. 1. Toronto: M. F. Feheley Publishers Limited, 1976. [Text ¶ 3, 18, 19]
Danzker, Jo-Anne Birnie. *J. Fenwick Lansdowne.* Vancouver: The Vancouver Art Gallery, 1981. [Pages 89, 90]

Reproductions:

Missed, courtesy of The Greenwich Workshop, Inc., Trumbull, Connecticut. All other photographs courtesy of the artist and Feheley Fine Arts, Inc., Toronto, Canada.

Roger Tory Peterson

Sources:

Interview, April 1990.
Devlin, John C., and Grace Naismith. *The World of Roger Tory Peterson.* New York: Times Books, 1977. [Page 33]
Gorner, Peter. "Birdman: Your field guide to Roger Tory Peterson." *Chicago Tribune* (25 September 1986). [Text ¶ 23]
Hume, Christopher, ed. *From the Wild: Portfolios of North America's Finest Wildlife Artists.* Richmond Hill, Ontario: GWA Group Publishing Company, 1987. [Text ¶ 9; Page 32]
Peterson, Roger Tory. Introduction to *The World of Owen Gromme* by Michael Mentzer. Madison, Wis.: Stanton & Lee Publishers, Inc., 1983. [Text ¶ 15, 16]
______. Introduction to *The Bird Illustrated: 1550-1900,* by Joseph Kastner. New York: Harry N. Abrams, Inc., 1988. [Text ¶ 21]
______. "Evolution of a Bird Artist." *Birder's World,* April 1989. [Text ¶ 1, 5, 6, 14, 25, 26]
______. *The Field Guide Paintings.* Boston: Houghton Mifflin Company (to be published). [Text ¶ 10]

Reproductions:

Gyrfalcon, collection of the Leigh Yawkey Woodson Art Museum. All other photographs courtesy of the artist and Mill Pond Press, Venice, Florida.

Maynard Reece:

Sources:

Interview, April 1990.
Birds in Art Master Wildlife Artist lecture, September 1989.
Reece, Maynard. *The Waterfowl Art of Maynard Reece.* New York: Harry N. Abrams, Inc., 1985. [Page 123]
Van Gelder, Patricia. *Wildlife Artists at Work.* New York: Watson-Guptill Publications, 1982. [Text ¶ 14]
Wechsler, Chuck. "'I've Been There' with Maynard Reece." *Wildlife Art News,* November/December 1984. [Text ¶ 15]

Reproductions:

Over the Marsh, collection of the Leigh Yawkey Woodson Art Museum. All other photographs courtesy of the artist and Mill Pond Press, Venice, Florida.

Peter Scott

Sources:

Burnham, Sophy. "A Walk on the Wildlife Side." *New York Times* (27 April 1980). [Text ¶ 12; Page 51]
Harrison, Kit, and George H. Harrison. "Sir Peter Scott." *Sports Afield,* September 1987. [Text ¶ 4, 10; Page 49]
Scott, Peter. *The Eye of the Wind: An Autobiography.* Boston: Houghton Mifflin Company, 1961. [Text ¶ 2, 7; Page 46]
______. *Observations of Wildlife.* Oxford, England: Phaidon Press, 1980. [Text ¶ 5, 6, 8, 9, 11, 12, 14, 15, 16, 17; Page 50]
The Waterfowl Foundation, Inc. "Peter Scott Memorial Appeal for Conservation." The Waterfowl Foundation, Inc. (1989). [Page 48]

Artist's Photo:

J. F. Leach, courtesy of the Wildfowl Trust, Slimbridge, England.

Reproductions:

Honkers Against a Cumulus Sky, collection of the Leigh Yawkey Woodson Art Museum. All other photographs courtesy of the estate of the artist and Mill Pond Press, Venice, Florida.

Keith Shackleton

Sources:

Birds in Art Master Wildlife Artist lecture, September 1986.
Hammond, Nicholas. *Twentieth Century Wildlife Artists.* Woodstock, N.Y.: The Overlook Press, 1986. [Text ¶ 10]
Kosier, Cathy. "Keith Shackleton: The Depths of Sea and Soul." *U.S. ART,* July/August 1988. [Text ¶ 2, 3, 4, 8, 9; Page 97]
Shackleton, Keith. *Wildlife and Wilderness: An Artist's World.* London: Clive Holloway Books, 1986. [Text ¶ 1, 5, 12, 13, 18, 20, 22; Pages 94, 95, 96, 98, 99]

Reproductions:

South From New Zealand, collection of the Leigh Yawkey Woodson Art Museum. All other photographs courtesy of the artist and Mill Pond Press, Venice, Florida.

Arthur B. Singer

Sources:

Text based on notes from *Birds in Art* Master Wildlife Artist lecture, September 1981; and interviews conducted by Dale Gregory (1982) and Joel Cook (1988).

Artist's Photo:

Courtesy of Leonard Eiger.

Reproductions:

Caroni Swamp at Sundown, collection of the Leigh Yawkey Woodson Art Museum. All other photographs courtesy of the estate of the artist.

George Miksch Sutton

Sources:

Auer, James. "Art Has Wings at Wausau." *The Milwaukee Journal* (September 1977). [Text ¶ 16]
Graham, Frank, Jr. "Signals from the Wild: The Art and Science of George Miksch Sutton." *Audubon,* July 1981. [Text ¶ 1, 19, 20; Page 24]
Hammond, Nicholas. *Twentieth Century Wildlife Artists.* Woodstock, N.Y.: The Overlook Press, 1986. [Text ¶ 17]
Sutton, George Miksch. *Mexican Birds: First Impressions.* Norman: University of Oklahoma Press, 1951. [Text ¶ 2; Page 22]
______. "Is Bird-Art Art?" *The Living Bird,* 1962. [Text ¶ 14, 21, 22, 23, 24, 27]
______. *At a Bend in a Mexican River.* New York: Paul S. Eriksson, Inc., 1972. [Page 23]
______. *To a Young Bird Artist: Letters from Louis Agassiz Fuertes to George Miksch Sutton.* Norman: University of Oklahoma Press, 1979. [Text ¶ 7, 9, 10, 11, 12, 13, 15, 18, 25, 26]

______. *Bird Student: An Autobiography.* Austin: University of Texas Press, 1980. [Text ¶ 4, 8]
______. *Birds Worth Watching.* Norman: University of Oklahoma Press, 1986. [Text ¶ 3, 6]
______. ". . . Forever and Ever, Amen." Norman: University of Oklahoma Press (Western History Collections), no date. [Page 27]
Wexler, Mark. "Wildlife Art Comes of Age." *National Wildlife,* October/November 1980. [Page 25]

Artist's Photo:
Courtesy of the *Norman Transcript*, Norman, Oklahoma.

Reproductions:
Sutton's Warblers, collection of the Leigh Yawkey Woodson Art Museum. *Red Knot and His Brood* courtesy of John S. Shackford. All other photographs courtesy of the University of Oklahoma Foundation, Inc., Norman, Oklahoma.

Kent Ullberg

Sources:
Interview, April 1990.
Birds in Art Master Wildlife Artist lecture, September 1987.

Reproductions:
Eagle Rock Monument, collection of the Leigh Yawkey Woodson Art Museum. All other photographs courtesy of the artist.

Production Notes

Design:
Earl J. Madden, Madison, Wisconsin

Color Separations:
Lithographics, New Berlin, Wisconsin

Printing and Typography:
Marathon Press Company, Marathon Communications Group, Wausau, Wisconsin

Binding:
Nicholstone Companies, Inc., Nashville, Tennessee

Typography:
Goudy Oldstyle Handtooled, Goudy Oldstyle Bold, Goudy Oldstyle, Palatino, Palatino Italic

Paper:
Dust jacket, 100 lb. Centura Enamel Gloss Text, White;
End paper, 80 lb. Strathmore Grandee Text, Navarre Blue;
Fly sheet, 70 lb. Tuxedo Text, Chardonnay; Text, 100 lb. Lithofect Plus Enamel Dull, White

Printing:
Dust jacket, one match color, gloss varnish, foil stamping;
Text, four-color process, one match color, gloss varnish

Binding:
Smyth sewn, case bound, foil stamping

Printed in the United States of America

Artwork Dimensions

All measurements given in inches in the following order: height x width x depth.

Acknowledgments

The authors wish to thank the Master Wildlife Artists for their generous donation of time and energy to make this book possible. We extend a special thanks to Kathy Kelsey Foley, Marcia Theel, and the staff of the Leigh Yawkey Woodson Art Museum. We also wish to thank the following people for their valuable assistance: William Bunce; Don Celing; Cecily Clark; Joel Cook; Alice and John Forester; Cyrus Y. Hagge; George H. Harrison; Bradford Koplowitz; Carol Krieg; David M. Lank; Mark E. Lefebvre; Robert L. Lewin and the staff at Mill Pond Press; Earl J. Madden; Robert A. McCabe; Jill Odegard; Carol Ray; Dale Singer; Alice Fisher Smith; David J. Wagner; William B. Webster and the staff at Wild Wings; Randy Westgate and the staff at Marathon Press Company; June H. White.

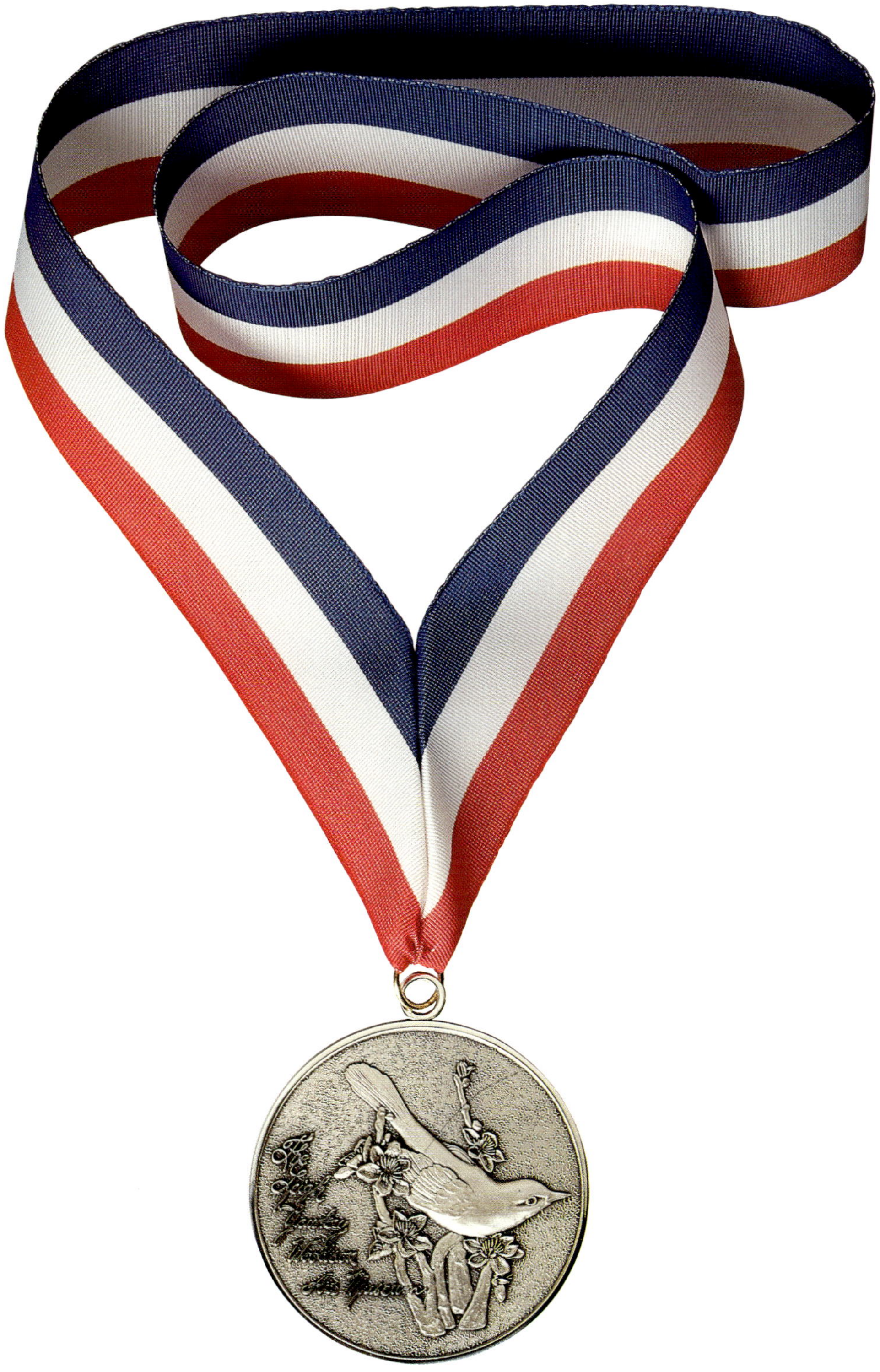